THE FICTION OF GARTH ST OMER

A CASEBOOK

THE FICTION OF GARTH ST OMER

A CASEBOOK

EDITED BY

ANTONIA MACDONALD

PEEPAL TREE

First published in Great Britain in 2018
Peepal Tree Press Ltd
17 King's Avenue
Leeds LS6 1QS
England

Thanks are due to *Caribbean Quarterly*, *Bim* and
the *Journal of West Indian Literature* for allowing us
to reprint articles first published in those journals

ISBN13:9781845233570

Supported using public funding by
ARTS COUNCIL
ENGLAND

CONTENTS

ANTONIA MACDONALD

INTRODUCTION

St. Lucia is seen as having a major poetic tradition; no doubt this is because of the international reach of the Nobel laureate Derek Walcott, followed by a generation of award-winning poets. Kendel Hippolyte and Vladimir Lucien have won Bocas literary awards – Lucien having the distinction of being the only poet, apart from Derek Walcott, to have won the overall BOCAS prize. Adrian Augier has been awarded an ANSA Caribbean award for Arts and Letters, and poets such as John Robert Lee, McDonald Dixon, and Jane King have all garnered strong regional reputations. The novelists have not made as large an impression: Garth St. Omer – a contemporary of Derek Walcott – is the most renowned. A generation after him came Earl Long, Michael Aubertin, Anderson Reynolds and McDonald Dixon, a poet who also writes novels.

Biographical information on Garth Timothy St. Omer, though scant, is readily available – both online and in print. He was born in Castries, St Lucia in 1931, was educated at St. Mary's College (at that time, the island's sole secondary school for boys), and upon completion of his secondary education became a junior teacher there. St. Omer taught at St. Mary's College for seven years and in 1956, entered the University of the West Indies (UWI) in Jamaica, where he read for a B.A. (Honours) in French Literature. After graduating from UWI in 1959, St. Omer spent two years teaching in France, after which he moved to Ghana where he taught French and English. In the early 1970s, he migrated to the USA and completed doctoral studies in Comparative Literature at Princeton University in 1975. Until his retirement in 2006, Emeritus Professor Garth St. Omer taught in the English department of the University of California in Santa Barbara.

It is important to note that during the earlier 1950s, St. Omer was part of the St. Lucia Arts Guild, a cultural group dedicated to the promotion of the creative arts. This group, founded in March 1950 by the Walcott brothers, Roderick and Derek, and the artist Dunstan St. Omer and friends soon became St. Lucia's most renowned theatrical society. Unfortunately, there is no available researched record of Garth St. Omer's role in this

period of St. Lucia's creative fervour, though an interview with Roderick
Walcott remembers Garth St. Omer and Derek Walcott as being the
intellectuals in that group, in distinction to himself and the painter
Dunstan St. Omer (unrelated to Garth) whom he saw as closer to "the
people".[1] There is an interesting piece written by Garth St. Omer in 1968,
which is a quasi-review of witnessing a St. Lucian audience's response to
a joint performance of Derek Walcott's *Dream on Monkey Mountain*, and Eric
Roach's more populist (and more appreciated) play, *Belle Fanto*. The article
reflects on the difficulty the St. Lucian audience appeared to have with the
sophistication of Walcott's play, and the dilemma this posed for the St.
Lucian writer who wanted to reach such an audience without indulging its
taste for comic folksiness.[2]

St. Omer's first novella, "Syrop," was published by Faber and Faber in
1964 in an anthology entitled *Introduction (2) Two: Stories by New Writers*. In
the following eight years, St. Omer had five works published (in four
books), some in the same year or within a year of each other, suggesting that
they were submitted to the British publishing house, Faber and Faber, at
around the same time. *A Room on the Hill* (1968) was his first novel. It was
followed by *Shades of Grey* (1968) which comprised two novellas – *Another
Place, Another Time*, and *The Lights on The Hill*. The following year saw the
publication of *Nor Any Country* and three years later, in 1972, *J—, Black Bam
and the Masqueraders*. St. Omer wrote *Prisnms* in the mid 1980s – a novel
which was different from his earlier works both in its North American
setting and in the cosmopolitanism of its themes – though the main
characters are implicitly St. Lucian. *Prisnms* failed to find a US publisher;
it was published by Peepal Tree Press in 2015.

When St. Omer started publishing, his short stories and novels gener-
ated a fair amount of critical interest. He was heralded by literary reviewers,
both regional and international, as a writer who would leave his mark.
There were many critical interventions by Caribbean scholars: Edward
Baugh, Michael Gilkes, Patricia Ismond, Clifford Lashley, Kenneth
Ramchand and Gordon Rohlehr all contributed reviews and essays on St.
Omer. These were important figures in West Indian literary criticism –
university lecturers who by their selection of teaching texts were themselves not only helping in the promotion of certain texts, but were also
involved in shaping a West Indian literary canon. However, in spite of the
reviews and critical essays, notwithstanding Edward Baugh's classification
of St. Omer in "the Sixties and the Seventies" as having "considerable claim
to our attention on the basis of a combination of output and quality" (*West
Indian Literature*, 63), none of his novels has gained a place of permanence
on the syllabi of the departments of English of the University of the West
Indies. The Caribbean reading public of that time remained small, and with
the flourishing of literature in the late 1960s and early 1970s meant that St.

Omer was only one of the many writers competing to secure a prolonged place in the literary spotlight. Moreover, at a time when some Caribbean critics were preoccupied with the positive role and responsibility of literature in the transformation of Caribbean societies, St. Omer's less-than-optimistic portrayal of the Caribbean's political leadership, and what some critics saw as his unceasing return to the themes of inevitable defeat and existential meaninglessness, was dismissed as nihilistic. Comparisons to V. S. Naipaul were frequent, except that Naipaul, though similarly uncomplimentary about the Caribbean, had the advantage of being one of very few Indo-Caribbean writers; hence his exploration of the role and fate of the Indo-Caribbean protagonist needed to be included in the Caribbean's narrative of self-fashioning.

By the turn of the twenty-first century, Garth St. Omer had joined the ranks of forgotten, and out-of-print Caribbean writers such as John Hearne, V.S. Reid, Jan Carew, Roger Mais, Andrew Salkey, Orlando Patterson and Geoffrey Drayton. From 2012, Peepal Tree Press, as part of its Caribbean Modern Classics series, has reprinted *A Room on the Hill*, *Shades of Grey, Nor Any Country and J—, Black Bam and the Masqueraders.* Each text includes a very useful scholarly introduction by Jeremy Poynting. Amongst other things, these introductions argue that St. Omer was uncommonly perceptive in recognising that the legacy of colonialism in the Caribbean psyche was far more deeply embedded than critics swept up in the enthusiasms of the independence years were prepared to admit, and that in all the novels there is a layer of metaphor that works as a counter-balance to the pessimistic reflections of the main characters, signalling a Caribbean capacity to surpass the dead-ends that St. Omer's protagonists, through their self-imposed and socially learnt limitations, find themselves in. Poynting's introductions note, for instance, St. Omer's critical honesty about race and class, the way that a protagonist such as Peter Breville expresses himself as a radical man of the people whilst being glamoured by wealth and whiteness.

The fact that for a long time Garth St. Omer held the distinction of being St. Lucia's only accomplished novelist made the reality of his descent into literary obscurity that much more difficult to fathom. Given that Derek Walcott has long enjoyed an international reputation as a major Caribbean poet, it would seem natural that critical attention would also be given to Garth St. Omer, the other St. Lucian writer who emerged from the same historical period – if only because it would provide a point of comparison between the two artists.

The Fiction of Garth St. Omer: A Casebook maps out St. Omer's critical reputation from his first published work until the present time. The casebook comprises ten early reviews of St. Omer's novels, four critical articles published by Caribbean critics during the heyday of St. Omer's critical attention, and seven essays written specifically for this collection. Directed at a varied community of readers, this collection aims to give its readers a heightened sense of the vitality of St. Omer's writing and the range of critical responses it has provoked. Additionally, our hope is that this casebook will bring St. Omer's novels out of obscurity and will help make a place within the Caribbean canon for this distinguished St. Lucian novelist.

The backstory behind the collation of this book is an interesting one. Garth St. Omer was slated to be a featured writer at the 2013 ACLALS conference in St. Lucia in an event billed as: *Plenary Conversation: Garth St. Omer and Jeremy Poynting*. However, due to unavoidable personal circumstances, St. Omer was unable to attend the conference. Given that his inclusion on the programme had already been formalized, Poynting organized and moderated a St. Omer panel discussion comprising Edward Baugh, Antonia MacDonald, Milt Moise, Velma Pollard, and Malica Willie. The range of ideas covered and the enthusiastic and lively response to the panel discussion spurred us on to continue engaging with St. Omer's oeuvre, this time in print – in the form of an edited collection of essays.

★

The primary aim of this book is to provide an interpretive and analytical framework for understanding and appreciating Garth St. Omer's novels. A necessary part of that scaffolding is an historical overview of the early critical responses to St. Omer when he made his debut as a writer. Included in Section One are reprints of reviews and critical commentaries on St. Omer's novella, *Syrop*, and of his novels during the period when they were first published. The range of response presented here indicates the lively critical conversation that these works generated.[3]

The first review is Edward Brathwaite's response to St. Omer's first published novella, *Syrop*. While Brathwaite's book review was on *Introduction 2: Stories by New Writers*, the collection in which this novella appeared, he devoted the majority of attention to *Syrop*, drawn as he was to its "accuracy and pitiless[ness] of the depiction of poverty" (p. 25). Brathwaite had read the original typeset manuscript of "Syrop" and noted in his review that in the published version, the St. Lucian *kwéyòl* dialogue had been, unfortunately, translated. A further Brathwaite review of *Nor Any Country* hints at some of the debate concerning St. Omer's perceived negativity, but the review acknowledges that his approach is in reality far more nuanced. Following Brathwaite's review is Clifford Lashley's review of *A Room on the Hill*, St. Omer's first published novel. It was a valuable insertion into the discussion, recognising that St Omer was an "enabling" rather than a "prescriptive" writer, a truth-teller rather than a writer who told the Caribbean reader what they may have wanted to hear. In his review of *A Room on the Hill*, Lashley also responded to St. Omer's use of creole

language and expressed regret that St. Omer had not chosen to continue to
explore the literary limits of the francophone language of the folk. One
notes that Brathwaite and Lashley were both drawn to the accessible style
and to St. Omer's experimentation with form. Both these reviews were
published in *Caribbean Quarterly,* one of the oldest journals in the English-
speaking Caribbean and a flagship publication of the University of the West
Indies.

   In 1969, the Barbadian columnist and critic, John Wickham, reviewed
Shades of Grey for the Barbadian journal *Bim.* Wickham's review formed
part of a larger review of new books and included in this collection is the
section of the review that relates specifically to *Shades of Grey.* Only
fourteen lines long, Wickham's review is oddly disenchanted by what he
saw as the unbelievable quality of St. Omer's narration. He deemed the
characters as lacking credibility and where previously Lashley and Brathwaite
had praised St. Omer's economy of language, Wickham relegated it to
"dreary and pretentious verbalizing"(32). Alongside Wickham's review is
Kenneth Ramchand's commentary on *Shades of Grey* in the *Journal of Commonwealth Literature.* While not a formal review, the relevant section of
Ramchand's (1969) critical commentary shows that St. Omer was gradually
taking a notable place alongside writers from throughout the Commonwealth. Far more positive than Wickham, Ramchand commended St. Omer's
"delicacy, control and economy of style" (33) and praised him as being in "the
first ranks of twentieth-century novelists" (p. 34). Wickham' review, unlike
Ramchand's, suggests that some Caribbean critics were not comfortable
either with literary modernism or with honesty about sexuality.

   Although not included in this section, Charles Larson of Indiana
University also reviewed *Shades of Grey* in *Books Abroad.* Larson's review
was quite brief, focusing specifically on St. Omer's exploration of education as something external to the lives of his young male protagonists and
ultimately as an alienating force. It is a focus I pick up in my own essay.
Where many other reviewers had commended St. Omer for his deft
handling of the novella form, Larson criticizes St. Omer for his fragmen-
tary development of characters. Less drawn than most to *The Lights on The
Hill*, Larson saw this novella as proof that St. Omer would be better served
by concentrating "on a larger work next time" (605). It is important to note
here that already St. Omer was receiving mixed reviews. Larson's review
also suggests that some non-Caribbean readers felt left at a loss by St.
Omer's reluctance to explain the social background of his characters, rather
than, as he does, hint at their social and racial location through more
oblique clues. For other non-Caribbean reviewers this evidently did not
matter.

   When *Nor Any Country* was published in 1969, its first reviews came
from British weekly magazines[4]. John Hemmings' review for *The Listener*

was published on May 8. Hemmings read St. Omer as less concerned with making broad statements about the Caribbean, but rather with exploring the inner sensibilities of his characters, of what it is like to be "hard, brilliant and conscience-ridden". Meanwhile, in the May 9, 1969 edition of *The Spectator*, Maurice Capitanchik gives most attention and praise to *Nor Any Country* in a five-book review entitled "Private Lives'. Capitanchik draws attention to the recurring St. Omerian persona – the isolated protagonist who operates on the margin of his community, and he describes *Nor Any Country* as a novel that attempts to understand the human predicament. Interestingly, in his reference to the "self-pity" of *Shades of Grey,* Capitanchik seems to think, mistakenly, that there is some autobiographical element to St. Omer's novels.

Though brief, these reviews have been reprinted here so as to demonstrate the international regard that St. Omer, having published three novels in quick succession, was now enjoying.

Edward Baugh's review of *Nor Any Country,* one of the lengthier of the reviews included here[5], like Ramchand's, Brathwaite's and Lashley's, again praised St. Omer's "commanding talent". Baugh read *Nor Any Country* as the maturation of St. Omer's style as evidenced in his earlier works, and drew attention to the masterful way in which St. Omer handles the colonial past, and the deft economy with which he manipulates "the possibilities of quintessential prose" (p. 42). Already, there was the sense that the St. Omer that British reviewers responded to was rather different from the novelist as read by the St. Lucian/ Caribbean reader. Whereas some international reviewers had been quick to criticise St. Omer's extreme economy of language, Baugh's review took care to point out St. Omer's parsimonious employment of the kind of detail that places characters in their social and cultural setting ("the method is one of implication and innuendo"), whilst leaving the alert Caribbean reader enough clues to make their deductions.

However, when it was published in 1972, *J—, Black Bam and the Masqueraders* did not generate the same volume of review interest as had its prequel, *Nor Any Country*, though it was reviewed in June and July of that year in major British newspapers and regionally, in the August 20th edition of *Sunday Gleaner* of Jamaica. Included here is the anonymous review that appeared in the *Times Literary Supplement* in August 1972. More importantly, in February 1974, *Tapia*[4] published a review essay, "Peter Plays For Paul", written by the St. Lucian poet and critic John Robert Lee. This was the first published work by a St. Lucian critic and is the final review included here. One comment worth making about Lee's perceptive review is that in his close reading, as a fellow St. Lucian, he shows very well how St. Omer simultaneously manages a mean economy of description and a highly specific analysis of St. Lucian society.

The paucity of reviews notwithstanding, in the seventies and eighties

J—, Black Bam and the Masqueraders had its fair share of critical attention. Many of the essays written on St. Omer made specific reference to that work, and reading this sequel alongside *Nor Any Country* often effected a comparative analysis and in one or two instances – unlike Lee's – a negative judgment of the latter. For example, in the listing of St. Omer's oeuvre, Gerald Moore, writing for *Contemporary Novelists*, dismissed this novel as less successful than *Nor any Country* in so far as it lacked the descriptive merits of St. Omer's earlier works. Moreover, St. Omer's return to the recurring theme of personal failure was judged by Moore as proof that St. Omer was "a talent desperately in need of an entirely new subject" (569). On the other hand, Michael Gilkes in *The West Indian Novel*, praises the experimental quality of this work, finding virtue in St. Omer's interlocking of two story lines –the epistollary backstory to Paul's disgrace and subsequent descent into the pretence of madness, and Peter's various attempts to withdraw from the consequence of his actions and inaction, and the failures they breed. For Gilkes, Paul is at the centre of this novel and in his unblinking confrontation of his society's hypocrisy; his refusal to succumb to its propagation of guilt and its demand for punishment, he stands as a polar opposite to his brother Peter. In its reconstruction of memories, Gilkes posits that Paul's confessional letters to his brother were a necessary, though "traumatic return to origins" (113). At the same time, Gilkes argues, Paul's 'return' was not enough to circumvent failure. Instead, it is in Peter that St. Omer locates the possibility of emancipation from self-contempt and bitterness. Reading the symbolism of Peter's child clambering successfully over his barrier of his body and its cries of pleasure when Peter plays with it as a hopeful note on which the novel ends, Gilkes suggests that freedom from guilt and genuine return to community can only occur when the individual takes responsibility for himself, and for his actions.

Whilst St. Omer's reiteration of certain themes – alienation, classism and discrimination – have been read as unmoderated pessimism by some reviewers, few paid more than passing attention to the deliberateness with which the novels and novellas all worked together to form one unified narrative. Male characters reappear in different books – older, younger, hopeful, disabused. For example, Derek Charles is introduced in *A Room on the Hill* as the successful lawyer who has returned to the island with a white wife, and as the ex-lover of the main female character, Ann-Marie; in *Another Place, Another Time*, set almost a decade before, he is the protagonist and the reader is given his story as a secondary school student who longs to leave the island. Derek Charles is also briefly mentioned in *The Lights on The Hill* by Stephenson, the main character in that novel, who reappears as a minor character in *J—, Black Bam and the Masqueraders*. Peter Breville appears in three of the novels. First he is witnessed as a drunken, wife-beating university lecturer in *The Lights on the Hill* by Stephenson, then is fully developed as the protagonist of *Nor Any Country* when he returns to his island after study in Europe, and then in *J—, Black Bam and The Masqueraders*, where the wife-beating scene is presented from another perspective. The title of *Nor Any Country* comes directly from *Another Place, Another Time*, and relates specifically to the outlook of the scholarship recipients whose loyalty is primarily to self, rather than the community from which they emerged. The title of the second story in *Shades of Grey* comes from a phrase in *The Lights on the Hill* where Stephenson yearns to escape his sense of entrapment: "He dreamed on his feet of walking through the night and emerging into another place, another time" (99). *Another Place, Another Time* is about embracing exile as the means of escape.

Simply put, *Another Place, Another Time* is a partial prequel to *A Room on the Hill*; *J—, Black Bam and The Masqueraders* is both the paraquel to *The Lights on the Hill* and the sequel to *Nor Any Country*. Together these novels allow for what Forrest Ingram, in *Representative Short Story Cycles of the Twentieth Century*, defines as a linking that allows "the reader's experience of each [to be] modified by his experiences of the others" (13). For instance, in the first part of *J—, Black Bam and the Masqueraders*, which presents Peter Breville and his long-abandoned wife, Phyllis, trying to salvage their marriage, the reader who is familiar with *The Lights on the Hill* is painfully attentive to the cracks appearing in this process. In his creative reworking of the short story cycle in his novels, St. Omer deliberately and self-consciously engages with form and structure. Bruce King, in his essay "Garth St. Omer: From Disorder to Order," struggles to classify St. Omer's style and form, and resolves his difficulty with a commentary that "the effect is rather a carefully constructed, sensitive, artfully-shaped *brooding over memories than story*" [italics mine] (57). Characterizing the novels as "guilty meditations" (57), Bruce King's focus is concentrated on the relationship of structure to character and plot. My perspective is different. I wish to suggest that what all these works allow for is the author's revisiting of St. Lucia's social landscape – a revisiting that, while it does not necessarily amplify character, provides additional layers of complexity and dynamic to a small-island Caribbean setting. The "delicacy, control and economy" (p. 34) that Ramchand had attributed to St. Omer can be seen in his quiet excavation of the behaviour and attitudes of his protagonists to reveal the essence of small island colonial society – the heart of which beats with narrow circumspection, a place from which one is constantly trying to escape, but one which one continues to carry into exile. Ultimately, it is the particularities of place, space and time that remain constant and integral to the experiences of St. Omer's characters. This manipulation of his novel cycle provides St. Omer with a very useful structure for what Ramchand had, in 1969, recognized as his probe into the psyche of the modern West Indian male. But here I would qualify Ramchand's statement and insist that it is a probe that is as much about place as it is about character. The essays in the following section bear this out.

★

Section Two comprises four critical interventions on Garth St. Omer written by Caribbean critics and published in Caribbean journals during the 1970s and 1980s.

Read alongside the reviews in Section 1, these essays constitute seminal criticism on St. Omer and provide an important barometer for measuring the historical state of St. Omer scholarship in the region. Although two of these four essays are readily available online, they have been reprinted in this book so as to not exclude readers with limited internet access or those who are not comfortable navigators of the online terrain.

John Robert Lee's survey of St. Omer's novels is a deliberate attempt to return St. Omer to the literary attention of the St. Lucian reader. In making the case that St. Omer was and remains revolutionary in his critique of colonial small island societies, Lee establishes relevance and topicality. The St. Lucia that St. Omer depicts has not changed substantially – it is still a society that forces compliance, that insists that its citizens, be they educated or uneducated, know its place. The status quo remains entrenched and the efforts of intellectuals who attempt to challenge it are soon reduced to pappyshow – worthless masquerades. In his depiction of this "self-limiting society" (57), Lee's intervention dovetails with Patricia Ismond's essay on the St. Lucian background in St. Omer's novels. When it was published by *Caribbean Quarterly* in 1982, Ismond's essay served a very important role in delineating the political and social specificities of colonial St. Lucia, an island that was in many ways different from other Caribbean islands.

Attentive to the peculiarities of place, Ismond looks at the factors that shaped what she dubs the "private orientation" of both Walcott and St. Omer. In her explanation of how St. Lucia creates the bias towards the "private" of both writers, Ismond outlines the ways in which Catholicism, in its permeation into every sphere of life in that island, forced its citizens into a prison of conformity. She argues that sin and punishment are constant themes in St. Omer's novels and traces the different strategies that the St. Omerian protagonists use in order to free themselves from the weight of guilt that the Catholic Church has bequeathed them. Exile, Ismond posits, was the only escape from its stranglehold. In her description of the St. Lucian space depicted by St. Omer, Ismond's essay is heavy in its use of words such as "sterility", "malaise", "paralysis", "madness" and "death". This drives home her point that these two St. Lucian writers were producing their art as a reaction to a debilitating social environment. She is careful, however, to show that while St. Omer focuses on negation, Walcott is more affirmative. Ismond suggests that Walcott's ongoing preoccupation with the role of the imagination in the creation of an artistic sensibility insulates him from the despair that haunts St. Omer. Instead, Walcott draws on nature, the folk, and St. Lucia's oral traditions as sources that can sustain the artist and move him to productive brilliance. Ismond's essay is important in its locating of St. Omer as a humanist – a writer who portrays the bleak truth about his society in order to apply a literary corrective. The mirror he holds up, while it shines a harsh and unforgiving light, allows us to understand the particularities of this small mid-twentieth century Caribbean society.

Jacqueline Cousins' essay, "Symbol and Metaphor in the Early Fiction of Garth St Omer", is included in this casebook as a rare critical intervention on St. Omer's short stories. This was the work that appeared in regional journals such as *Bim* or were aired on the BBC's *Caribbean Voices.* To date, these stories have not been reprinted either as part of a St. Omer collection or as part of a Caribbean prose anthology. Cousins scholarly engagement with these stories helps to bring them into discursive view. In her essay, Cousins compares them with Joyce's *Dubliners.* Arguing that St. Omer is influenced by Joyce in his creation of character as "symbolic construct" (p. 72) and in what Joyce, in describing *Dubliners*, had characterized as the "scrupulous meanness"[7] of his prose style, Cousins is careful to establish St. Omer as a deeply moral writer who engages with the notions of freedom, choice and responsibility. Analyzing his short stories as an unsparing exposé of the individual's struggle for social validation, Cousins shows that although St. Omer does not provide any easy solutions, what he validates is the ongoing human struggle to cope with the psychic malaise engendered by society. In her detailed reading of "No Second Chance", "It will Last forever", "The Old Man" and "The Revendeuse," Cousins establishes that death is a constant thematic thread developed through symbols such as the sea, darkness, light, and the Catholic church; and, like Ismond, she traces the ways in which the Catholic Church can be read as a symbol of corruption and corrosive family relationships. Cousins, in her analysis of these works, is careful to show how the themes explored in St. Omer's short stories are reiterated in his novels and cites Edward Baugh's description of St. Omer as a writer who is in search of "perfective fiction" (p. 71).

The final essay reprinted here is the much-referenced article, "Small Island Blues: A short review of the novels of Garth St. Omer" by Gordon Rohlehr. Published in 1969, a few months after the publication of *Nor Any Country*, Rohlehr's essay focuses on St. Omer's exploration of the experiences of an emerging middle-class in a small Caribbean island society. Paralysis and purposelessness, isolation and irrelevance are, for Rohlehr, recurring themes in St. Omer's works. In this regard, and like Cousins, Rohlehr compares St. Omer to James Joyce, seeing in both writers the same "scrupulous meanness of style" manifested in their "careful, tightly economical prose and almost bleak detachment" (p. 89). In his discussion of St. Omer's *oeuvre*, Rohlehr zeroes in on the passivity that appears to define his protagonists and reads this tendency to submit rather than fight against the forces that seek to repress them as part of what he sees as St. Omer's fatalist philosophy. Acknowledging St. Omer as a careful and conscious artist, Rohlehr is nonetheless concerned that the "small-island blues" that St. Omer sings tell the one-sided story of men who have given up the struggle to shape a new society, without showing the reader how this failure relates to a committed and ongoing engagement with that struggle. Conceding that St. Omer's novels are proof of considerable talent, Rohlehr's article ends with the warning that this recurring theme of disillusionment, and St. Omer's tendency to tell, rather than demonstrate, to intellectualize rather than dramatize, may well lead this novelist to a "dead end" (28).

In the same way that the reviews of St. Omer's books were both regional and international, there were also seminal articles written by non-Caribbean critics. Though these essays are not included here, Jacqueline Kaye's "Anonymity and Subjectivity in the Novels of Garth St. Omer" was published by *The Journal of Commonwealth Literature* in 1975 and two years later, *Ariel: A Review of International Literature* published "Double Identity in the Novels of Garth St. Omer," an essay by John Thieme. From its inaugural issue in 1965, *The Journal of Commonwealth Literature* was a major critical forum in the field of commonwealth and postcolonial literature. Similarly, *Ariel* was, from its inception, committed to the study of Commonwealth literature and the ways in which literature written in English, emerging from the colonies, intervened in or entered into dialogue with the "great" imperial tradition. Given the international reputation both journals enjoyed, and active role each played in the production of knowledge about West Indian literature, these two essays did an excellent job in bringing Garth St. Omer to the attention of commonwealth scholars. It was shortly thereafter that article-length essays appeared in regional journals, adding now to the growing intellectual conversation.

A prolific writer on Caribbean literature, namely the creative writing of Derek Walcott, V.S. Naipaul, Samuel Selvon and George Lamming, Thieme's essay explored the existential quality of St. Omer's novels. He provided a close reading of each text, and was careful to show the interconnectivity of themes and character. He also compared St. Omer's "large ironic vision" (96) to Naipaul's and posited that for both writers, "West Indian life is all too often poisoned by its mimetic quality and colonialism is primarily a psychological condition" (95). Kaye's essay, like Thieme's, explores the existential quality in St. Omer's novels and uses Fanon's *Black Skins, White Masks* to discuss the impossibilities of the choices facing St. Omer's educated black protagonists. For Kaye, madness – pretended or real – "hides despair and total collapse"(46) engendered by colonial malaise, which is the ultimate fate of St. Omer's protagonists. Marked by self-absorption and subjectivism, hiding their real selves from themselves, Kaye reads these protagonists as gradually disintegrating into anonymity. The focus in this essay is primarily on Stephenson from *The Lights on the Hill* and the two Breville brothers in *J—, Black Bam and the Masqueraders*. Reacting to what she describes as "the farce of anonymous egotism" (52), she sees these characters as failing to move beyond the painful and unshakeable consequences of slavery. Both Kaye and Thieme seem to be less than impressed by the sensitivity and thoroughness with which St. Omer's probes the choices available to the educated colonial.

★

The third section provides a view of St. Omer as man, and a personal account of the social world within which he was attempting to carve out his niche. Velma Pollard offers us a portrait of the artist as a family man – a very useful intervention because St. Omer is an intensely private writer. Pollard's personal narrative – "The Man at Home" – returns St. Omer to our Caribbean literary community. Moreover, there is always the tendency to read the Caribbean novel as an autobiography and, in the St. Omerian protagonists, all unaccommodating unsympathetic men, one might mistakenly believe that these are characteristics of the novelist himself. Pollard in humanizing St. Omer – the man and the writer – debunks this perception. Meanwhile Jane King's "Rereading St. Omer: Some Very Personal Thoughts" is an intimate portrait of the "brown-skinned" St. Lucian – the mulatto group that is so much a feature of St. Omer's novels. King's portrait of the social life of that group: their insecurities, their prejudices, their class anxieties, and domestic politics that drive them, adds an important dimension to the context of St. Omer's novels. In her weaving of her own life story – as the daughter of a white expatriate woman and a "brown-skinned" man – King is able to show how certain recurring tropes in St. Omer's works: death, love, sex, exile were integral to the fabric of St. Lucian life at that time. King's personal piece provides an excellent counterpoint to Ismond's essay in so far as it gives us another vantage point from which to view the St. Lucian background in St. Omer's novels. It is a piece that fruitfully follows in the space that Cliff Lashley's important review opens up.

The final section – Part Four – constitutes five scholarly interventions on St. Omer's corpus. The essays by Milt Moise and Malica Willie and Jeremy Poynting focus on specific works: Moise on *Another Place, Another Time*, and Willie on *The Lights on The Hill* (the other novel that constitutes *Shades of Grey*) and Poynting on *Prisnms*. Edward Baugh and Antonia MacDonald are general in their exploration of form and meaning in St Omer's novels.

In her essay, Willie makes the case that in *The Lights on the Hill*, St. Omer's main character, Stephenson, quite clearly resembles Albert Camus' Monsieur Meursault in *The Stranger*, a character who feels like an outsider in his native land and responds by recoiling into a state of somnambulism. Willie goes on to establish that St. Omer utilises Existentialism in order to evoke the Caribbean experiences of forced exile and colonialism that have produced a society suffering from inferiority and a crippling malaise. However, she proposes that instead of exposing our maladies only to put us to shame, St. Omer's *The Lights on the Hill* serves as a template for the individual journey to enlightenment. Core to Willie's argument is that rather than existing in a state of terror and passive helplessness, St. Omer's existential text proposes a Sartrean solution: that while exile acknowledges the precariousness of our being, it also demands of us responsible action.

Moise looks at the representation of the Castries fire of 1948 as it is represented in Garth St. Omer's *Another Time, Another Place* and in Derek Walcott's poem "A City's Death by Fire". Moise argues that whilst the latter has become *the* definitive literary representation of that event, St. Omer's portrayal helps fill in some of the blanks that the poem leaves behind and offers a distinctively different and bracing response to the event. Using trauma theory as his discursive base, Moise reads St. Omer's depiction of the 1948 fire as a "holistic and terrifying diachronic snapshot of a society's response to a disaster" (p. 110). Further, Moise argues that the exclusion of the St. Omerian version in the St. Lucian literary imagination is a function of its "frightening, counterdiscursive" nature. That is, it exposes a pain for which the reader is not prepared.

Poynting's essay is similarly concerned with counterdiscourse. In his exploration of St. Omer's most recent novel, *Prisnms*, Poynting highlights the metafictional quality of this US-based novel, but establishes the similarities in theme and characterization between it and St. Omer's previous works. Poynting focuses on the duplicity of Eugene Coard, the protagonist and unreliable first person narrator of *Prisnms*. He makes the case that, in Coard's character, St. Omer extends and deepens the exploration of the psychoses which contoured his earlier novels. Coard manages his dividedness like a novelist, by projecting it outwards into the world within which he operates in a manifestly fictive way. In his problematizing of the reliability of accounts that are generally regarded as "truthful", St. Omer, Poynting argues, is highlighting "the porous divisions between different kinds of storytelling" (p. 183), and the masquerading that is core to human performances, especially in contexts where disclosure has become fetishized.

Whereas the first three essays focus on particular works, the final two essays concern themselves with a more generalized discussion of the style and structure of St. Omer's novels. In "St. Omer's Word Craft", Edward Baugh devotes himself to the analysis of narrative style. Arguing that "the overall impact of St Omer's novels is inseparable from the quality of the prose style", Baugh makes the point that the simplicity and clarity of St. Omer's style is deliberate, and that in his bid to present St. Lucia dispassionately and objectively, he elects to write in a style that does not call attention to itself. Further, using evidence from both *A Room on the Hill* and *The Lights on the Hill*, Baugh in his essay discusses St. Omer's style as one which highlights, in ironic counterpoint, the self-deceptive personalities of some of his protagonists (p. 166). Baugh's essay is particularly important in its tracing of the maturation of St. Omer's style from its early awkwardness, as evidenced in his stories read on the BBC's *Caribbean Voices* (and as critiqued by V. S. Naipaul, the then programme editor). Through careful historicizing of reviews, Baugh maps out a critique of what was seen as a mannered sparseness of style and its perceived Hemingwayesque quality, but shows how St. Omer's "tone of distance" becomes more fully realized and sure-footed in later works such as J–, *Black Bam and the Masqueraders*. And indeed, with the publication of *Prisnms*, Baugh's thesis is all the more on point. St. Omer's voice has continued to be one that is thoroughly modulated by dispassionate inquiry.

While Baugh's essay engages primarily with St. Omer's narrative voice and its critical reception, my intervention focuses on the theme of education and its relationship to the history of the period he writes about. Entering into dialogue with Rohlehr's "Small Island Blues", I take issue with his claim that St. Omer's characters are passive and unengaged in struggle. Instead I am suggesting that they are involved in a very personal struggle, the articulation of self and that this individualism is a function of and, in some instances a reaction to the colonial education they are receiving. In the exploration of what I call St. Omer's quintet of stories, I argue that these works can be read as the literary representation of the first stage in pre-independent, Caribbean socio-political life – the desire for self-advancement through education. The socio-historical reality in developing societies is that poverty continues to be a barrier to schooling and an impediment to social and political development. Accordingly, education is not only the escape from poverty but also the means of separating the emerging black middle class from the entrapment of this stultifying past. I go on to suggest that the narrowness of vision and the self-centredness that St. Omer represents in his main characters is part of the reality of his time and that what makes his novels remarkable is the relentless honesty of this portrayal. Applauding the frankness with which St. Omer depicts the malaise of his society, I argue that this quintet deliberately provides an antithesis to the optimistic narrative of nationalism publicly circulating at that time.

In their exploration of the economy of St. Omer's style, his manipulation of the structure of interconnectedness in his novels, and his approach to social issues, the reviews and essays that make up this collection reinforce the importance of his contribution to Caribbean literature. Although one can find correspondence both in themes and literary techniques between St. Omer and the French existentialists, the essays included here demonstrate that St. Omer's particular blend of philosophy and style is both unique and ground-breaking and deeply rooted in the Caribbean.

In conclusion, the new availability of St. Omer's novels is a very valuable contribution to his re-emergence as a notable contributor to the body of Caribbean writing. But availability does not necessarily translate into readership. St. Lucian and Caribbean scholars can play a role in promoting the novels of Garth St. Omer so that these reprinted works do not soon fade into obscurity. This casebook, in the range and scope of its interventions, hopes to assist St. Omer's books and their reflection of a particular moment in St. Lucia's social history to resonate well into the twenty-first century. In making St. Omer scholarship more accessible, we can secure him a place not only on the St. Lucian literature curriculum but also in the Caribbean literary canon.[8] No longer preoccupied with righting historical wrongs, twenty-first century Caribbean readers find it easier to accept that a writer does not need to be overtly political, and that the work does not have to be explicitly ideology-driven. St. Omer's themes remain current: alienation, marginalization of women, the paradoxical nature of love, ambition, race and class are issues that continue to constellate in twenty-first century Caribbean society. In bringing Garth St. Omer back to readers' attention, we hope he will be appreciated not only for his meticulous rendering of St. Lucia's social history but also for the incisive style that defines his narration.

Works Cited

Anonymous, Review of *Nor Any Country* by Garth St. Omer. *Times Literary Supplement* 3509 (May 29, 1969): 589.

Anonymous, "Brothers in Inaction". *Rev. of J—, Black Bam and the Masqueraders* by Garth St. Omer. *Times Literary Supplement* 3678 (August 25, 1972): 985.

Baugh, Edward, Rev. of *Nor Any Country* by Garth St. Omer. *Bim* 13:50 (January-June 1970): 128-130.

——, "The sixties and seventies". In *West Indian Literature*. Ed. Bruce King. London: Macmillan, 1979. pp. 63-75.

Brathwaite, Edward. Rev. of "Syrop" by Garth St. Omer. *Caribbean Quarterly* 10:1 (March 1964): 68-69.

——, "West Indian Prose Fiction in the Sixties." *Black World* 20:11 (September 1971): 15-20.

Capitanchik, Maurice, "Private Lives". Rev. of *Nor Any Country* by Garth St. Omer. *Spectator* 222 (May 9, 1969): 620-621.

Cousins, Jacqueline, "Symbol and Metaphor in the Early Novels of Garth St. Omer". *Journal of West Indian Literature*, Vol. 3, (September 1989). pp. 20-38.

Gilkes, Michael, *The West Indian Novel*. Boston: G.K. Hall, 1981.

Hemmings, John, Rev. of *Nor Any Country* by Garth St. Omer. *Listener* 81 (May 8, 1968): 656.

Ingram, Forrest, *Representative Short Story Cycles of the Twentieth Century: Studies of a Literary Genre*. Paris: Mouton, 1971.

Ismond, Patricia, "The St. Lucian Background in Garth St. Omer and Derek Walcott". *Caribbean Quarterly*. Volume 28, Numbers 1&2, (March – June 1982). Pp 32-43

Kaye Jacqueline, "Anonymity and Subjectivism in the Novels of Garth St. Omer", *Journal of Commonwealth Literature* 10 (August, 1975): 45-52.

King, Bruce, "Garth St. Omer: From Disorder to Order", *Commonwealth Essays and Studies* 3 (1977-8) , pp. 55-67.

Lashley, Clifford, Rev. of *A Room on the Hill* by Garth St. Omer. *Caribbean Quarterly* 17:1 (March 1971): 58-59.

Lee, Robert, "Peter Plays for Paul". *Tapia*. Vol. 4, No. 5, (February, 1974). pp. 6-7.

Moore, Gerald, "Garth St. Omer". In *Contemporary Novelists*. Ed. James Vinson. New York: St Martin's Press, 1972. pp. 1084-1086.

Ramchand, Kenneth, *Journal of Commonwealth Literature*.

Rohlehr, Gordon, "Small Island Blues: A short review of the novels of Garth St. Omer". In *St. Lucian Literature and Theatre: An Anthology of Reviews*, eds. John Robert Lee and Kendel Hippolyte, Castries: Cultural Development Foundation, pp.15-19.

St. Omer, Garth, "Syrop." In *Introduction Two: Stories by New Writers*. London: Faber, 1964.

——, *A Room on the Hill*, London: Faber and Faber, 1968.

——, *Shades of Grey*, London: Faber and Faber, 1968.

——, *Nor Any Country*, London: Faber and Faber, 1969.

——, *J—, Black Bam and The Masqueraders*. London: Faber and Faber, 1972.

——, *Prisnms*. Leeds: Peepal Tree Press, 2016.

Thieme, John, "Double Identity in the Novels of Garth St. Omer". *Ariel*, Volume 8, (July 1977). pp. 81-97.

Wickham, John, Review. *Bim*, Vol. 13, No. 49. July- December, 1969. pp. 63-64.

Williams, David, "Mixing Memory and Desire: St Omer's *Nor Any Country*" *Journal of West Indian Literature* 2.2 (1988): 36-41. Web.

Endnotes

1. Olivier Stephenson, *Visions and Voices: Conversations with Fourteen Caribbean Playwrights*, Leeds: Peepal Tree, 2013, p. 371

2. "Dream, but not, please, on Monkey Mountain", *The Voice*, 2 Nov. 1968, reprinted in *St Lucian Literature and Theatre: An Anthology of Reviews*, Compiled and edited by John Robert Lee & Kendel Hippolyte, Castries, 2006, pp. 195-197.

3. The texts of review articles have not been edited in any way (other than correcting obvious typos), but layout follows the style of the book.

4. *The Listener* was a BBC broadcast magazine that not only reproduced literary and musical programs but also reviewed new books. *The Spectator* is one of the oldest, continuously published British magazines. Conservative in its orientation, its principal subject areas are politics and culture.

5. Baugh had previously reviewed *Nor Any Country* for the *Sunday Gleaner* (Jamaica), July 13, 1969, p.4. The review was entitled "A Graceful Wisdom".

6. *Tapia* was a weekly newspaper published by the Tapia House Movement in Trinidad. It became *The Trinidad and Tobago Review*.

7. Writing to a prospective editor of *The Dubliners*, Joyce explained: "My intention was to write a chapter of the moral history of my country, and I chose Dublin for the scene because that city seemed to me the centre of paralysis... I have written it for the most part in a style of scrupulous meanness and with the conviction that he is a very bold man who dares to alter in the presentment, still more to deform, whatever he has seen and heard." Source: Herbert Gorman, *James Joyce*, New York, 1940, (pp.v-iv.)

8. St. Omer currently enjoys a modest online presence. I remain hopeful that digital editions of his works will be one day available. Perhaps, we can start of the digital production with single chapter excerpts – a modern-day serialization of the novels. And given the important social history that these novels contain, perhaps the chapters can be linked to images of colonial Castries. Additionally, those who know St. Omer, speak often of the length of time he devoted to editing his stories. It might well be a worthy project to collect facsimile reproductions of MS pages for the purposes of archiving Caribbean writers at work in the perfection of their craft.

REVIEWS

EDWARD KAMAU BRATHWAITE

INTRODUCTION 2: STORIES BY NEW WRITERS,
Caribbean Quarterly 10:1 (March 1964): 68-69.

For those interested in recent developments in short story writing in English, this is a useful introduction. There is a great deal of well written, if somewhat irrelevant 'psychological realism'; equally well written, straightforward material like Sheila MacLeod's *One Day* and Tom Stoddart's *The Story* – a dispassionate account of the cynicism behind Sunday rag journalism; and Angus Stewart's *Brown God in the Beginning:* a mythepoeic account of childhood.

But from the point of view of readers of *Caribbean Quarterly* – and also on its own account – Garth St. Omer's *Syrop* is what makes *Introduction 2* really worthwhile. St. Omer, a St. Lucian contemporary of Derek Walcott, graduated from the University of the West Indies in 1959. He is at present teaching in Ghana. *Syrop* must have been written about 1957. I remember seeing it in typescript and being quite excited about it. Over the years, the story – of poverty and futility in a small St. Lucian fishing village – kept haunting me; the beauty and the terror of it. Too long for an anthology-type short story, too short for a novel (it is about 50 pages long), it has only now been published. It seems a pity, though, that it should be lost in the kind of collection that *Introduction 2* is; in a few years, who will remember it? Let us hope that Mr. St. Omer will be at work now on more stories so that we may again have *Syrop* in a more formidable presentation, for it is, in my opinion, one of the finest bits of writing in this genre to have come out of the West Indies so far. Its delineation of poverty is as accurate and even more pitiless than Orlando Patterson's *Children of Sisyphus* (reviewed elsewhere in this issue), and its climax – an illustration of Camus's absurd – is almost unbearable in the impersonality and compassion of its art.

My only regret is that it appears that in seeking a publisher, St. Omer has had to remove (if my memory of the original typescript is to be trusted) the marvellous mixture and flavour of French creole speech and English narrative from the story, and provide instead what amounts to a translation of the creole. The result is rather like the folksy, unconvincing simplicity of the speech of Hemingway's Spanish Civil War characters:

'Why Pappa? I have of two years smaller than sixteen. One does not always have to wait to be sixteen for one to become a man'

or

'I am glad this thing about having a child is going to be over...'

From the publishers' point of view, this kind of compromise is no doubt necessary for the sake of intelligibility; but it must pose a very real problem for the creole writer, especially a non-English creole writer. I still hope that when Mr. St. Omer gives us his full collection of stories, the 'original' *Syrop* will be included.

EDWARD KAMAU BRATHWAITE

"WEST INDIAN PROSE IN THE SIXTIES AND
SEVENTIES: A SURVEY"
Black World 20:11 (September 1971): 15-20.

III

...Garth St. Omer's work, on the other hand, though consolidating
the tradition of frustration, has also introduced certain significant variations,
though it is still too early to say whether these will result in an alternative
way of seeing. Like Patterson, St. Omer is one of the few West Indian
novelists who have, for some time at least, returned to the islands.
But since *Syrop* (1964), written before he first left the region, St. Omer
has so far eschewed the 'peasant' for a more 'middle class' *persona*. 'Each
generation has its *angst*, but we has none', his friend and fellow St.
Lucian, Derek Walcott, had written in *In a Green Night*. With St. Omer
and his generation, this is no longer the case. St. Omer's (anti-) heroes
are deeply worried men, expressing a worrying sense of *nothing*. In *The
Gulf and Other Poems* (1969), it is again Derek Walcott who puts it neatly
in a poem dedicated to St. Omer ('Homecoming: Anse La Raye'):

> You give them nothing.
> Their curses melt in air.
> The black cliffs scowl,
> the ocean sucks its teeth
> like that dugout canoe
> a drifting petal fallen in a cup,
> with nothing but its image,
> you sway, reflecting nothing.
>
> (*The Gulf*, p. 51)

Or, as one of St. Omer's own characters puts it at the end of *Nor Any
Country*:

> It was easy. I discovered the absence of responsibility. I pretended I did
> not exist. It was better to be nothing than to be what I knew I could
> only become thinking always of what I might have been. I became nothing.
> I am nothing. (p.107)

This is the kind of pessimism that has been increasingly haunting the conventional West Indian novel (It is present, too, in Walcott's verse) since the end of Samuel Selvon's *The Lonely Londoners* (1956). It is a mood which reflects the continuing West Indian sense of political and cultural rootlessness and failure. But in *Nor Any Country*, despite the pessimism, we begin to discern (it is there even in the short passage quoted above) the outlines of a new hope, of possibility. This is most clearly expressed – indeed realized – within St. Omer's reticent prose. In the long, sustained passage (pp. 86-102) where Peter (the anti-hero) meets Father Thomas, a priest and countryman of his own age who, unlike Peter (the Biblical connotations of the names are clearly reversed) is consciously and emotionally committed to his island, despite its apparent deprivations:

> '... I decided it must be better to go to France and become a priest over several years than to remain as a teacher here. I went away.'
> 'And you've come back.'
> 'Yes. And have discovered how much easier it was for me to take the decision to become a priest than to return as one to this island.'
> 'How so?'
> 'I suppose I could be dishonest, pretend that the church must mean for me the same thing that it means for my French colleagues, the older ones especially. And yet...'
> 'And yet?'
> 'Let us say that it is more complicated for me to be a priest here than it can be for them...'
> '[Yes]... The Church demands loyalty that is absolute. It does not allow loyalty to it to be shared with anything or anybody else. One can only serve or leave her...' [...]
> Then he added, 'I can't leave, of course.'
> 'I don't suppose you can.'
> 'Merely by wearing this cassock I'm doing something. The people here saw me bathe naked on the beach. A lot of them bathed with me. Their attitudes to priests can never be the same again.' (pp. 96-98)

Father Thomas is here facing the problem of Faith and Authority within the post-colonial West Indian context; a problem posed also by Earl Lovelace in *The Schoolmaster* (1968). Lovelace in *The Schoolmaster*, however, does not get beyond signalling the problem; his concern was more specifically with the story he was telling. But St. Omer, with his sense of *nothing*, is still, paradoxically perhaps, very much aware of the dangers of the void; or at any rate appears to have grown to this awareness after *A Room on the Hill* and *Shades of Grey*:

> 'Being a priest seems somehow abortive. I should have been a bridge, like you, a link between our parents and the children you alone will have.'
> Peter said nothing.

'Now you alone, of the two of us, are that bridge. I am like one side only... I project from one bank and I end over the chasm. But you can go to the other side. You will join what you have known to what you will never know...' (p. 101)

CLIFF LASHLEY

A ROOM ON THE HILL — GARTH ST. OMER
Caribbean Quarterly 17:1 (March 1971): 58-59.

I promptly read Garth St. Omer's novel *A Room on the Hill* and his earlier novella *Syrop*. I have since read his novellas in *Shades of Grey* and his crowning achievement, the novel *Nor Any Country*. I wrote to thank and congratulate St. Omer, with whom I had been at university, and I spoke with him about his work in New York.

Every writer, I hear, dreams of his ideal audience who will read his work in the spirit in which it was written. I have always dreamed of the ideal writer who would write of my experience in such a way that I could focus and understand it. St. Omer is that writer; the subtle probing delineator of my generation of West Indian "been-tos." Faced by my ideal writer, shocked by self-discovery, I find the old critical clichés inadequate. You see, our literary education did not prepare us for evaluating literature at first hand or for evaluating literature which deeply engaged us. I couldn't understand why some critics feel that final literary judgement had to wait on time, maybe even on a later generation. I am beginning to understand because all I can say now is that St. Omer's work is excellent and is about you and him and me: our generation. Until I learn to deal directly with literature about my experience I cannot say more.

Or at best I can point out how the books fit my case and make a few simple comments. These may at least serve to bring these notable books to a wider readership. St. Omer is very readable. His is a spare, very controlled though colloquial style. *Syrop* is a tour de force because St. Omer manages to convey the flavour of St. Lucia French creole in English. How he achieves this must await further study. To my regret, but at no cost to literary effectiveness, he abandoned this experiment in the later books. Instead he translates the occasional creole phrase he uses almost as if he were writing for a foreign audience. When I tackled him about this, he said he felt free to use the wide gamut of language which is naturally his and didn't wish to be confined to the expressive limits of a creole. (Or something tantamount to this.) St. Omer's readability is enhanced by a very good ear for dialogue and considerable powers of selection allowing him to isolate the single incident or remark which tells as much as many other writers whole chapters. So his books are powerfully concentrated.

St. Omer's plots can be abstracted as the struggle of the young to survive and thrive in the economic and spiritual swamps of the small West Indian island. We are always made aware of the high cost of any success; particularly the cost of the scholarship route which by a combination of luck, charity, ability and parental self-sacrifice takes the naive black boy through secondary school and university to one of those "ruins we became". St. Omer's wide-eyed, dry-eyed vision of this process is not simple, either/or. There are no answers offered.

When I read his books, St. Omer led me unfalteringly to the quicksand edge of my typical life history and left me to my own devices. This is as much as I ask of an imaginative writer. St. Omer is not a prescriptive writer: he is an enabling writer, giving me my life in such a way that I am better able to live it.

What is lamentable about all this is my trained incapacity before this body of creative writing. This is possibly the final point of St. Omer's work: that the price of success in the West Indies through the usual scholarship route is the psychic and spiritual survival of the individual. If there is any inference I would want to make from St. Omer's work it is that we need to look very closely at how our educational system – in the widest sense of the term – has made and marred us. As people connected with the university (survivors of the English department in particular) we can focus our concern on what and how literature is taught at the university. Before St. Omer's work I am unable to find anything in my university study of English literature that is useful in helping me to comprehend and, as is claimed for English studies, deepen my experience of the work. We must see to it that our literature professors begin to pay attention to the reading of our own literature, to providing some of the climate in which our writers can fulfil their promise, by encouraging our scholarship boys to read our own writers, to react to our own experience at first hand.

JOHN WICKHAM

REVIEW: SHADES OF GREY
Bim vol 13, no. 49

On the other hand, the boyhood and young manhood recorded in Garth
St. Omer's *Shades of Grey* are unbelievable [the contrast is with Ian
McDonald's *The Hummingbird Tree*]. The book is really two short novels
–*The Lights on the Hill* and *Another Time, Another Place* but they might
easily have been one and better. They both present main characters
who are victims of a youthful frustration in a poor island society. The
facts of these characters' lives are recognizable but the whole picture
is confused and lacks credibility. One feels that although the events
which have been related may have happened (perhaps 'taken place' is
a better way of putting it) they are not true in the sense in which truth
resides, or ought to reside in any creative work. Abortion, casual and
meaningless sexual intercourse, introduced one suspects in an effort
to shock, succeed merely in boring. The thought processes of the characters
amount to no more than a dreary and pretentious verbalizing:

> He lay on the wall. It was good not to have to pretend, nor to inflict,
> unsubtly, the grossest pain and afterwards cover it with the salve of
> sentiments of a consideration he did not really feel. He saw how clearly
> the confession about Calixte and Peter, which he had never forgotten,
> had qualified his attitude to her, how insidiously it had worked to induce
> in him the conflict of malice, desire and revulsion. His entire relationship
> had been one repeated act of revenge as if the frequency of his visits
> were the whetstone he sharpened his vengeance upon, watching its blade
> become narrower, if keener, until there might be none left. But not even
> an extreme brutality of gesture or of word had been able to consume it.
> And he had gone to Berthe again and again like a penitent with the same
> sin, unforgiven, to the confessional. He had come out of that small room
> in her friends' house just as he had entered it, unable to find the release
> he sought there, in the depths between Berth's legs where he pushed
> to hurt, and returning always to push ever more deeply seeking for a
> calm and a release he should never find.

KENNETH RAMCHAND

"THE WEST INDIES"
The Journal of Commonwealth Literature,
December 1969. No. 8, pp. 80 -81

....A critique of island society and a sense of the impoverishment of
the new West Indian middle class are implicit in Garth St Omer's two
volumes, *A Room on the Hill* and *Shades of Grey*. But St Omer turns the
social situation inwards, following in an unspectacular but rhythmic
prose the twisted lines of the under-consciousness, the perverse fluxes
and refluxes of feeling, the tangled coils of history, culture, and personality
in the inner life of the benighted islands. In *A Room on the Hill*, John
Lestrade becomes increasingly uncertain of what men live by and for,
as he examines his own ambivalent feelings to his mother and best
friend, is surprised by his own cruelty and perverse emotions, and is
disillusioned by the cynicism and defeat of his countrymen now returning
with their degrees from metropolitan institutions. In 'The Lights on
the Hill', one of the two novels in *Shades of Grey*, Stephenson comes
to a West Indian university after years of drifting in the smaller islands
only to find an air of unreality and irrelevance at this centre of learning.
As he reviews his own life and meaningless liaisons he begins to question
the value of that achievement he has come to pursue at the University,
when compared with the possibilities of unthinking contentment in
his little island. The novel ends pessimistically with the tortured and
self-torturing Stephenson breaking with his girl friend Thea, and numbing
himself into a passive spectatorial role in an indifferent world. In 'Another
Place Another Time', St Omer turns to an earlier period in the history
of a young colonial: the selfless struggle of Derek's mother to get him
through secondary school never remains quite in the background as
St Omer explores the relentlessness with which Derek himself pursues
his ambition. At the end of the novel, he wins a coveted University
scholarship, and St Omer leaves the young man impatient to start a
new phase in his life. St Omer's growing pessimism is moderated by
an increasingly critical attitude to his inward-turned and self-concerned
heroes. And the flashback technique within each novel parallels the

way the *oeuvre* develops – each novel being set further back in the past. Derek's determination to *achieve* strikes the reader as bitterly ironic coming after both Stephenson's disillusion and Lestrade's vision of the returning scholars' frustration, cynicism, and imitativeness. The probe into what makes the modern West Indian (thematic level) and what makes a man (psychic insights) that St Omer is conducting with such delicacy, control, and economy must surely place him in the first rank of twentieth-century novelists…

JOHN HEMMINGS

"IMPOSSIBLE LOVE"
The Listener, May 8, 1969

… Quantitatively a short novel, qualitatively a short story, *Nor Any Country* tells of a West Indian's return from London to his native island, to his wife to whom he has grown indifferent, to his mother with whom he is no longer at ease, to his elder brother who has turned out a failure. There is little more to it than that: the discomfort of the repatriated expatriate, having 'no cause nor any country now other than himself'. Peter has made good, has 'had the best of two worlds' as his friend Colin tells him, but belongs to neither. Mr. St Omer has made a statement this time, not so much about contemporary Caribbean society, nor even about the psychological strains of displacement, as about what it is like to be hard, brilliant and conscience-ridden.

CAPITANCHIK, MAURICE.

"PRIVATE LIVES"
Spectator 222 (May 9, 1969): 620-621.

As the external world becomes more complex, and individuals more isolated, our chances of understanding each other become increasingly dependent on the communication of individual perceptions, the mutual intelligibility of our private worlds. It is perhaps for this reason that some of the most interesting of contemporary novels are in the form of confessional, either first person narrative or stemming from a main character, and it may not be quite accidental that the best two of this week's books are, respectively, in these forms.

Garth St Omer's short novels are distinguished by a quiet and unpretentious simplicity in which the situation of one man is precisely defined. His previous book, *Shades of Grey*, contained a story about a young man alienated by education from his people, the inhabitants of a small West Indian island; and Peter Breville, the central character of *Nor Any Country*, is a variant of the same person. In this deceptively undramatic story, Peter, having completed his studies in Europe, returns from the tension and hostility of the cities to the more relaxed, but almost as problematic, situation of home. As with the previous work, there is a haunting atmosphere of sadness, but the main weakness, a tendency to self-pity, has been eradicated. Through portraits of the subsidiary characters, Peter's discarded possibilities are gradually defined. He rejects his vivacious girlfriend Anna's hatred of European condescension; he realises that had he refused to marry his wife when she became pregnant, his brother's pathetic fate, failure and half-pretended madness, might have been his own. He is aware that he can never give himself, never really belong. Knowing he has "no cause nor any country", he nevertheless accepts his responsibilities.

Certain stylistic faults continue slightly to mar this author's work – an attempt to elaborate a naturally simple style makes the opening pages unclear – but on the whole this novel represents an advance in the development of a modest and honest author with little illusion about himself, whose patient wish to understand human predicaments is both interesting and significant.

ANON

BROTHERS IN INACTION
GARTH ST OMER:
J—, BLACK BAM AND THE MASQUERADERS
Times Literary Supplement 3678 (August 25, 1972): 985.

J–, Black Bam and the Masqueraders, in keeping with Garth St Omer's previous novels, is an ordered and circumspect book, deliberately understating its case and using a dry, spare prose which organizes the narrative line with precision and coolness. As before, Mr St. Omer sets his book in the Caribbean, though it is not his purpose to spend long on the evocation of place: the sort of colourful, touristy details which a visiting novelist might want to make use of. The islands make their mark, rather, in the effect their seclusion, their poverty, the narrowness of their culture and their social oddities have on the principal characters – two brothers, each afflicted by his background, each apparently about to be brought to grief. Paul, the elder of the two, remains trapped in the land of his birth, bitterly resentful and possibly approaching madness. Peter, who escaped, but to little purpose, has returned and is attempting to pick up the pieces of a shattered marriage, only to find that his emotional weariness is greater than his dexterity.

The novel is divided between Paul's letters to Peter – confessions, painful memories – and accounts of Peter's failing relationship with the wife he had abandoned. The passionless speech of these two, and the persistent sense of inaction, invests them with the notion of an emotional nullity: they have about them the air of men who see that the roof is about to collapse on them, but lack the willpower or concern to raise a protecting arm. The pointless but dogged persistence of both Peter, in his affair with a white girl, and his wife, in her jealous and desperate hounding of him, is well developed and perceptive in its emotional implications; it serves as a neat counterpoint to Paul's own disastrous involvement with a local girl; but there are times when reserve and nicety in language can manufacture their own kind of misjudgment, and a finicky way with language can produce chronic lapses in style. These are traps which Mr St Omer all too often falls into. We are told that a girl "played superbly the piano", of "a bar they sat on high stools before at three or four in the morning", of towns which seem "transformed by the wand of a fairy"; Paul writes on the "complexional variation" of the islanders, and tells how "maids made up our beds".

In a narrative which is trying to be remarkable for its orderliness and quiet sensitivity, that sort of carelessness stands out; and in the same way, the author's desire to circumvent action in order to sustain the investigatory tone of the book results, at times, in an accidental and jarring melodrama, as when Peter's wife is driven to violence by his adultery: "She put on a record then moved through the curtained doorway into the bedroom. Phyllis was there sitting on the edge of the bed. In one hand she held a stick..." The chapter ends on the ellipsis, the intention being, one assumes, to exclude the climactic. Instead, the expression given is of a burst of discordant music followed by an invitation to tune in to next week's gripping instalment.

EDWARD BAUGH

NOR ANY COUNTRY: GARTH ST. OMER
Bim 13:50 (January-June 1970): 128-130.

Those who have read Garth St. Omer's *A Room on the Hill* and *Shades of Grey* will know that, within the space of a year, a commanding talent has established itself. Now, in quick succession comes *Nor Any Country*, which, in certain ways, carries his craft nearer to perfection and assists in the bodying-forth of his view of things.

Those who have read the earlier works will also know, when they come to *Nor Any Country*, that they must not expect much in the way of plot or action. In this respect the novel is even more lean than its predecessors. There is next to nothing that would "make" the newspapers and hardly more that would attract the attention of the grapevine. The tremors and crises are all within and have to do with understanding and indifference, adjustment and isolation, desire and necessity, will and apathy, and so on. The excitement is in the weaving of the net which is the complex and inescapable tyranny of these abstractions. The method is largely one of implication and innuendo.

St. Omer scores his points with deft, delicate strokes, as in the last sentence of this brief paragraph:

> His glimpses of the rude Atlantic were more frequent. They were on the coast. They passed through small villages consisting of huts on either side of the main road. The big car, unwieldy in the hills, sped over the flat, coastal road and, passing through the villages, was as obvious, and as prestigious, as a priest's cassock.

The resonance of that sentence (we shall not carp at "prestigious") sounds, sharply but without noisiness, not only through this book but also through *Room* and *Shades*. For one of St. Omer's preoccupations is with the influence of the Church in those islands of the Eastern Caribbean which are, like his native St. Lucia, almost exclusively Roman Catholic. The equating of the cassock with the big American car, so incongruous in such a setting, provokes the thought that the priests, regarded by the society as being so much a part of itself, are also incongruous. The simile, too, equates priest and car as images of "the bitch-goddess Success" which the society worships to its discomfort and which is another theme running through these novels.

Later, in *Country*, the car will take us into a village where we shall meet a young native priest, a good and humble man, who drifted into the priesthood by default as it were, in order to avoid a complete frustration, and whose mother, for whom he represents Success as much as anything else, obsequiously calls him Father, while she speaks to him about his father.

Another fine example of the St. Omer touch occurs when the chief character is reliving his feelings of relief at having left Europe:

> Already, he was aware of an absence of tension and of strain. He had left the city and the special anonymity it conferred behind him. And the unknown woman, who did not know him, but who yet had recognised him sufficiently to whisper her greeting ("I see the niggers are here again") conspiratorially, out of tight lips before the Supermarket shelves, would have to look now for others to whisper her special greeting of recognition to. Peter smiled. For a long time he had believed he had remained personally inviolate within the skin he wore which everyone recognized, and that, in the anonymous city, he, too, could have remained anonymous.

I shall remember that whisper of hate long after I have forgotten whole novels about racial prejudice.

But I have nearly forgotten the "story". Peter Breville, Ph.D. ("not a real doctor," he has to explain to the worshipful and befuddled peasant woman), returns for a brief visit to his native island. He had been able to "escape" some years before, thanks to a scholarship to the university "in the larger island to the north." From there he had gone on to Europe for post graduate studies. Now he is en route to a post at the university where he had been an undergraduate.

In the first chapters he reflects on what life in Europe had meant for him, on the nature of the release which it had afforded him, but which was not enough to negate the sense of alienation which makes him eventually leave it. This reflection is effected through reminiscences of the two women whom he had loved there. They and the city in which he had loved them serve to highlight his reactions to the island when he returns.

After this point, the return, I experienced, initially at least, some disappointment. The first two chapters were fully in the dominant mode of *Room* and *Shades* – the protagonist very introspective, shuttling backwards and forwards in time, lifting layer after layer of memory. In this mode the consciousness of the protagonist is, in effect, as much an object of our scrutiny as is the environment, which we experience through that consciousness. But after Chapter 2 of *Country*, the focus is almost exclusively on the society, and we lose most of the interest of probing with the protagonist into his own self.

The bulk of the novel, then, is simply a record of Breville's observations and feelings during his few days on the island. He is now able to distinguish most clearly the complex of pressures and weaknesses, in the society and in himself, from which he had fled. He looks squarely at his responsibilities and involvement, at his fears and guilt: but the main impulse of the writing is towards a portrait of the island society. The truthfulness of his view of the island is evident as much in the compassion which informs it as in the sharp-edged exposure of the society's faults.

The compassion is alive in the very fact that the complex nuances of the problem are so astutely realised, without any facile diagnoses or anxiousness to prescribe. We are made to think constantly about blame and responsibility, but it is never easy to station them decisively. The characters, in contrast with one another, manifest the multiplicity of choice possible in the given situation. And each choice, however opposite to that of the protagonist, however pathetic or selfish, is viewed with a cool sympathy. Each has a validity of its own. Consequently, although there is no attempt at comprehensive or detailed characterisation, we are left with a sense of each character's innate individuality (even in succumbing to convention).

I suppose that what I am trying to say is that St. Omer's view of the West Indies is ultimately more sensible, more "real" than most of the views of the propagandists and pundits whose novels I have read. His approach to his subject is a welcome relief from the usual ostentatious, self-indulgent, "angry" exorcising of the ghosts of the past. I cannot get out of my head a passage in which Breville, as he drives through the countryside, reflects on a former governor of the island:

> The rough Atlantic, almost continually glimpsed now, soothed a little his remembered uneasiness. It might have been by the sudden precipitous lift of rock at one end of the small beach they had just passed that a Colonial Governor of slave times had sat, alone, on his horse, in the desolate and early morning majesty he described in his diary, lamenting his loneliness and yearning to look again at the Channel coast of England. Duty, so he had written, compelled him to stay on the island, a bachelor, pacing the verandah of Government House night after night, unable to sleep, alone, forced, for administrative reasons, to keep himself aloof both from his compatriots whom he commanded and with whom he had more than a skin in common and from the creole landowners and businessmen with whom, he had written, a skin was all he shared. And he had died, that dutiful and principled man, worn out by disease and by his efforts to preserve justice on the island, ironically, within the sphere of a greater injustice he had nowhere in his diary questioned.
> The road turned inwards again and began to climb once more.

Whatever is meant by wisdom is in that passage. It loses nothing of the many-sided reality of history. Here is compassion which is not achieved at the expense of honesty or rage. It was a fine insight which made Breville identify with the governor, without detracting from his awareness of the governor as other than an enemy. Separated by great gulfs of time, of class and colour, they are yet bound together by a deep humanity. I am reminded of the closing lines of Walcott's "Ruins of a Great House":

> And still the coal of my compassion fought:
> That Albion too, was once
> A colony like ours...
> All in compassion ends
> So differently from what the heart arranged:
> 'as well as if a manor of thy friend's...'

But I could commend St. Omer enough simply by saying that he writes a rare and masterly prose. He is one of the few people who can exploit the possibilities of quintessential prose. Prose, when it is most itself, is capable of rhythmic subtleties which are quite alien to verse. Most prose which catches the ear and has the stamp of personality is something which is on the way to being verse. For example, when we delight in the prose of the Authorized Version of the Bible, we are delighting in it because it is to some degree "poetic". Consequently, it is not surprising that poetry is popularly thought of as being a higher form of writing than prose. Some people would no doubt distinguish between the two by saying that poetry is prose-and-something-more. This could well be true; but the fact that most people who write can write passable prose, while few of those who attempt poetry achieve even passable verse, is no reason for prejudging the question.

I recently read an undergraduate paper in which the writer, ostensibly explaining Wordsworth's theories, writes: "There is an excitement received from poetry which is not in prose." True; but there is also an excitement received from prose which is not in poetry. St. Omer's prose can generate that excitement. He has been assiduously refining his style and getting rid of the marks of strain, the clumsy, contorted postures which sometimes result from his effort at simplicity. He is so much in command of himself now that there are even faint hints that he is in danger of indulging himself. I hope that I am mistaken.

JOHN ROBERT LEE

"PETER PLAYS FOR PAUL"
REVIEW OF J—, BLACK BAM AND THE
MASQUERADERS
Tapia, Vol 4 No. 5, February 3, 1974

J—, Black Bam and the Masqueraders is, without doubt, Garth St. Omer's finest achievement to date. The promise showed in *Syrop* (a novella published by Faber in 1964) and in the first three novels finally comes to mature fruition. The other novels were *A Room on the Hill* (1968), *Shades of Grey* (1968) and *Nor Any Country* (1969). In evidence immediately in *J—, Black Bam and the Masqueraders* is maturity, great control, highly developed technique. Here the themes of the first three novels find a unique fusion.

There is that continuing concern with the West Indian growing out of his society through his education, the resulting crises in personality this colonial education produces; there is his examination of the role of the church in the society; there is, too, exploration of the class/colour prejudice that grew out of the effects of the education received and the result of having white French priests in positions of power in the church. All these themes play out the pattern of the novel which goes on for only 109 pages, a technical achievement.

As usual in St. Omer there is no conventional story-line, plot or characterisation. But by the end of the novel one has a strong sense of situation and individuals. It carries on where *Nor Any Country* left off, is an essential epilogue to the other three novels, but can stand firmly on its own.

In *J—, Black Bam and the Masqueraders* our two main protagonists are Paul and Peter Breville. Paul is the brother of promise who never escaped from his island society, and Peter is the brother who escaped and later returns. At present, Peter is working at the university on another island. He has taken there with him his wife Phyllis and his brother's son, Michael, and together they are trying to pick up the threads of an existence they had barely had together before he left for Europe.

As we saw at the end of *Nor Any Country*, his return only symbolises a further and perhaps more important departure into self, which has now become a dominant theme in the progression of St. Omer's writing. The search for self is a hard one as we see husband and wife facing the turmoil of disenchantment, extramarital excursion, professional frustration, age.

Paul's failure leads from one depth into another. His escape has also been into himself. But it has led only to despair, the masquerade and madness, his only means of survival:

> '...we need to perform. Otherwise our world ends. For we have become both actor and audience and to end our performance is to remove the need for both and annihilate ourselves.
> 'They say I'm mad. I know it's only that I have chosen a way to live with my confusion and with the pain that results from my inability to resolve it'.

St. Omer's early major theme of frustration in a small society governed by a strict triangular code of sin/guilt/punishment is fused here in Paul. This is again enhanced by the tone of the confessional, now given final, climactic presence in the form of letters from Paul to Peter. (Letters which, of course, will not be sent). His whole life now is one of expiation for the sin of defiance he had made to the society several years before. Too proud to give in, his letters trace his downfall and his search for a way to live with himself and his society.

The first chapter of the novel, labelled 'Paul to Peter', shows the young Paul asserting his confidence after victory of a sort. Dissatisfied with the meal his mother has prepared, he rails unkindly at her. We can be certain that this kind of thing must have happened several times, in whatever different forms.

Paul, like the other St. Omer protagonists, has been created anew by the educational requirements of his society. Even his stern father has to acknowledge the forces at work on his sons:

> ...college had given us a special immunity against his disapproval. The initiative was passing away from him to you and me. Increasingly, our loyalties, our obedience, were not to him, but to something else, a new authority that existed outside of the house and which he, too, respected but apprehended only vaguely.

Contempt for his fellows, which is essentially a self-contempt, grows quickly. His education (preparing him for codes and values foreign to him) separates him quickly from them.

> They were not professionals – not doctors nor lawyers – and they were not white. And I did not therefore wish to become what they were. (p. 34/ 56)

He refuses to play in the school steelband, aware the negative values it represents to the society. It was local and therefore inferior. He does not want to share these values with former elementary school friends to whom he no longer speaks.

> And daily I walked the streets, and measured my potential distance above, and my growing superiority to them. I would not play in the steelband to be enclosed by them, or by their friends. (p. 34/ 56)

The self-contempt that is below the contempt for those around him is well illustrated in the example of the usurper ejected from the church pew. Already there are potentially dangerous schizophrenic signals in Paul's dual identification with usurper and usurped:

> ...it was always with regret that I watched the usurper get up and walk away. I wanted him to continue to be defiant, to refuse absolutely to move. I wanted to see him carried bodily out of the pew by the church orderlies, perhaps be clubbed by the truncheons they carried and which I have never seen them use. For I know, sitting in the pews reserved for us, that I, like him, was a usurper, and it was my own defiance that I wished had been total. It was myself that I watched going shamefacedly down the aisle.
> I was always disappointed. No matter how long he remained obdurately sitting in the pew, the usurper always got up in the end and walked sheepishly away. And, always, it was myself that I watched self-justifiedly taking the place he had vacated for me. I knew that, in a few years, I would insist, even more forcibly than those I observed, that every usurper remove himself to make room for me. (p. 38-39)

There is already too, in Paul, that desperate need to gain favour from the whites and mulattoes of Columbus Square; not at any cost to be identified with the black mass following the steelband his brother Peter plays in.

Growing recognition as a sportsman brings a fierce desire for acclaim, especially from his parents. But it is only the failures that are taken notice of. (A feature of W.I. society already given prominence by Naipaul.) Like the society around him Paul's father's

> notions of success and failure could only be based on standards that were not his own. And for him, it was the public response to my performance that became the determinant. But neither he, nor the public, had the knowledge which made all performance relative. For me to appear to fail, therefore, no matter what the circumstances, was always to incur his and the public's disapproval, and his sarcastic comments in the house. (p. 50)

His relationship with Patsy, commencing after his return from a neighbouring island where he has been a success, is one of vented frustration and anger. Patsy is for him, like the others, only an object of contempt. He admits that 'it had always been her body, only that I wanted'. The sordidness of his short uninvolved affair leads to the beginning of disaster. On the 'threshold of success,' all is lost as Patsy becomes pregnant. The sin is committed and the triangle closes around him.

It is the notion of respectability shared by Mr. Breville and Patsy's mother that makes her demand marriage from Paul. His confidence in his ability to move beyond the old ready-made solution makes him refuse. But getting no help from Patsy, who sees no other way of solution but the old and time honoured, he is doomed to failure. Before he leaves Patsy's mother's house, to which she had summoned him, he asks her daughter to come and live with him.

> It was a sudden and impulsive suggestion. But, and I can see that even more clearly now, it held out more hope for the survival of the two of us. Patsy hesitated. (p. 83)

And she chooses her mother. Because his pride will not let him change his mind, he is now at odds with society, and threatening it. We are reminded here of Stephenson in *Shades of Grey* who, in a similar situation, likens himself to a runaway slave in the hills.

> They had been fighting (for their freedom) a system that had seemed no less logical than the one he saw himself, in his dreams, fighting now. They had been defeated because, being against the system, they had to be. And he, too, since he could see no way of escaping, would have been defeated as well. (*Shades,* p. 106)

Stephenson, in a sense, is lucky, where Paul is not. For Paul never escapes, caught by his own pride and contempt; but in a larger sense, caught in the greater closed circle the society itself has created, since his education in the society provided the contempt and pride that destroys him.

Losing his job at the Catholic college where he teaches, he refuses jobs he considers below his worth. Finally, there is nothing more to refuse. He feels humiliated, blackmailed, and punished. And he becomes aware of the value system used by the totally Roman Catholic society to judge itself:

> I saw that the whole town accepted the idea of sin, guilt, punishment. (p. 97)

He succumbs to the 'squat, ugly edifice crouching in middle of the town' and goes to church every day a year. It is after one of the masses he has attended that he comes upon J— and Black Bam who provide him the way to live with himself.

In his last 'letter', we discover how Paul learns live with 'his confusion and the pain that results his inability to resolve it'. He tells us that:

Eager to convince, we intensify our posturing until the impersonation we intended as reality for others begins to assume reality for us. We play less and less for those who watch us and, in the end, it is ourselves that we fool. It is then that, more than ever, we need to continue to perform. Otherwise our world ends. For we have become both actor and audience and to end our performance is to remove the need for both and annihilate ourselves.

He begins the masquerade of madness:

When I decided to become mad, it was to preserve my identity whole for myself that I reflected its bits for others to look upon. (p. 93)

Paul identifies with J—. Both have been college boys, well educated, with all the attributes of that education such as contempt for those 'below' them, and both have become, in their own way, failures. (We are not told why J— has failed). It is through the degradation of Black Bam, as black as his name, that J— earns his money. And Paul, watching the drama being played out, understands,

the extent of his [J—'s] contempt for all those whom he performed for. They, nor I, existed for him. (p. 102)

To Paul is revealed an actor and his audience, both contained in the one man. An exclusion of everyone outside himself is the mark of supreme contempt.

It was if I had come face to face with contempt suddenly and for the first time. I who thought I knew it so well. (p. 102)

And he decides

I felt that I too, to survive, would need to be as contemptuous as J— had been.

For Peter, Paul's brother, the journey to self-discovery that commenced in *Nor Any Country,* continues. The past of that novel has given way to a present that is ugly. His wife, Phyllis, single-minded in her possessiveness of him, follows him everywhere, waits for him outside his mistress' home, allows herself to be brutalised by him. His entreaties to her to return to their island home, taking their child and nephew with her, have no effect.

Phyllis is a creature of instinct created by the narrow island society. A mulatto, unreleased by education, she knows only her simple basic desires of self-preservation; hers is an unsophisticated approach to her desire, which here is directed solely at Peter.

Yet their early days on the university island had been happy together. Becoming more and more discontented with his job, Peter begins to see his purpose in life as that of making Phyllis happy. But gradually, the relationship disintegrates as their differences in educational achievements begins to make itself felt. Phyllis is 'impatient with ideas and unwilling or unable, to deal with them'. Her unconcern with events in the world around and beyond them makes him begin to regard her as 'incomplete and ill-equipped' to be his wife. More and more he becomes irritated by her claim on him.

> He was struck by a quality he thought he detected that was much like arrogance in the assurance with which she had waited once before, and waited again now, for him to come to her. p. 70

His relationship with Jeannine, a French lecturer, begins. Phyllis' pregnancy only makes things worse as she refuses to abort. Things finally come apart when he decides to move into a room by himself. From then on, their life consists of quarrelling and fighting. At the end, with age making itself apparent, the situation is unchanged, and hope seems to rest for Peter and Phyllis in the baby suckling at her mother's breast.

Peter's continuing awareness of the limitation in the society around him is one of the indications of a deeper search within himself for something valid to him. Early in the novel, he says of Emancipation and Independence:

> The slaves had not acquired one, nor the island governments the other. But they had made of another's expedient concession their own achievement and were proud of it. We are like children... mindlessly imitating adults, informing our fantasy with total and high seriousness. We not only make cakes out of mud. We eat them as well. We are so busy imitating others that we have no time to do anything of our own. p. 14

At the end of the novel, this theme returns. Standing in front of a mirror, he suddenly becomes aware of the ravages of time on him. He remembers an opera he had been to see two days before, done with the island's black performers. The incongruity reminds him of a picture he had seen of slaves dressed up in their masters' old clothes.

> Peter had the sense of an absurdity, of children gathering about them the adult clothes they wore and hobbling smilingly about in too-large shoes, pleased with themselves. (p. 109).

Peter and Paul Breville are, finally, portraits of the greater West Indian dilemma. Each recognising the shortcomings of the society, a direct heritage of the colonial experience, and each, working his way toward resolution of the great psychosis. Paul, representative of one kind of West

Indian, 'copping-out'; Peter, not copping-out, but unable to find, within himself, the resources necessary to see beyond the obstacles.

St. Omer's novels are all portraits of the West Indian dilemma, viz., that lack of true, meaningful identity. All his characters, major as well as minor, seek in their ways to live with an emptiness that has always, in their experience, been there. St. Omer himself seems unable to offer anything more than hope for a better future; and nowhere is that primary vacuum filled. A change of society, a 'change of mind', babies, are all only hopeful efforts.

In the most intense sections of this intense novel, one senses strongly the presence of the author. Attacks on the church, on the selling of land which means that the people have now even less than before, these are vehement protests registered by St. Omer himself. But generally, the style and technique of the author is tightly controlled, allowing the characters and subjects to present themselves to the reader. Whatever solutions that seem offered are proposed almost casually, and as a logical progression of the novel's development.

As in so much else, St. Omer here has achieved a virtuosity in style that should put him among the top craftsmen in the West Indian novel. His favourite technique, that of the flashback, is no longer exasperating in parts as formerly. Evident, now, is a clear transition between events and time boundaries. The form of 'confession' that was evoked through the flash-back sequence reaches perfection in the letters of Paul to his brother.

A kind of total involvement is acquired with chapters being headed with the names of characters. As their chapters are part of the whole of the novel, so are the characters inseparable components in one scheme.

His prose, (made almost 'poetic' in its excursions into the human condition of suffering 'for the sins of the fathers') makes the harsh reality of these islands almost romantic in its telling. There is compactness. St. Omer wastes no words as he sketches directly, and without fuss, his particular portraits of these wretched of the earth.

One wonders whether a symbol is at work in the names Peter and Paul. From the beginning, St. Omer has been strongly anti- the Roman Catholic Church that has dominated the lives of his people; and here one can perhaps see irony in the fact that this Peter and Paul are certainly no saviours of men or holders of the keys to any particular heaven. If this is to be so, as they move through trauma after trauma, then it will be in the future. But one is not given much encouragement here. They can hardly survive day-to-day living themselves.

The baby suckling at Phyllis's breast seems a symbol of hope residing only in the future generations, a very pessimistic view.

He heard her footsteps begin to follow him and the sound of the baby suckling her breast. (p. 109)

The sound of Phyllis footsteps, terrifying in their persistence, is almost deathlike in its echoes, and this gives sombre tones to the possible symbol of hope suggested in the baby. So even the future (perhaps depending on the devil's child) is seen pessimistically.

Drawing as it does so completely on the author's own island, St. Lucia, it should make interesting and revealing reading to St. Lucians. Perhaps even more than to many other West Indians who have not the peculiar form of Catholic society that is in St. Lucia. The novel, and Garth St. Omer's earlier work, can be found in bookstores around the island.[1]

Endnote

1. A sad reflection of negative change is that in 2018 St. Lucia has very few functioning bookshops, and even sadder that these bookshops (carrying only school textbooks) do not carry St. Omer's novels.

SURVEYS

JOHN ROBERT LEE

GARTH ST. OMER: AN INTRODUCTION TO HIS NOVELS
The Voice (Artbeat), 27th April 1985

Garth St. Omer's novels made their unobtrusive appearance in the West Indies during the late sixties and early seventies, years of great social upheaval in the English-speaking West Indies. Up now, they have been largely ignored, despite the fact that they examined the very aspects of the society that young intellectuals and revolutionaries were revolting against during those years.

In a unique way in West Indian literature, St. Omer examined honestly and courageously the kind of culture that produced the rebels of the seventies. St. Omer, in an uncomfortable way, laid bare the very roots of the colonial society that had caught up with itself by the early seventies. Despite the fact that his novels were set in the late forties and fifties, the revolutionary fervour of those years had done little to change the essential condition that he had explored. And if today, in the eighties, much has changed externally, there still remains the exploration of the small-island psyche which the sensitive reader will recognize as truthful.

These novels show the West Indian intellectual growing out of his colonial education, carrying with him the self-contempt, the envy of the upper and whiter classes, the desire for recognition and acceptance by them, which were the direct results of that education. The characters he selects as his protagonists are men from the 'roots', the very masses that the black powerists had claimed they were trying to liberate. They have all had a chance to get a secondary education and in some cases have attended a university which places them at odds with their society, which has not prepared itself for the kind of person it has made into one of its foremost status symbols – the educated man. Not just the degreed social climber, proud of his own place among the new middle classes, but the truly educated individual, who is determined to apply what he has learned at university towards bringing real change to his community. This kind of graduate destroys the safe view of conservative power structure and threatens it. As well, he frightens the simpler folk, who demand that he hold the traditional place reserved for him.

In the novels of St. Omer, this dilemma lies at the roots of frustration and pessimism, and as one character puts it, behind "the relentless pursuit of futility". Part of the reason for this trapped situation is fact that the society will not allow its educated, its symbols of the "bitch-goddess Success," to be otherwise but what they have become. Stephenson in *Shades of Grey* (1968) speculates:

> He had told himself that he was merely that which, ever since his birth and without his having any say at all, he had been tending to become. Now, talking actually to himself as he walked, he wondered whether it was not too simple an explanation.

In the later *J—, Black Bam and the Masqueraders* (1972), probably his finest novel, the character chides Peter "for wanting to pretend that he was what he was no longer and, after the education he had received, would never again become."

St. Omer remained obsessed throughout his four novels with this type of colonial product, the West Indian intellectual, of which each different protagonist is a facet.

In his novels the strong influence of the Roman Catholic Church is obvious. This priest-influenced society was the place from which his characters try desperately to escape. The church society (much more influential then than today,) provided those triangular barriers that all the characters in the novels found themselves caught within: sin, guilt and punishment. It is so all embracing that Paul in *Black Bam* is forced finally to realize:

> I saw that the whole town accepted the idea of sin, guilt and punishment.

Pervasive also were the class and colour prejudices. In the setting of St. Omer's novels, the true holders of power were the white French priests, the people with the big houses who could afford to pay their sons' way to university, who could afford first-class funerals, who (in those days) lived around Columbus Square, who were white and mulatto.

The teachers at the secondary schools were also white in those days, but Irish, Brothers and Sisters who had no qualms about putting expediency before morals. The educational system of these schools, structured originally for white boys in England, created the now-stereotyped white men in black face

During the period in which St. Omer's novels are set, they were very much a power, no matter how idiosyncratic, in West Indian society. In St. Omer's work, this colonial education prepared the destruction of every character. It created the famous figure of existential literature, the alienated man. The system created contempt for former classmates left behind in the elementary schools. It created, destructively, a fatal self-contempt. These things seem distant now. Those prejudices have been exchanged for other kinds of separation.

St. Omer's novels are an intense exploration of the psyche of West Indians at a particularly painful period of their colonial history. It was the twilight of Empire and the dawning of the era of Independence. It was a time of death and the frustration of his characters, their lostness, their deliberate, self-conscious madness, become in retrospect, a powerful and sad metaphor of that time.

Saint Lucia (never mentioned by name,) is the source of the experiences that the novelist has observed and himself experienced, as a sensitive child of that past age. In our local literature, St. Omer is our international novelist. It is perhaps of some significance that most of our newer writers have chosen verse as their medium rather than prose. St Omer's work is a valuable fictional record of the past, but patient rereading of his work will probably reveal that his concerns with the human frustration of potential in our self-limiting societies still remain relevant and revealing to a new generation of readers.

PATRICIA ISMOND

THE ST LUCIAN BACKGROUND IN GARTH ST OMER AND DEREK WALCOTT
Caribbean Quarterly, Vol. 28, No. 1/2,

This paper examines the influence of the St Lucian background in the works of Garth St Omer (1931-) the novelist, and Derek Walcott (1930 -2017) poet and dramatist – the two important writers that island has produced. In taking this approach, I begin from the following premise: while the West Indies constitute one region, sharing the issues of history, race and the colonial legacy, the various islands were left each with its distinct, local variety of the general predicament. From one to the other, varying factors combined to leave each with its own colonial mould. This distinct character of each writer's native territory goes a long way towards explaining the particular leanings and imperatives which distinguish the individual talents of our writers.

A close attention to the influence of their respective island origins, for example, sheds important light on one primary area of difference between West Indian writers: the difference between those who give priority to the public, collective engagement; and those for whom the private mission takes precedence. Brathwaite and Lamming of Barbados are examples of the first, while the two St Lucian writers fall into the second group. It is precisely this 'private' orientation – an original link between the two St Lucians – that I hope to trace back to its origins in their island background. I am not concerned with the critical polemics of the question of 'public' versus 'private'; but I hope to suggest that this kind of attention might yield a sensitive critical appreciation of the relevance and value of both strains.

The private bias is conspicuous in both writers, and underlies their positions, although obvious differences in scope and preoccupation distinguish them from each other. Walcott remains committed to an interiorised, self-exploratory quest, despite his recent departure into full-scale public and social comment. St Omer speaks through a protagonist who, reappearing in various permutations of one essential crisis, is an alienated consciousness turned inwards on itself. Within this self-reflective context, national and political concerns are either absent or at best secondary. Both Walcott and St Omer, in fact, assert their priorities with a controversial thrust. Shabine, the Walcott persona in "The Schooner *Flight*", takes flight with this resolve: "I had no nation now but the imagination."[1] St Omer's protagonist in *Another Place Another Time* makes this defensive assertion of selfhood: "He had no cause nor any country now other than himself."[2] This characteristic position has left both writers open, in varying degrees, to the charge of non-involvement.

In order to properly "place" these emphases in St Omer and Walcott, it is necessary to begin with a brief survey of the character of the society in which these writers grew up, and the specific historical and sociological forces that helped to mould it. The single most dominant shaping force was Roman Catholicism: St Lucia remains over 90 per cent Catholic from colonial times to the present. Poverty, colonial neglect, isolation – the typical small island package – conspired to give the Catholic Church a monolithic, disproportionate presence. The Catholic Church got a head-start from the very first effort at settlement, which was undertaken by the French in the 18th century. A contingent of French priests accompanied the planters to inculcate discipline in the slave population. The subsequent course of the island's history, from which it emerged a British colony, helped in many ways to consolidate the Church's position. Throughout the 19th century, the English and French fought for possession of the island, prized as a strategic military base, in the imperial, naval battles of the period. It changed hands between them thirteen times.[3] The island had, however, seen its longest spell of development while in French hands, and the French legacy survives in the patois which is still the language spoken by the majority of St Lucians. The final settlement on the British was, in this respect, an anomalous situation. But, more critically, the British had inherited a liability which had long outlived its sole value. The island was thus relegated to neglect, and to the more tepid, nondescript forms of colonial administration.

What remained of the white imperial presence found its exclusive repository in the Catholic Church; a small French creole elite secluded itself, and lived close under the shelter of the Church. To all intents and purposes it was the Catholic Church that played the key role in transmitting and establishing the codes and values of the alien culture. Its main business was, of course, to institutionalise religion: the island was indentured to religion primarily, and its effects on the mentality and predispositions of the people have died hard, as St Omer's works illustrate most fully. It was Catholicism at its most conservative and paternalistic. With it came a rigid code of orthodox morality, which regulated the manners and mores of the small community.

The influence of the Church extended to every sphere of the island's secular life, its public and domestic affairs. St Omer sums up the entire picture when one of his characters rails against French priests who, in an

English colony, never bothered to learn to speak the official language properly. To fully appreciate this monopoly, we need to refer back to the other missing half of the equation. Under the Crown Colony system, which virtually amounted to a kind of political absenteeism in the poorer islands, political life in St Lucia remained virtually neuter, nil. St Lucia is among the very few islands which produced none of the political tremors, labour unrest, which characterised the social climate of the late forties and the fifties. The Church fitted readily into this vacuum: theocracy arrogated the role of political and civic system, to govern over its few essential institutions and general social conduct.

It held absolute control over the Board of Education, for example. Both primary and secondary education were in its hands; the only two secondary schools, a College and Convent, were run by Irish religious orders. While the pattern is not peculiar to St Lucia, it is significant that the situation obtained well into the seventies. Education in the hands of the Church meant a heavy content of religious and moral instruction. From this base, its censorship extended into the limited cultural activity in the island. As late as 1958, the Church was in a position to prevent the production of Roderick Walcott's play *The Banjo Man* (1976),[4] which had to wait until 1971 for performance at Carifesta. The Church guarded jealously its prerogatives. In these circumstances, it is not surprising that the revivalist sects which sprang up in islands with a significant Protestant component never took root in St Lucia.

It is within this context – the stranglehold of religion in the life of the island – that we are to understand the common orientation of both writers. Walcott, growing up as a Methodist, belonged to a marginal Protestant minority. This fact only served to sharpen his awareness of the Catholic stronghold: his work provides ample evidence of this. St Omer is himself of Catholic background. Both start with an iconoclastic mission, compulsively aimed at the religious establishment. They enter the mainstream of protest in a direct quarrel with the betrayals and deceptions of the religion of the master: what Walcott terms "one race's quarrel with another's God".[5] Religion becomes the first battlefront of the fight for freedom (the affinity to James Joyce's *Portrait of the Artist* has been well noted in both cases). Thus Afa, the hero of Walcott's *Sea at Dauphin* (written *circa* 1952), declaims against the religious servitude that keeps the small village resigned to "dirt and prayers". St Omer's returning professional meets its sinister shadow in every scene he revisits: the wasted lives of the poor, the series of strained, disordered relationships in a small community bemired in its customs and codes.

The converse of this quarrel with religion is of utmost importance. The confrontation with the imposed religion impels both writers to the quest for a liberating faith, in a basic preoccupation with the wider crisis of belief. And, as men of their times, they find its sole battleground, access, in the individual consciousness. They set out committed to an interiorised quest to reclaim self. Obviously, they have no new or exclusive preserve on this particular access. My argument is that this is where they stake their first claims.

So that, in a sense, it is possible to see them as never having recovered from their island's religious dispensation. Throughout the early stage represented by *In A Green Night* (1962), Walcott's concern with the various facets of colonial oppression resolve into the issue of belief, and it is implicit in his conception of his role as castaway. This explains a lasting reluctance to accord first place to public imperatives (until he becomes well-seasoned in the Trinidadian climate). St Omer's fictional heroes maintain a defensive solipsism which is one of the symptoms of their traumatic route through unbelief. The St Lucian Catholic, non-political combination outlined above does lie at the root of this bias. We find, significantly, an opposite tendency in the writers from a primarily Protestant background: they lean towards a public/political, collective approach. This approach assumes an integral bond between the individual and communal growth, the latter being an inbuilt principle of the Protestant ethic. I intend no value judgments or apologia, but advance this merely by way of explanation. We turn now to St Omer and Walcott in turn to examine their approach, where it leads, and the ways in which it remains "engaged".

St Omer

There is one representative figure behind St Omer's four interlinked works of fiction, *A Room on the Hill* (1968), *Shades of Grey* (1968), *Nor Any Country* (1969), and *J—, Black Bam, and the Masqueraders* (1972). He is one of the first generation in his small island to make a breakthrough by way of secondary education and a scholarship which enables him to study abroad, and he is returning as the educated professional to take his "place" in the society. *Room on the Hill* presents its protagonist, John Lestrade, prior to departure, in a kind of anticipatory disillusionment with the prospect of achievement; and in *Another Place Another Time*, one of the two novellas in *Shades*, we go further back to the College days of Derek Charles to trace the growth of the single-minded determination to "escape" through education. Essentially these stories function as flashbacks in the total scheme, projecting the predestined course of one essential crisis – that of the professional returning home. The implicit effort to reconnect with his past environment is baulked at every turn, and he returns to a sense of acute exile at home. From this condition of isolation, he assumes the role of spectator, this twofold motif being expressed in the first title, "room on the hill".

Thus, he becomes enmeshed in a close network of family relationships, friendships, past associations. He moves in the flesh, incapable of quite cutting himself off from the ties that bind, but in spirit he lives and inclines elsewhere. From his position as spectator. However, the St Omer persona surveys the "several postures" of his small island with a clinical precision, which Gordon Rohlehr has aptly compared to Joyce's "scrupulous meanness".[6]

St Omer has the rare novelistic skill of deploying an introspective drama through a texture of sheer, stark, social realism. He presents a full portrait of the social, cultural, moral condition of the St Lucian environment, though the island is in fact never named. We get a close-up view of the small, cramped community of Castries, sharing its few, spare essentials – school, Church and its various observances; of its narrow range of occupations, small vendors/domestics, civil servants, teachers. The milieu is pervaded by a sense of privation. The one cultural force binding all classes together is conformism to religious custom, the norms and codes of Christian morality – which makes for a prevailing atmosphere of constraint.

The lower class, the stratum from which most of St Omer's characters come, is in the foreground. The familiar picture of unmarried mothers, bearing the brunt of child-rearing as best they can, prevails. The ill-effects of a life rigidly circumscribed by poverty and religion are accentuated in the characteristic postures of this class: passive endurance in degradation, conditioned to the norm of sacrifice, and dedication to the routines of piety. In the opening scene of *Room,* John Lestrade, visiting his mother's grave, meets the prototype of this class in the figure of Miss Amelie. Miss Amelie, an ageing spinster and something of an institution in the town, is still engaged in her lifetime's effort: selling Sweepstake tickets ("every booklet she sold entitled her to two free tickets"),[7] and praying. She is like the ghost of his bedridden mother, who had lain passive and prostrate in her lot, with her eyes averted in prayer, looking solely to the dim promise of the afterlife. Such images evoke the final spirit of a place where life-purposes are obviated, or curiously suspended, in a waiting for death. The mood is one of stasis, proneness. Poverty has a peculiarly 'ascetic' flavour in this setting, contrasting with a kind of vibrancy we find amidst the seething, violent desolations of the jungle and backyard scenes elsewhere in the region.

The Catholic code of sin and expiation exerts a strong, pervasive pressure, adding constricting and repressive influences. Guilt and shame dominate both private and public morality. Old Desauzay, another of the town's "characters" in *Room,* is one of the extreme casualties of the code. The middle-class mulatto had been dismissed from the Civil Service for theft, and had retreated since then from public disgrace to take up a permanent post: sitting still and vacant at his window, virtually lobotomized, immobilized in his "perpetual and unnatural expiation". Old Desauzay's weird paralysis is at the extreme end of the general malaise and deportment of the community: inwardly stifled, failing and succeeding according to the strenuous mores of respectability and propriety. St Omer's overall image is of a society of "robots", "automatons".

There is, however, a glaring discrepancy between these abstemious norms and the pattern of disordered, ill-assorted family arrangements, man-woman relationships, from which St Omer's protagonists originate and to which they return. It comes to the fore in his major concern with sons, mothers and fathers, and lovers. Pulling against the stringent sanctions of marriage, legitimacy, and the taboo against sex, we find a great deal of "irregularities". There is the common feature of fatherless homes already referred to members of the white privileged class often avail themselves of the right to keep two separate families, one legitimate, the other illegitimate and half-black, love relationships, courtships are forced into becoming mainly degrading, brutal affairs. The repercussions of the system have backfired, in effect to disrupt and despoil fundamental human ties – the links between the parent generation and the younger one, relations between men and women. John Lestrade, a "fatherless" son, grows up deeply and violently estranged from his father. The latter's image remains permanently tainted by the shame and rebuking tone with which his mother had treated his night-time visits: "You have your wife. You have no right here" (p. 30). This is one of the many cases of alienation between fathers and sons; and sons are no less alienated from their mothers, torn between dutiful pity, and revulsion at their condition. It is one of St Omer's major themes.

We get another kind of casualty in the case of Anne-Marie, who has broken away from her white upper-class background and now moves with the new elite of educated blacks. Her French creole father had adopted this illegitimate daughter by a black servant, and proceeded to buy her the privilege of legitimacy at the Convent, where the nuns maintained a system of double uniforms – one for legitimates, and the other for illegitimates. Anne-Marie's early discovery of the sham meant a violent break with her background, and she has drifted into the role of the hedonist, a lone, unlikely figure in St Omer's world.

The most obtrusive sphere of damage and disarray is in the love-sex relationships, which, driven underground, issue in primarily debased, unsavoury affairs, and in the series of failed, abortive marriages which recur in St Omer. We get the early pattern in the case of Derek Charles (*Another Place Another Time*). He becomes incapable of anything but a compulsive sexual aggression on his girlfriend Berthe, once he discovers that he has been cheated of her virginity. He persists defiantly against the threat of an unwanted pregnancy, despising both himself and Berthe for it. The institutionalization of the sex-taboo is the root cause of the double tragedy of the two brothers in *J—, Black Bam and the Masqueraders*. The Church, standing behind the education system, maintains a policy of firing young men in education who are responsible for unwanted pregnancies. Paul loses his teaching job and the chance of a future for refusing to marry the girl he made pregnant; Peter, who conformed to retain his chances, ends up trapped in a disastrous marriage. Other unnatural, sinister effects of the system are seen in the grotesque business of trying to give Ann-Marie a decent burial. Anne-Marie, who dies by accident while pursuing pleasure, is refused a Church burial. The situation registers in passing the absurd climate of a setting where funerals are the strongest index of privilege and status. The number of bells – and they resound from one end of the town to the other – announce first and second class citizens, and no bells, the ignominious status of the public sinner.

It is to this kind of environment that the St Omer protagonist returns to find little possibility of re-entry, and his implicit mission thwarted from the outset. Rather, the wretchedness and disfigurement he surveys seem to bespeak an essential hopelessness, and make one weary of all faith in the possibility of dignified, worthwhile, human endeavour. He borrows from Walcott to extend this overarching burden in his first epigraph: "Only the gulls, hunting the water's edge/Wheel – like our lives, seeking something worth pity" ("A Careful Passion"). These fatalistic intimations answer quite closely to the basic physiognomy of the setting: a place reduced to the elementals of poverty, distressed and abused by the errors of misguided 'civilizing' norms.

But, for the St Omer persona, it is not a matter of assuming the burden of the environment. The concern is with his subjective state, his psychic disability, and personal failure. Returning means disturbing the stigmas, stirring up the old propensities of his roots in an unchanged environment, and the maturation of these in his present inclinations towards futility. Stephenson, the representative hero in *The Lights on the Hill* (*Shades*), articulates this viewpoint: "You did not choose the circumstances of your birth, to be born, your parents or their condition. And yet nothing in your entire life could be more important" (p. 116). Memory, which accounts for a great deal of the action in St Omer's plotless works, is the main dynamic behind the persona's concern with his own maladjustment. In *Room*, John Lestrade sums up its central, informing purpose: "From his memory he had exhumed corpses of his old self, probing them with the scalpel of his new awareness, lifting his motives delicately out of their integuments to look at them" (p. 37).

Congenital insecurities and complexes rear up with these corpses. Stephenson coldbloodedly destroys the prospect of a hopeful relationship with Thea, his only stay in the general aimlessness of his life as a postgraduate student. He rakes up the most painful, humiliating details of a childhood of abject poverty, of theft and a jail sentence, intent on shocking her into disaffection. These abrasions remain unappeased. What is dredged up with Stephenson's action are the root-sources of a psyche preconditioned to failure, left with distrust of the prospect of happiness, and a pathological fear of the responsibility of happiness. It becomes perverted into a will to hurt. All St Omer's representative protagonists suffer from this deficiency, prefer transient relationships, and use sex for expediency or as temporary solace.

Yet, it is his very education – in the finest sense – equipping the St Omer persona with his "new awareness", that has served to sharpen his sensitivity to these "old corpses", ultimately to presage the various strains of his pessimism. St Omer gives a searching insight into the complex, ironic facets of education for our new class of intellectuals. He reflects both the pluses and the minuses, which are critically intertwined. Intelligence opens a huge gap between the new class and the mental bondage of their parents. This carries a positive, but is fraught with various shades of alienation. Not the least of these has to do with the acquired metropolitan prejudices which make the St Omer figure uncomfortable with the crudeness of the native accent, sensitive to the lack of etiquette and polish to which he returns. But its real burden for him is this: Intelligence puts him well in advance of his parents, to whose faiths he can, rightly, "never go back"; while, the same time, the strains of the past which he carries within himself hinder him from finding a route to the future. St Omer goes to Walcott for another epigraph to sum up the burden: "Irresolute and proud/I can never go back" ("Crusoe's Island").

Quietly monitoring the symptoms of his own paralysis, the St Omer persona withdraws into anonymity and non-involvement, which constitute his operative stance in his works. It leaves him capable of only inauthentic, externally dictated actions, or of such destructive actions as in the case of Stephenson cited above. The posture serves, on or level, as an insulation against the burden of responsibility. It is at the same time a morally determined choice, dictated by his inward preoccupation with futility. Speculation is his most purposive 'action' this affords him, and behind the impersonal tone of the spectator we hear the strains of "contemplative evacuation", to borrow Walcott's description of his role as Crusoe-castaway figure.

The burden of defeat, futility, which absorbs him, orients him towards a fatalistic view of existence in general. This philosophical strain in St Omer comes to the fore in a almost obsessive concern with death, which often intrudes into the world of his protagonists, to impinge on their consciousness. Commenting on this feature Rohlehr speaks of: "Contingencies that have nothing to do with environment... death, guilt, meaninglessness".[8] They are not, however, altogether extrinsic. Walcott's own words are pertinent here: "To be born on a small island, a colonial backwater, meant a precocious resignation to fate."[9] The signs are there in the early Walcott's precipitant concern with generic issues; and the roots of St Omer's 'death-sense' lie in the very psychology and climate of the environment, as should emerge from his own rendering of the scene. The deaths which confront St Omer's protagonists are all untimely, deaths of the young, from among their friends – all of promise and talent. Death endorses the sense of an indifferent irrational and even malevolent fate. Indeed St Omer's earliest novella *Syrop* (1964),[10] deals with this theme. Syrop is the one generous, loving spirit in a desolate family, the one taste of honey (which is what his name signifies in the local French patois) sweetening the bitterness around him. He goes diving for coins in order to give his brother, who returning from jail, a good homecoming, and is mutilated by the ship's propeller – one touch of goodness squashed and refuted by ultimate contingency.

We are all the time aware, to return to the St Omer persona, that the spirit withdrawn into this cocoon of anonymity, remains unappeased. He betrays the tensions and stresses of all his sterile, despairing sentiments and attitudes. He is, in fact, a victim, invalid, no figure of revolt. The malaise is expressed in strong impulses towards anaesthesia, and nonentity, a power-ful recurring motif in the works. St Omer extends this in few outstanding images which point to strong intuitional, even lyrical levels encompassed by this consciousness. These images are associated mainly with the sea. It serves, as Walcott, as a place of retreat from the human landscape. The image of "driftwood floating on the ocean" reappears in *Room* and *Shades* to sum up the protagonists' view of their plight: aimlessness, restlessness, inertness. The sea exerts a more potent influence, however, John (*Room*) and Stephenson (*Shades*) yearning to be "drenched in sea and sun" long for an atonement with the sea, to pass into its pure vacuous motion, free of human thought and emotion. Their sea is an ideal of a pre-human, insensate mode of infinity where they locate peace, freedom and the paradisal. It really amounts to a sublimated death-wish. There, at the extreme-limits of the will to inaction, where every negative is revised to a positive, we find the final fragility of the St Omer figure – the internalized absurdity that threatens his world, and the precariousness of the passive poise he maintains.

Thus, signals of madness and breakdown always hover at the edge of the world encompassed by this consciousness; and insanity becomes a central crisis in the last novel. The signals are placed with St Omer's usual tact. In *The Lights on the Hills* (*Shades*), Stephenson, busy arranging his own safety, is alarmed every so often by the solitary, strident scream from the lunatic asylum on the encircling hills. In *Room*, the overheard commotion of masquerading children clashes with the deepening stasis of John's situa-tion. It connotes delirium, and sounds like the furies. What emerges out of all this is that St Omer's hero is a figure vitally in need of cure and rehabilitation, too disoriented to begin to undertake his responsibility as a pioneer. This seems to me St Omer's overarching point of view, as the artist behind, while in, his creations.

St Omer's purpose, then, in dramatising this private drama, is strictly diagnostic and confessional. It is not prescriptive, and offers no solutions. His exposition highlights the problem and need for the individual liberation in relation to environment; and he does so with the inwardness and authority of one who himself belongs to an important contingent of the region's pioneers, the class of returning professionals/scholars. He presents with honesty the personal chaos of those awakening for the first time, and in their own innards, to the full nightmare of past and environment, and the difficulty of coping adequately with it. The message emerging is of houses that need to be set in order (quite literally in St Omer), before any viable contribution to change and a better society can be made. It is from this standpoint that Stephenson (*Shades*) expresses general scepticism towards *all* "group endeavour" (he is reacting to the then-current squabbles over the Federation); and he is speaking for St Omer.

In this context, it is important to note that there are definite positives against which St Omer adjudges this failure. This serves to sharpen the perspective. Peter Breville in *Nor Any Country* returns to confront the anachronism of that past to which the small community is still tied. It calls to mind the burden of an earlier discussion: "Your past as a people, shall have only begun with you, now." The void of the past from which he comes is featured in the total gap between himself and his parents. By the same token, the situation consigns him to a duty to a son, to father a legacy of intelligence, self-respect, creative relationships (none of which his own past could provide). Peter Breville drifts impassively into resuming his obligations to Phyllis, the girl who had trapped him into marriage, had been waiting eight years in his mother's home, and from whom he is totally estranged. The sequel, dramatised in *J* —, *Black Bam and the Masqueraders*, underlines the dialectic. The child who comes out of this abortive marriage is destined to be no better adjusted – which is the bleak, tragic image projected at the end of that novel. Critics so far have linked St Omer with Naipaul, in their common concern with exile and alienation. St Omer seems to me to start from an opposite end of the spectrum. Ralph Singh looks back from his position of exile to review the cultural morass that foredooms all action to fraudulence and self-deception. St Omer is concerned to expose the weight of a past that frustrates the very necessary will to action.

St Omer's final intention in probing this dilemma is humanistic. At a very integral level it is the search for a finer human possibility that has motivated the effort. This humanistic base remains the implicit frame of reference, obliquely invoked, of his essentially tragic resolutions. The pattern emerges complete in *J* —, *Black Bam and the Masqueraders*, his greatest achievement so far. The novel presents a new formal organization of his typical method and content, which work together to crystallize this humanistic intention. It consists of the alternating case-histories of the two brothers, Peter and Paul Breville. Paul, whose prospects of achievement had been dashed by the society, had remained behind to go mad. Peter, the successful brother lecturing in "the larger island to the north" is undergoing another kind of collapse in a mutually destructive life with his wife, Phyllis. The latter personifies all the most intractable "skeletons" of the past; she is devoid of any ambition or resources, save a single-minded pursuit of salvation in "marrying well". Paul's story unfolds in his letters to his brother, which serve mainly as personal release, and will never be sent. The style is emotionally charged and intense. Peter's is third person narration, characterised by the impersonal tone of St Omer's withdrawn protagonists. Both in tone and situation, the two brothers are doubles of each other. In the scheme of the novel, these two tragic alternatives are reduced to one basic crisis.

Paul, punished for defying the society's code, opts out into despair and social contempt. He comes to depend on a pose of madness to assert an identity, and ends up its victim: "I know now that it is only we, the serious uncertain masqueraders... who commit excesses... the impersonation we intended as reality for others begins to assume reality for us" (p. 93). We hear, in the case of Peter and Phyllis, of silently violent beatings, as Phyllis deliberately immolates herself against him in retaliation for his affair with an expatriate colleague. She closes in and weighs upon him at every turn, even in the toilet. We sense the inward, psychic dissolution of Peter, under this pressure. The outer excesses of madness in the possessed Paul, the inner disintegration of the St Omer persona predisposed to impassiveness, both end in a tragic disorientation. The reverberations are of terror and pity, rather than absurdity. St Omer's protagonist returns in fact full circle to Walcott's "A Careful Passion" to invoke, in tragic awareness, the power of compassion: "All in compassion ends/so differently from what the heart arranged."

St Omer comes to this humanistic affirmation via an oblique route, but he shows in the process a lucid perception of the potential tragedy of the particular dilemma he explores. This humanistic base, reflected in his close familial contexts, represents a seminal link with Walcott. Walcott comes through all his complex explorations to settle for a faith in a renewed humanism. Indeed St Omer might well serve to put some perspective on the native origins of Walcott's humanism, which is usually branded "literary".

Walcott

St Omer serves as a good guide into the St Lucian component in Walcott's work. There are obvious and substantial differences between the two. Walcott presents a much broader cultural-historical canvas; his range is more inclusive and regional. More strikingly, Walcott's dynamic is quite different from St Omer's. It turns on an interplay between negation and affirmation, and bears a celebratory thrust totally outside St Omer's medium.

The St Lucian content, however, remains an important substratum in his work, and a vital part of his sensibility. He begins from there to posit the private, individual approach to the mission. The position of Afa, the fisherman hero of *Sea of Dauphin* is an early expression of this approach. Afa is embittered and outraged at the wretched plight of his small St Lucian fishing village. He sees in race and oppression the instruments of a cosmic injustice levelled against the black man. He rails against the white man's God:

> God is a white man. The sky is his blue eye,
> His spit on Dauphin people is the sea.
> (*Dauphin*, 11.67-68)

He cuts himself off from the resigned villagers, who find solace in religion, and opts for combat with the greater but more rewarding hazards of the sea. There he looks to forge self in courage and bravery: "This piece of coast is make for men like that" (1.459). A private tournament with the "all" of existence (the sea) which has always seemed too strenuously stoic, and lonely. Walcott's own persona is absorbed in the fisherman's – as is the case with all his main heroes – and he is already positing his speculative role as a castaway figure.

Dauphin and *In a Green Night* are among the few works in which Walcott deals directly with the social realism of his native island, with the exception of *Another Life* (1972), where he recaptures certain snapshots of the society in his return to his formative roots. This leads us to a significant difference between the two writers. Walcott and St Omer are in fact drawn to different aspects of the St Lucian landscape. St Omer dwells on the social realism of its small urban milieu. Walcott is primarily drawn to the rustic landscape, both human and physical, to intuit more mythic, symbolic influences. The climate of St Omer's St Lucia is "spinster-like" and bears all the marks of sterility and despoliation; Walcott's St Lucia is more 'virginal', capable of natural, elemental energies. In Walcott, the 'virginal' approximates to the primeval.

They both come, however, from the urban environment of the capital-town, Castries. Seen from this angle, it is almost as if Walcott had been spared the claustrophobic conditions which St Omer internalizes. Here, I think, personal biography comes into play to account for Walcott's case. The latter started out with a particular advantage in a personal bequest which set him apart. His father had been an aspiring artist and the guiding light of a small cultural "circle of self-civilizing, courteous people in a poverty-ridden… colony"[11] – a rare phenomenon in that setting. As he puts it, it was natural for him to "simply continue where (his) father left off".[12] This early, inherited vocation shielded and left him secluded to a large extent (perhaps even more than his mulatto, middle-class background). It is an important background to his early, overriding commitment to Art. It helped to foster his sense of a solitary effort, and his lasting loyalty to Imagination.

Among West Indian writers, Walcott professes a very special pledge to the Imagination. Defending his assimilative approach, he affirms the power of a "shared" imagination, which traverses and transcends cultures and times. He describes it in "The Muse of History": "There is a memory of imagination in literature which is, in fact, another life, and that experience of the imagination will continue to make actual the quest of a medieval knight or the bulk of a white whale, because of the power of a shared imagination."[13]

Thus, the St Lucia he retains in memory preserves a primarily enhanced image, imbued with the "amber glow" he describes in *Another Life*. Walcott himself is concerned to admit that this "amber glow" was imparted by the borrowed hues of the metaphors of the Western imagination. He was most strongly inclined to "look" through the mirrors of its literature and art, and this no doubt served as a buffer against a more brutal contact with its harsher outlines. Thus, an entire portrait-gallery of the small town's derelicts reappears in Greek classical guise – to reveal all kinds of incongruities, while at the same time attaining truly tragic stature. He himself, moreover, points to the general tendency we are considering here. Commenting on one of his first attempts to render the scene as an apprentice painter, he says:

> In its dimension the drawing could not trace
> The sociological contours of the promontory. (*AL*, 1, ii).

He was, of course, soon to become aware of the contradictions and ambiguities opening out of this, as is explored in the complex burden of the "divided child" in Book I.

This brings us back to a closer look at the nature and significance of the St Lucia to which he is more powerfully drawn. Circumventing the bleakness of its sociological contours, he goes rather to the rustic, peasant landscape for inspiration. This is most clearly illustrated in the drama. His seminal and arch-heroes – they are mainly St Lucian – are figures outside, or on the fringes of society: outlaws, like the ex-convict Chantal (Malcauchon), for whom his Makak evolves; Makak himself, the Wood-cutter 'in hiding'; or the legendary Ti-Jean, who comes from the forest of the folk-imagination. They are figures beyond the pale of the organized society, and outside the constrictions of the peculiar conformism St Omer writes about. They belong instead in a realm of contact with organic, unimpaired natural energies, with its accesses of terror, violence and power. Walcott's rustic heroes come, in their own reduced circumstances, imbued with those potential resources. He recalls the St Lucian figure who inspired his Makak in these terms:

> My Makak comes from my own childhood. But there was no king, no chief, no warrior for a model. So the person I saw was this degraded, humble, lonely, isolated figure of the woodcutter. I can see him for what he is now, a brawling, ruddy drunk who would come down the street ... and let out an immense roar that would terrify all the children in the street. This was a degraded man, but he had some elemental force in him that is still terrifying.[14]

This provides the model for the tribal, heraldic figures who become Walcott's prime revolutionary vehicles. They come doubly equipped. Their basic degradation is loaded with history and its despair; their elemental energies provide the dynamic for combat. Walcott sinks his own poetic persona in theirs to probe the tensions between these two poles, and extend their meanings and resolutions. Makak, his arch-hero, is all that. I locate the particular climactic moment of self-discovery in *Dream* here: Makak, having taken the necessary step of militant action, comes, in his interiorised quest, to an awareness of his capacity for inner power even unto hubris – and, on its other side, his capacity for being humbled (Part II, Sc. 2). This is when he awakens to a revolutionized consciousness in acceptance of self, and self-responsibility. It enables him to shed and exorcise the false disfiguring images imposed by history, which had alienated him from himself. Walcott, then, arching through his shared imagination, returns to these roots to find "first principles", and possibility of a reinvigorated humanism. Both he and St Omer, though through different routes, end on common ground.

Endnotes

1. Derek Walcott, "The Schooner Flight", *The Star-Apple Kingdom* (New York: Farrar, and Giroux, 1977), p. 8
2. Garth St Omer, "Another Place Another Time" (novella) in *Shades*

of Grey (London: 1968), p. 222/ Peepal Tree ed. p. 190.

3. See the following works on the history of St Lucia: (i) Rev. C. Jesse, *Outlines of St Lucia's History* (St Lucia: St Lucia Archaeological Society, 1970) (ii) Henry H. Breen, St Lucia: *Historical, Statistical, and Descriptive* (London: Longman, 1844).

4. Roderick Walcott, *The Banjo Man*, in *A Time and a Season*, ed Errol Hill (Trinidad : Extra-Unit, 1976).

5. Walcott, "What the Twilight Says", *Dream on Monkey Mountain and Other Plays*, Farrar, Straus and Giroux, 1970), p. 13.

6. Gordon Rohlehr, "Small Island Blues", *Voices*, vol. 2, no. 1, Sept. - Dec. 1969. In this *Casebook*, pp. 89-94.

7. St Omer, *A Room on the Hill* (London: Faber, 1968), p. 15/Peepal Tree, p. 30.

8. Rohlehr, "Small Island Blues", p. 90 (this volume).

9. Walcott, "What the Twilight Says", p. 14.

10. St Omer, *Syrop* (novella), in *Introduction 2* (London: Faber, 1964).

11. Walcott, "Meanings", *Savacou*, no. 2, September 1970, p. 45.

12. Loc. cit.

13. Walcott, "The Muse of History", in *Is Massa Day Dead?*, ed Orde Coombs 1974), p. 25.

14. Walcott, "Meanings", p. 50.

JACQUELINE COUSINS

SYMBOL AND METAPHOR IN THE EARLY FICTION OF GARTH ST OMER

Journal of West Indian Literature, Vol. 3, (September 1989). pp. 20-38.

Edward Baugh has described St Omer's consistent reworking of the same themes from one work to the next as motivated by the search for a "perfective fiction".[1] This examination of five short stories and two novel extracts published in *Bim,* or broadcast on the BBC programme *Caribbean Voices* between 1951 and 1957,[2] attempts to show that these themes recurring in the novellas and novels have their roots in this early work. It is also argued here that in these stories and extracts St Omer evolved a system of symbolism and a basic stock of symbolic motifs to articulate his central thematic concerns. In this regard I think there is little doubt that James Joyce's work, especially *Dubliners,* had a profound influence on the development of his art.[3] Further, I believe that an analysis and appreciation of the moral pattern that informs these stories and extracts, and which is represented by the use of symbols, can enlarge and enrich our appreciation of the later work.

St Omer has been criticized by a section of his West Indian audience on the grounds that he has failed to provide any answers to the West Indian dilemma. If this is taken to mean that he does not provide any facile, overtly aphoristic solutions to the communal and individual tragedies with which he is concerned, then certainly St Omer cannot be considered a prescriptive writer. However, as this analysis of his early prose will try to show, he is a deeply moral writer whose subject matter is the social and psychic dislocation of individuals and whole communities who endure the colonial condition against a backdrop of an inimical universe. His work derives from the impulse to create meaning out of the chaos of the universal and colonial experience and to ascribe value and significance to the struggle to live authentically and ethically in the face of the certainty of death.

The issue of whether or not St Omer is an overtly instructional writer – and the irritation aroused in some of his readers and critics who reject the work because it does not provide any easy solutions – is raised indirectly in a review of *A Room on the Hill* by Cliff Lashley, who notes:

There are no answers offered. When I read this book St Omer led me
unfalteringly to the quicksand of my typical life history and left me to
my own devices. This is as much as I can ask of an imaginative writer.
St Omer is not a prescriptive writer: he is an enabling writer, giving me
my life in such a way that I am better able to live it.[4]

St Omer's analysis and diagnosis of the psychic malaise that is the
legacy of the colonial experience goes beyond the merely descriptive.
As Lashley suggests, it is "enabling" and thus – in the broadest sense
– morally prescriptive. Close analysis of the symbolic method and
motifs in these short stories will reveal that St Omer's art involves
the positing of basic human values, which can be termed prescriptive,
alongside his diagnosis of the individual and collective condition.
Furthermore, it is argued here that the great existentialist moral questions
of freedom, choice and responsibility, which reflect the *angst* of his
protagonists in the work published after *Syrop*, are foreshadowed in
these stories.

St Omer's attitude is not one of "precocious resignation to fate"[5] but one
of uncompromising engagement with the existential nature of the divisions of class and race created by colonialism. His art involves an unsparing
analysis of those negative factors which inhibit human happiness. He is
concerned with psychic independence from the master's culture, and with
an exploration of the states of being which facilitate the perpetuation of
colonial order. All of this is coupled with a basic sense of the value of the
human struggle to create moral order in the face of death.

One can only speculate whether St Omer's sense of the tragic that
inheres in the human condition was sharpened by the existence in the St
Lucian setting of physical reminders of death, like the proximity and
location of the Catholic graveyard, or created by such reminders. However,
we do know that St Omer has used aspects of St Lucian landscape, social
reality and experience, and developed these within the psychological and
narrative framework of his fiction as elements in a highly organized
complex of symbols to advance his perceptions about the colonial experience and the human condition.

The method he has used when forging these physical realities into
symbols that advance his themes is closely patterned on Joyce's method in
Dubliners. Such a comparison suggests that St Omer found concretized in
those stories his own intuitions about the spiritual sterility of St Lucian
communal life and a means through art to advance his prescription for the
revitalization of the communal soul. His treatment of character as symbolic
construct, the manipulation of dialogue to serve a thematic purpose, the
investment of selected details from the totality of the St Lucian environment and experience with symbolic/thematic resonances, the refinement
of his prose into the style of "scrupulous meanness"[6] that characterizes

Joyce's prose style in *Dubliners,* signify the profound influence that Joyce has had on the development of St Omer's art.

The degree of correspondence between the narrative method and the thematic concerns in Joyce's stories and St Omer's "Boy", "The Meeting", "The Revendeuse", and "The Departure" is great enough to suggest that perhaps St Omer had set out to write a St Lucian version of *Dubliners.* They have – like Joyce's stories – a central unifying concern with the question of communal morality. The narrative in most of St Omer's early pieces is channelled through the consciousness of a boy, as are the first three stories in *Dubliners.* In each instance, the boy's response to his world carries the writer's thesis about the cultural and moral inheritance his society offers. Both writers articulate their concern with communal morality through an analysis of the prevailing moral order of the society. This involves an iconoclastic assault on the failure of the Catholic Church, the official guardian of moral order, to foster those basic human values which are symbolized by the Host. Like Joyce, St Omer characterizes the male/father-figures as morally bankrupt victims of the colonial order, with sons involved in a struggle to preserve the integrity which has already been destroyed in their fathers, and without which life is envisioned as living death. St Omer also shares Joyce's fundamental concern with the corruption of the relationship *between* man and woman. The carnality and degradation involved in many of these relationships symbolizes the corruption and betrayal of those human values that ought to be at the base of communal life. Further, all of these concerns are expressed with the same quality of compassion for his people that we identify with Joyce.

However, although St Omer can be said to share Joyce's conviction about the purpose of his art – that of "creating the conscience of his race" – his existentialist vision of the absurdity of the human condition is a component of his work that has no thematic parallels in Joyce. The symbol of the sea is woven into St Omer's work with an ever-increasing complexity and concentration, signifying his view of life as inherently tragic and indicating his obsession with the fact of death. His treatment of the symbol of the sea is complicated by the connections he makes between the sea as a metaphor for the most final of all human limitations and the restrictions dictated by a given social order. A state of death-in-life is shown to be the direct result of a breakdown of individual and collective moral order. Such implications of the symbol of the sea, evident in his early work, are the basis of extended reworkings of this metaphor at the centre of his subsequent writing, suggesting that St Omer has never become reconciled to death.

The first story discussed here, "No Second Chance" is an account of a Hemingway-like meeting with the forces of fate in a setting that is not as clearly particularized as in the other stories, and displays none of the engagement with collective morality and the community that is a basic component of St Omer's work. The tide of the short story encapsulates St Omer's fatalistic perception of the nature of human existence. All the events in the narrative conform to the central idea that human effort is expended in an innately inimical universe that is as oblivious to evil as it is to right action.

The wartime confrontation between two "enemies" brought together to illustrate the absurdity of war and the perception that men are no more than pawns in this universal game is highly contrived. From the beginning we know that this journey will be the island Captain's last. The reader's sympathy is evoked for him because he is a good man motivated by the need to fulfil his role as provider for his family. He is prepared to take on the immensely risky task of transporting empty oil drums to another unnamed island where they will be filled with oil for use by the allied forces. This father is presented as an understanding and responsible male and is one of few such fathers in St Omer's work. Fate, however, has already injured this man – he has a wooden leg, the result of an accident on board his ship earlier in his life. Ironically, fate has therefore contributed to his desire to take his chances on the sea and try to earn as much as he can while he can, as his earning power will always be limited by his handicap. The reader is forewarned that fate is conspiring to take away the means of his livelihood altogether when, early in the story, his fearful wife asks if he has not heard that the Germans have sunk another ship in local waters.

The German submarine captain functions as St Omer's mouthpiece when he injects into the narrative his thesis about the innate absurdity of war. Both captains are conventional characters modelled on the Hemingway-type men who do what they have to, despite the odds against them, and who endure stoically. Nevertheless, despite the heavily plotted climax and the rather flat characterization, St Omer does evoke our pity for both men as victims in this universal catastrophe, which forces men to act in a way that is basically repugnant to them.

It is in the series of images involving the opposition of light and darkness, and in the manipulation of symbolic levels of meaning associated with the sea, that we find St Omer using metaphor to convey his perceptions about the human tragedy. His perception that fate is inescapable is intimated by images of water "striking the body of the ship" and the "rustled shearing off of a wave top in the darkness." These images and the detailed description of the body of the white man found floating off the West Coast, with the flesh of his face and feet eaten away, are the rudimentary forms of major symbolic motifs which characterize St Omer's work.

In this story, the descriptions of the sea and the drowned man are imposed on the work rather than integrated within the framework of the rest of the story as if, in fact, they belonged to a quite different narrative voice. They indicate St Omer's creative exploration of the technique of investing the physical world with metaphorical implications.

In the love story "It Will Last Forever", St Omer uses the sea and landscape as metaphors to suggest the ultimate impossibility of a love which crosses race and class barriers. His use of light and darkness as symbols of the couple's love and their certain unhappy fate is not particularly innovative. When the story begins they have become lovers. Their affair is acted out either on the beach or in the woman's hilltop home, when her husband is away. It is the couple's movement, or journey between these settings of hill and sea's edge, with shifts between night and day, dark or bright skies, which St Omer uses as metaphor to suggest that their love is doomed:

> It was night and there was a moon but there were plenty of clouds so that one saw the moon only at intervals. But all over there was a subdued effect of the moon through the clouds and it was not dark anywhere. The night was warm and they lay on the beach in their trunks and he could feel the throb of her heart through the temple resting on his breast.[7]

The intensity of their love cannot vanquish the social and universal forces which militate against human happiness. At the end of the story the woman returns home, leaving her lover behind. Both know that she is going to commit suicide, as it is impossible for her to bear the child she is carrying for him.

The motif of the triangular journey from the sea's edge, to the town, to the home on the hill recurs in most of St Omer's work as a symbolic paradigm for the realities that his protagonists want to shield themselves from by retreat to a room, or a house, on the hill – a retreat into self in an attempt to become inviolate. But ultimately this strategy proves futile as each protagonist is drawn from his hill to the sea's edge.

The couple and their unborn child are doomed because they have transgressed their society's codes of class, race and morality. The price for their transgression is death; it is exacted as ineluctably as each individual's death on the universal plane. The way in which ascendant codes of morality and the barriers of class and race predetermine the nature of human relationships in a more clearly defined colonial context – a central concern in the later work – is foreshadowed in this relationship. Their child, who cannot be born, is the first in a series of aborted or stillborn foetuses found in subsequent work, signifying the power of the life-denying forces within the society to subvert self-realization among the colonized. Like Walcott's Bolom, it represents the West Indian cultural identity that waits to be given life.

The two extracts, "Boy" and "The Meeting", as well as the stories "The Old Man" and "The Revendeuse", are linked by a deepening engagement with the colonial urban proletarian experience and are informed by the impulse to provide a moral analysis of this experience. St Omer's treatment

of character and the use of symbol to articulate this experience provides us
with a thematic coda to the novels.

"The Meeting", although subtitled "extract from work in progress", is
as complete a short story as any other of St Omer's stories.

Derek, the boy protagonist, finds his Araby in a wonderful garden
inhabited by a dream-girl who is brown-skinned and has "pretty white
teeth and soft dancing dimples". The language of the extract is marred by
excesses that are in total contrast with the terseness and elliptical quality
that are the hallmarks of St Omer's mature style:

> Oh, how pretty, how very pretty she was! An almost irresistible longing
> overwhelmed him; he wanted to feel her to touch her clothes to stroke
> her long black hair to caress her slender brown legs as brown as doves.
> How shapely they were, what silky smoothness they possessed. His soul
> subsided sibilant within him in a gentle sussuration of longing.[8]

A comparison of the language of this extract with the language of "Boy"
shows the development of St Omer's prose style towards the "scrupulous
meanness" of Joyce, a quality suggested in the last sentence of "The
Meeting": "And they went out. The wind was rising, and scraps of paper
blew along the street".[9]

The boy is called back to the reality of his life, a complete contrast to all
the garden holds. Except for the contrast between the Eden-like nature of
the garden, the real world and the boy's yearning for beauty in a world that
is hostile to it, this extract does not exhibit the symbolic range that
distinguishes "Boy".

In "Boy: An Extract", a number of the symbols associated with St
Omer's central concerns (that reappear later in more concentrated form)
are developed at length. When the boy, Derek, comes awake, he lies in bed
thinking about the "animals that were being slaughtered in the abattoir",
comparing how different animals meet death and relating the different
emotions these deaths have elicited from him. These descriptions establish
a sense of the boy's fascination with the fact of death in a way that suggests
that he has drawn an unconscious parallel between their deaths and the fate
that each man meets in his own death.

The image of the abattoir and the animals who wait for slaughter recurs
in "The Revendeuse", where it is also a signifier of St Omer's perception
of the duality of the tragedy that inheres in the colonial and human
condition. It acts as a metaphorical paradigm for the "slaughtering" people
inflict on each other when the moral base of a society has been destroyed
and when each individual is at the other's mercy in an environment where
compassion is scorned.

The descriptions of the slaughtering of these animals – with the metaphorical implications of universal death – are developed into a formulation

of the central metaphor that underpins all of St Omer's subsequent work: the colonial condition as a metaphor for the universal condition. This perception is developed through his arrangement of details about the physical setting and their interrelation with the narrative events. He establishes this by applying the values symbolized by aspects of the setting to events in the narrative. The details of the setting suggest a society and a quality of life characterized by extremes of both material and spiritual impoverishment. Between the descriptions of the scenes at the abattoir and the conversation between two unnamed women that reveals the degraded nature of the male-female relationship in this society, the omniscient narration focuses on the statue of the Madonna and Child near the small wooden chapel in the boy's yard, and on the religious statuary in his own home. These descriptions of the symbols of the Catholic faith suggest an ironic gap between the ideals of the faith represented by these devotional figures and the moral reality demonstrated by the members of the community. The light set before the four statues in the boy's home goes out after making a "final sustained rattle" and the statue of the Blessed Virgin that "looked down with sculptured tenderness upon the upturned face of her small son" is paired with the "bucket of filth that stood behind the low wall of bricks", not far from where the statue is positioned. The bucket is filled with human effluent that, like the blood of the slaughtered animals, finds its way into the canal.

This image of human effluent is one of the major metaphors that recur in different forms and permutations of meaning throughout his subsequent work. The "bucket of filth" positioned near the statue of the Virgin and Child in "Boy", signifies the corruption at the base of the communal soul, revealed in the conversation between the two women already referred to, as well as in the response to the lame fisherman's misfortune. The image recurs in other forms that redefine the terrible irony of death in more obvious existential terms. The Virgin and Child represent the promise of eternal life given to mankind, but the "bucket of filth" signifies man's mortality.

The latter half of the extract is seemingly a pastiche of incidents that typify the nature of human relations in this society. However, when the reader applies the symbolic values attached to the figure of the Virgin and Child to these incidents, and links them with the Christ imagery suggested in the description of the fisherman, the moral design that informs St Omer's narrative emerges. The "fighting and pushing" for water at the communal pipe stands and the conversation between the two women show a society where the basic decencies of life are absent and where men and women live in states of hostility.

One of the women relates the story of the beating that she got from her male partner the night before and her toughened friend chides her for not fighting back with blows. Perhaps the most distressing aspect of the whole incident is the boy's amusement at her story and at the exposition of "man's sins". The "furtive glances" that the boy casts at the beaten woman's face are in ironic contrast with the icon of the Blessed Virgin looking down on the upturned face of her son with "sculptured tenderness", and symbolize the breakdown in human relations. The boy's capacity to find amusement in the suffering of others is, however, tested when the lame fisherman falls and his ragged pants expose his nakedness, to the hilarity of the same women standing for water at the pipes. The description of his clothing and possessions – as well as his physical and spiritual bearing – are elements in a poignant symbolic laying-out of the basis of the communal tragedy revealed in the two women's conversation and the subsequent discussion of the long list of man's sins

St Omer's diagnosis of this society's moral condition is advanced alongside an analysis that offers an explanation for how this condition evolved and how it is maintained. This is achieved by the use of clothing as symbol. The fisherman wears ragged khaki pants and a policeman's cast-off jacket – the remnants of the uniform of those who maintained colonial order. Thus, St Omer suggests, the abandonment by the society of those principles that should ideally form the basis of communal life is a correlative of the colonial experience. The restrictions that colonial and neo-colonial conditions place on the establishment of true community – at both the individual and collective level – engage St Omer consistently in later work that is structured around protagonists who are in revolt against these restrictions and are involved in a search for a self that is undefined by colonial order.

St Omer's application to the lame fisherman of symbols associated with the crucifixion of Christ – like the long bamboo pole carried over his shoulder and the indentations in his hands – links the character to those values symbolized by the Virgin and Child. Structurally and thematically, these figures highlight the spiritual debasement that is a consequence of the communal disregard for the values of compassion, concern and respect for others. The laughter and obscene jokes that come from the people waiting for water are at the expense of the suffering of a member of their own community – the lame fisherman. Their response to his predicament signifies the extreme nature of the moral breakdown of the society, measured by St Omer in terms of the breakdown of the male-female relationship and the mother-son relationship. The description of the statue of the Virgin and her Son is in ironic symbolic counterpoint to the hostility and cruelty that characterizes the male-female relationship in the colonial context. When the fisherman accidentally reveals his body to the women standing at the pipe, their contempt for their men finds an outlet in the mocking of the physical symbol of his manhood.

Through the use of the symbol of Virgin and Child, who represent the values of true community, and the fisherman as Christ reviled and betrayed, as well as the symbolic associations with the sacraments implied by the narrative's emphasis on bread and water, St Omer advances his analysis of the moral chaos that characterizes the colonial condition in terms of the ironic gap between the love of mother for son and the moral confusion characterising the male-female relationship.

The ambivalence of the boy's response to the fisherman's predicament foreshadows St Omer's extended analyses of the moral and social forces that soon separate the colonial son from the nucleus of communal values represented by the icon of Virgin and Child. However, the boy does feel stirrings of compassion for the fisherman, as shown in the way he moves to help the fisherman recover his possessions:

> Derek returned to the pipe. The people were making obscene jokes about the fisherman but he felt a slight guilt as if he had deliberately trespassed on the man's privacy.[10]

Although already hardened to the real nature of the "tragedy" of the corruption of relations between his society's men and women, the boy still reveals a capacity for compassion, however overlaid with the moral attitudes acquired with the colonial experience that resides potentially in each member of this community. The fact that the guilt he experiences is only "slight" suggests the possibility that the boy may succumb totally to the moral nihilism that inheres in the colonial order. On the other hand, the fact that in such a moral climate he can still have such feelings attests that a restoration of those values remains possible. The task of repairing the breach in the male-female relationship created under the colonial order that informs Peter Breville's quest to create a family in *J—, Black Bam and the Masqueraders* and *Nor Any Country,* is adumbrated in the quality of the boy protagonist's response to the fisherman.

In "The Old Man", the character clichés of "No Second Chance" and "It Will Last Forever" are entirely missing and we find the two dimensions of St Omer's tragic vision revealed through symbol and metaphor in an exposition of the universal and colonial condition described in existential terms. Each physical detail and the memories that surface in the old man's consciousness advance St Omer's perception of life as a struggle of Sisyphean proportions.

The old man's heroic journey through the migrant labour centres of the Caribbean and Latin America – the consequence of exile as retribution for his "sin" of fathering an illegitimate child – brings him back finally to his island and to the "water's edge" and the sea, St Omer's symbol for death. Despite the vicissitudes of fortune and the threat to survival and personal

safety ever present in a malign and absurd universe, the old man has
preserved his integrity and a capacity to fulfil a commitment to another
human being. Nevertheless, his life's journey is ultimately a journey to
death. A sense of the cruelty and irony of the fact of death that obsesses St
Omer is apparent in his descriptions of the effects of the ravages of time and
fate on this old man's body:

> He sat with his legs before him and he passed his hands with the sand
> over the insides of his thighs but lightly because of the pain in them;
> and as he rubbed he watched where the doctor had shown him that the
> muscle was beginning to be atrophied. His great head showed a mane
> of straight very white hair with more of the Carib Indian than the Negro
> in it. His face was lined and folded and there was dignity in it except
> where the scar of the knife wound rose on the side and ran down his
> throat and under his shirt.[11]

Even though the old man had lived cautiously, the sudden anonymous
violence of the city streets and bars, the memories of which follow in quick
succession after he recalls the chain of events that had started with his first
"mistake" of fathering a child, has left its mark.

The old man's re-examination of his past experiences is triggered by the
pain from the injury sustained in an accident. He feels sharp pain from this
injury when he throws a ball of sand at a crab he had been watching for some
time:

> Before the ball of sand that he had been carefully shaping fell inches
> away from where the crab had *been,* there was a quick sudden movement
> and the hole was empty. And as he threw, the old man felt the pain in
> the shoulder and the jerk at the waist. He remembered.[12]

In the description of the crab we can see a symbolic prelude to the
history of the old man's vulnerability before fate. St Omer records
his perception of life's many contingencies and his sense of each man's
vulnerability in an innately malevolent universe. Despite the "dignity"
that the crab, like the old man, possesses, it too inhabits the same absurd
universe that produces "sudden" circumstances which can destroy all
security and whatever seems certain, in an instant, and from which
there is no protection. The incidents that the old man recalls from
the past are not only included in the old man's story to suggest the
scope and nature of twentieth-century urban social breakdown and
the arbitrary malevolence of fate, but are also treated by St Omer as
metaphorical equivalents to the depredation of the body by natural
process and the sudden manifestations of the universal and ineluctable
fact of death. The old man remembers the "maniacal" beating that he
had once seen four drunken sailors give an old man on a city street,

witnessed by the street's inhabitants from behind "locked doors". In particular, he recalls the "futile" attempts of the old man to parry the blows, the quick cessation of any kind of resistance, and the quick sudden burst of blood from the split head.[13] These details of the beating given to this old man parallel some of the details in the description much earlier of man's helplessness before the force of the sea.

The old man has come to the sea to bathe in the hope that it will help his condition, but he is rejected by the sea that will take no part in healing him. Its strong waves push him back "shoreward". However, when he stands up in the water, like a man, the sea asserts its total power over him, "wrenching" him from his daughter's hands and rolling him over and over and then almost smothering him with sand. His action of pouring sea-water over his head with "cupped hands" is in ironic symbolic counterpoint to the rite of baptism and its associations with cleansing, salvation and the promise of eternal life. When he then "plunges" into the water he comes up "floating on his abdomen", face downwards in the sea – an image that recurs throughout St Omer's work as an image of headlessness (actual physical decapitation) and the masquerade, associated with the themes of loss of identity, psychic masquerade, and alienation from self and total negation, as it does here.

The old man has never questioned the moral authority of the Catholic Church. However, this is exactly what St Omer set out to do in this story and in all of his subsequent work. The repercussions of fathering a child out of wedlock in a social system where basic life opportunities, such as an education, are controlled by the Church, are examined again and again. This basic situation broadens into an analysis of the role of the church as a prime agent in the maintenance of colonial order. This extended analysis is foreshadowed in the description of the priest whom the old man had known in Cuba:

> He remembered the priest, probably very old now and retired, or dead, but young then and very black. He had been trained in France, was tall, and the whiteness of his collar had stood out conspicuously against the blackness of his face and robes.[14]

The details of this portrait symbolize the priest's role in the maintenance of colonial order and prefigures the treatment of Fr Thomas in *Nor Any Country*. The knowledge of the old man's suffering, the quality of reverence of the narration when it touches this man, who has endured without bitterness the negative impact on his life of an inflexible and punitive social order, his capacity to feel compassion for another human being (when none has been shown to him) – all these are factors that shape the reader's critical appraisal of the nature of the authority of the Catholic Church.

Despite his rejection by the Church and by his family, the old man did not go into a moral tailspin during his exile but tried to maintain the practice of his Catholicism, avoiding the night clubs and the women he might have had, and carefully "saving for his bastard child at home". It is this commitment to his daughter – the assumption of the burden of responsibility for the life of the other – St Omer suggests, that is the only real test of a man's moral worth.

The relationship between father and daughter foreshadows other key father and daughter relationships in later work. Significantly, St Omer's focus throughout his work is on a number of basic relationships that are permutations of the archetypal family. These relationships recur in three basic forms that are intended to represent the collective destruction of the family into fragments, the consequence of the colonial experience. The icon of father and daughter is one of these fragments and functions in ironic contrast to the male-female relationship, which is fraught with conflicts and divisions of class and race, determined by that same colonial experience. Furthermore, this relationship – in which St Omer reposes the highest good that man can attain – is non-sexual, cannot regenerate itself and is finally negated by death. The old man regards his child, who shows him such offices of love, with a fondness reminiscent of the "tenderness" on the face of the Virgin in the extract "Boy", when she returns with the sea-grapes she has picked for him.

His feeling for his daughter, who has also suffered the burdens of time and circumstance, is a denial of the power of those forces in a colonial context that seeks to dictate the form that relationships should take. Such relationships, St Omer suggests, are what give life any meaning at all, though they too are finally negated by death. The old man rests against his daughter for support and she tries to hold him against the pull of the sea that finally sweeps him from her hands and does with him what it likes. She, too, is embraced by the landscape of sea and sand. At the same time, she is the butt of the wit of a group of cruelly stupid loafers whose obscene laughter at her appearance and her father's condition punctuates the narrative. Their obscenities are immediate reminders of the violent absurdities the old man has endured and the inimical universal forces that militate against human happiness. She is also dying and belongs to the sea.

In "The Revendeuse" St Omer explores the mother/father/son relationship while analysing the spiritual condition of the whole community. The pathos that he evinces for mother and son extends to all those individuals who are victims of extremes of material and spiritual deprivation, and who exist with their fellows in states of hostility in the climate of moral disorder characteristic of the colonial condition.

Joyce's stated purpose in *Dubliners* was to "write a moral history" of his country, and it is this same concern with collective morality that informs this story. St Omer's concern – like Joyce's – is to describe the prevailing moral order within his society as he perceives it. However, unlike Joyce or Walcott, St Omer does not posit any alternative for a debased faith like the new/old Religion of Art. He can only suggest the possibility of the attainment of a certain purity in the bond between parent and child, and a hope for the achievement of dignity and integrity in communal life.

In the setting described in the first paragraph of this story, St Omer achieves a level of narrative control and certainty in communicating a sense of the tragic rooted in a specific social milieu that merges with his perception of the innately absurd nature of the human condition that is characteristic of his later work:

> In the cold heavy darkness around the marketplace the scent of fish was dry and very stale. Their footsteps were loud on the hollow concrete pavement and he could not make out the animals that were standing and lying in the pen between the market and the abattoir. But in the street behind the abattoir it was light.[15]

Darkness and light carry thematic significance in the patterning of the story's meaning. The engulfing darkness symbolizes the spiritual abyss created by the absence of meaningful faith, and the artificial light source – the street lights – signifies those moral forces which subvert the genuine realization of self.

The darkness that envelops the mother and her son functions also as a symbol of the "nothingness" that St Omer believes finally engulfs all human endeavour and hope. The work-worn mother walks with her son in the early hours of the morning to the wharf to buy cheap fish which she will cook for resale at a small profit. These earnings contribute to her central goal in life – the education of her son. The "cold heavy darkness" which presses down on them, and which also covers the sleeping community of the town, the revendeuses, the fish vendors, the fishermen, symbolizes the ultimate negation of all human meaning.

The scent of "stale and dry fish" that permeates the dark air also symbolizes St Omer's perception of the society's moral condition. It also suggests the sterility and corruption of the communal soul. As they walk, the footsteps of mother and son echo "loudly" on the "hollow concrete pavement". The concrete and asphalt image is another recurring motif in St Omer's work, where it functions as a symbol advancing his concern with the impact on the community of development, the dross of materialism and the resulting breakdown in community values. The hollowness of their footsteps suggests the denial of individual human significance which is a basic to the colonial situation and to twentieth-century materialism.

In the darkness the boy cannot single out the animals penned in the abattoir. Similarly, he and his mother are indistinguishable from one another in the darkness. St Omer's use of the continuous participle in the description of the animals "that were standing and lying " ironically suggests continuity, but these animals are only waiting to be slaughtered. In the second paragraph, the narrative shifts to a description of the fish vendor and the revendeuses, who "were standing" under the artificial street lights, and who were "waiting to buy". The use of the same verb form links the revendeuses and the fish vendors to the animals who were waiting to be slaughtered. Thus, the journey towards the wharf (another permutation of the sea's edge) is a journey towards the only human certainty, that is death. The eye registers the meaning of the continuous suggested in the -*ing* endings of the animals "standing" and "lying", but in terms of the patterning of sound and the final tonal effect, the endings conform to the sombre and stark sound quality of the rest of the paragraph. Consequently, the mother's ambitions for her son are ironically linked to the fate of the animals awaiting slaughter.

In this story, St Omer frames his analysis of the role of the Catholic Church as a force in colonial society which actively works towards maintaining that order by creating an alienated intelligentsia. In "The Old Man", the moral authority of the Catholic Church is questioned and a concern is voiced about the obvious debasement of a faith that preaches forgiveness and yet practices retribution. In "The Revendeuse", the gap between the ideals represented by the Catholic faith becomes a bitter analysis of the Church as a power structure that determines and perpetuates the colonial condition. This is articulated through a number of metaphors developed and applied with a craft that marks the emergence of St Omer's distinctive voice.

In this unnamed Catholic society, the moral values of the faith are paid lip-service at the "daily early-morning Mass and Holy Communion". Communal charity, integrity, respect for fellow man are all absent. The atmosphere is permeated by the scent from the marketplace, which dominates the community's social relations. The fish, which symbolizes Christ and the Christian faith, is used ironically by St Omer to suggest the absence of the values of the faith in the members of this society and the sterile role played by the Catholic Church in this society. Madeleine, the economically and socially advantaged fish vendor, arbitrarily raises the price of her fish even though she must realize that the revendeuses make a minimal profit from the fish they buy from her, and even though she knows how desperately they need her fish to help provide for their children. In an ironic inversion of Christ's miraculous feeding of the five thousand, when one of the revendeuses asks Madeleine to show understanding towards them, she snarls: "I dohn have that, is only humans have it. I am animal". Her answer is indicative of the society's overriding stress on the principle of profit, the exploitation of the weaker and the absence of a humanising concern for others which characterize social relationships in this society. The ugliness of the quarrel which follows Madeleine's retort and the stranger's theft of the mother's fish indicate clearly how values such as fairness and charity are held in low esteem in the communal psyche.

St Omer's involvement with political and national issues that are peculiar to the colonial condition are advanced in "The Revendeuse" chiefly through his treatment of the male-female relationship. The old man who hovers on the perimeter of the scene is an allegorical figure of death, but at the same time he also functions as a symbol for the moral inadequacy of the male in this society. He is shown as "scratching through the hole in the bottom of the old police trousers he wore". In this, St Omer communicates through metaphor the moral sterility of men broken by the colonial experience. The pair of cast-off policeman's trousers not only indicates the level of material deprivation in the society but also functions as a symbolic correlative of the wearer's psychic condition. Here, St Omer suggests that the spiritual dereliction of the male is a direct consequence of the colonial condition.

This symbolic characterization of the male figure prefigures the treatment of the father figure in the novels, where we get expanded analyses of the psychic repercussions of the colonial experience. St Omer's fathers are an ironic inversion of the traditional father figure as repository of collective tribal wisdom such as Pa in Lamming's *In the Castle of My Skin*.

The thief/oppressor who comes out of the spiritual abyss wears a soiled T-shirt and shorts made from cut-off dungarees. These details of his dress are used by St Omer to suggest the thief's lack of manhood and the moral fitness required to bring about change in the society's condition. The threepence-worth of fish which he steals from Joe's mother – associated with the betrayal for thirty pieces of silver — is no simple theft, but a loss which signifies the enormity of Joe's father's betrayal to his wife and child. From St Omer's point of view, this theft symbolizes what he sees as the never-ending cycle of exploitation of woman/mother/island.

The characterization of mother and son and their relationship in this story takes on a complex of meanings, which is a fundamental feature of St Omer's subsequent work. Joe's mother, while firmly rooted in a given social reality, is also a symbolic figure representing country. Images and symbols associated with the Catholic religion are woven into the characterization of the mother in such a way that she can be seen as the repository of those basic human values with which the men have lost touch and which cannot flourish in this kind of society.

One of the activities associated with the mother is the preparing and serving of fish. The fish as symbol of the Christian values of love and sacrifice in their widest sense serves (through its association with the mother figure) to bring into focus one of the story's central ironies: the Catholic Church as a structure in the society that facilitates the continuation of states of hostility and division. Joe's mother invests the remainder of her emotional life in the Church. She subsumes the "promptings of Nature" in her acts of worship, as she cannot risk an alliance with another man after the death of her brutal and alcoholic husband. She belongs to the generation of the uncritical and the unquestioning which simply accepts the Church for what it says it stands for. The intellectual assessment of the Church's role in colonial society is left to another generation: the generation of the alienated, educated, colonial sons of the novels.

Endnotes

1. Edward Baugh, "Since 1960: Some Highlights", in Bruce King, ed., *West Indian Literature* (London, 1979), pp. 78-94.
2. "Boy: An Extract", *Bim,* 5.20 (June 1954), 261-3; "The Meeting: Extract from a work in progress", *Bim,* 4.15, 176-178; "The Revendeuse", *Bim,* 6.22 (June 1955), 121-125; "The Departure", *Bim,* 6.23 (Dec. 1955), 138-145; "No Second Chance", *Bins,* 6.24 (Jan-Jun 1957), 245-251. Broadcast on *Caribbean Voices:* "The Old Man" transmitted Sunday 21 Nov. 1954. "La Revendeuse" transmitted Sunday 19 June 1955. "The Departure" transmitted Sunday 23 Oct. 1955. "It Will Last Forever" transmitted Sunday 1 July 1956.
3. Edward Baugh, remembering St Omer when they were fellow students on the Mona Campus of the UWI in the late 1950s, says that Joyce's *Dubliners* was a book of which St Omer was particularly fond, and that he once recited the final sentence from "The Dead" as an example of "fine prose style". (Conversation with E. Baugh, 18 January 1988).
4. *Caribbean Quarterly,* 17.1 (March 1871), 58-59.
5. Quoted in Michael Gilkes, *The West Indian Novel* (Boston: Twayne, 1981), p. 103.
6. Gordon Rohlehr, "Small Island Blues: A Short Review of the Novels of Garth St Omer", *Voices,* 2.1 (Sept-Dec. 1969), 22-28.
7. St Omer, "It Will Last Forever", broadcast 1 July 1956. Quote is from p. 2 of the script.
8. "The Meeting", *Bim,* 4.15, p. 176.
9. "The Meeting", p. 178.
10. St Omer, "Boy: An Extract", *Bim,* 5.20, p. 263.
11. St Omer, "The Old Man", broadcast 21 Nov. 1954, p. 2 of script.
12. "The Old Man", p. 4 of script.
13. "The Old Man", p. 5 of script.
14. "The Old Man", p. 5 of script
15. St Omer, "The Revendeuse", broadcast 19 June 1955, p. 1 of script.

GORDON ROHLEHR

SMALL ISLAND BLUES
A SHORT REVIEW OF THE NOVELS OF
GARTH ST. OMER
Voices (Port of Spain) 2 (Sept-Dec 1969), 22-28

Within two years, Garth St. Omer, a St. Lucian writer, has published one novel and three novellas, in which he undertakes an examination of the experience of an emerging middle-class in one of the smaller West Indian islands. *A Room on the Hill* came out early in 1968, closely succeeded by *Shades of Grey*, a volume which consists of two short novels, "The Lights on the Hill" and "Another Place Another Time". 1969 saw another short novel, *Nor any Country*.

The four stories are linked together by cross references, and seem to be interrelated fragments of a single island saga. While St. Omer generally concentrates on a middle-class circle of civil servants, returned professionals, ambitious scholarship winners, teachers and so on, his vision includes a much wider cross section of the community. He recognises that lines of class distinction are generally blurred in the West Indies. A lower class skeleton resides in every bourgeois cupboard. The old aristocracy of whites, near whites and mulattoes, cannot escape the links that connect them in blood, history and psychology to the blacks at the bottom of the social greasy-pole. Hence all of St. Omer's people are bound together in a tight net of complex interrelationship, and the reader is like a stranger suddenly immersed in the tangled mosaic, at times losing his way completely, as the closed circle gossips incestuously about itself.

A Room on the Hill is the longest and the fullest of the stories. Its central figure, John Lestrade, is one of those who never had the opportunity to escape from the island. Bourgeois in a society which as yet offers little scope for a middle-class beyond the Sunday morning beach party, the nightclub circuit and the perennial lechery, Lestrade is earmarked for alienation. His friends return to the island as qualified professional men; the bonds which made even a superficial community of interest possible wear thin, and essential loneliness is all that is left.

This is, however, a simplification of the issue in the book. The story is more than that of a man seeking escape from a limiting environment which narrows choice to abject conformism or exile. It is not merely the record of one man's failure to ascend the social ladder. Indeed, in *Nor Any Country*, St. Omer is able to show that social and academic success merely creates another set of problems, and does not necessarily lead either to a new sense of commitment to society or to a resolution of the problem of existence itself. Lestrade is confronted with contingencies which have nothing to do with environment. He is bedevilled by the spectacle of death, and by the anxieties of guilt and meaninglessness. There was the death of his best friend, Stephen, who in despair of ever leaving the island commits suicide. Lestrade, who did not try to save his friend, is tormented by a sense of personal inadequacy and, like a Conrad hero, withdraws from a situation of guilt at his own cowardice to one of nihilism, and passive surrender to the scheme of things.

The book begins with the death of Lestrade's mother. She is one of these self-sacrificing black mothers, who suffer to ensure their children a future. Lestrade, who is never sure that he deserves her sacrifice, and whom we see becoming more and more detached from people and things, is also troubled by a sense of guilt when she dies. More frightening than her death, however, has been the example of her life, which, like the life of so many of the islanders, seems to the young people to have been merely the grim, fixed struggle of a trapped generation, no less lost than their own. In a way, everyone seems to be waiting for the end; and that is how we leave Lestrade himself at the end of the book.

Paralysis, inertia, a weird sense of stasis and purposelessness; a constant lack of grace, ease, or even relaxation; isolation of person from person, life from life; the failure of ambition and irrelevance of achievement – these are recurring themes in St. Omer, and I think I recognise a similarity, both in theme and treatment, to the James Joyce of *Dubliners*. Joyce, like St. Omer, was describing a small community immured in dead custom, just sufficiently small to deny individuality and sufficiently large to deny communion, and completely dominated by the Catholic priesthood. It may also be worth noting that Joyce was the product of a country which had suffered a most brutal period of colonialism under Britain, that he was acutely aware of what the British had destroyed in Ireland, and that he was torn between a fascination for his broken people, and a rejection of the colonial experience. His people, like St. Omer's, are constantly dreaming of escape, but are incapable of the effort of will demanded, and finally surrender to the tedious limbo around them.

In order to depict this grey life, Joyce adopted what he described as a style of " scrupulous meanness". Economy, starkly controlled feeling, an amazing variety of shades of tone, a delicate and most oblique irony, and a careful selection of images, combine to give Joyce's art in *Dubliners* its coherence and its relevance to the kind of experience he describes. There is in St.

Omer something of this same scrupulous meanness. He has fashioned a careful, tightly economical prose and an almost bleak detachment, which matches the cramped narrowness of the society, and the taut spareness of the lives he describes. This is what gives his work its inner intensity, even when the plot is at its slenderest, and even when, as happens too frequently, a simple catalogue of events replaces genuine exploration of their significance.

Though St. Omer lacks Joyce's virtuosity in subtly changing tones of voice, or the wealth of dimension which exists beneath the surface of the simplest story of Joyce, he seems to be well on the way to achieving his own blend of surface clarity and symbolic depth. Like Joyce, he is able to suggest that the lives and daily events he describes are in some way symbolic of a general fate facing people. Hence, the sick woman waiting for the end, old Dezauzay sitting in silent vacancy in the morning sunlight, listening to the church bells which lost their meaning for him when he was found guilty of embezzlement, old Antoine, the perennially drunk and occasionally demented shoemaker, scapegoat of all the children in the society, all suggest in their lives the weariness, paralysis, loss of faith, dry despair and slow subsidence into apathy and acceptance of meaninglessness, which Lestrade endures. Each life complements the other; and though each must endure his burden alone, it is strongly suggested that the individual fate illustrates the predicament of the group.

Early in the book there is the image of the river behind the dispensary befouled with bits of discarded dressing in which rats are drowned in steel cages. It is a rather obviously symbolic passage. The rats, engaged in their futile struggle to escape are like the people on the island.

> The frantic struggle of the rats to escape amused him. They clung to the steel wires. They fought each other for possession as if the wires did not confine them to death but led to liberty and life. They bit one another. They turned their sharp teeth even on themselves. He and his friends watched and laughed. Eventually, exhausted, they lost their grip and slowly, their grey bellies upturned, and the displaced air from their bodies rising in assorted bubbles to the sea's dirty surface. (p. 27/39).

The rubbish-heap image, a favourite with West Indian writers, also occurs. The point about this passage is that it *suggests* the futility, not only of the struggle for social significance, but of the existential quest for meaning of any sort. St. Omer's people never really confront existence. They simply are its passive victims. They resemble Naipaul's Mr. Biswas in their lonely struggle to escape from the steel wires of their cage, but they lack the quality of his rebellious spirit. They give up too easily.

Indeed, St. Omer's fatalist philosophy may well account for the frequent lack of symbolic dimension noted above. Starting from the position that phenomena have little meaning beyond themselves, not only does he not depict people trying to construct their own meaning out of a teeming variety of sense impressions, but he restricts himself to a careful cataloguing of phenomena, a fairly elementary impressionism. At times this is well done, as in the description of the funeral of Anne-Marie (ch. 12) where the blinding sun, the animal-drawn hearse, the masquerading children on holiday, the sound of flutes and drums, the figure of the drunk lunatic, the pain and distraction of Dennys all form part of the same scene. The effect is one of macabre delirium. It is as if the reader shares Dennys' grief-crazed vision. There is also the strong suggestion that the world is totally indifferent to the fate of the individual, that there is no dignity anywhere. The mourner and the drunken lunatic are one.

The trapped animal is one image of man in society, and man in existence. The robot is another, the mechanically wound-up toy, the sleepwalker. These references recur from time to time in St. Omer's work. In "The Lights on the Hill", Stephenson could easily be a John Lestrade who manages to escape from the island, but still faces the same problem of trying to find a meaning in life itself. Like Lestrade, he has moved from being a castaway on his island to being a spiritual drifter. Stephenson, like old Dezauzay in the first novel, becomes a moral exile from his society when he is caught smuggling. No one will give him a job. He becomes a sort of beachcomber, a drifter among the scenes and images. Eventually someone helps him to get a teaching job on another island. There he discovers no commitment. He simply accepts everything as it comes. A significant picture of him shows him floating on his back in the sea (pp. 34-35), regarding life as an illusion, a moving pageantry of images, limitless, pure present without past or future. It is therefore no surprise that his life at University in Mona should turn out to be a farce, that his relationships should prove tenuous, or that we should finally see him surrendering to a grey apathy after the sudden death of his friend.

Significantly, Stephenson at the end of the novel is shown walking away from a world where politics is *going* on. St. Omer's people have all turned their backs on politics of any sort. This leaves them no choice except the "gray light suffused with heat" which Stephenson moves through at the end of the book. They are all orphans of some sort, or have lost any meaningful contact with their parents. Derek in "Another Place Another Time" lives for the present:

> As though that life and the present he lived it in, did not spring out from, had no connection with the past nor with the lives of his forebears who had lived in it. (p. 129/118).

His high-school education separates him from his lower-class friends, and teaches him a sort of scorn for himself, his colour, and other people. "It was at college he discovered that she was ugly, too black, and that her hair was short and hard." (p. 161/ 143). It also teaches him to be cruel in his sexual relations with lower-class women. He lives through the day by day tragedy of transition from underprivilege to bourgeoism, and finally decides that "He had no cause nor any country now other than himself." (p. 222/190).

Nor Any Country examines the predicament of the West Indian who returns from the metropolis, self-conscious, accent-conscious, to try to resume a life in the tropics. Peter Breville, returns to the little island, to the wife whom he had married because he feared that the Church would have had his scholarship taken away if he had left the girl pregnant, to his brother who having failed in the eyes of the island, has become a moral outcast, to a life which will clearly be empty. At the end of the book he is leaving to take up a university appointment in another island. St. Omer has however anticipated this in "The Lights on the Hill" where he mentions the disintegration of Peter's life on the Mona Campus.

Nor Any Country is the slenderest of St. Omer's stories. It is too thin, too simply a catalogue of impressions to be sustained by the controlled nostalgic prose of reminiscence which St. Omer writes so well.

In this brief review, there has been little room for any detailed examination of technique, but it must be stressed that St. Omer is a most careful and conscious artist. One needs to be always conscious of tones of voice. In conclusion, I cannot help reflecting the distance between St. Omer's work, or a book like Orlando Patterson's *An Absence of Ruins* and an earlier work like Lamming's *In the Castle of My Skin*. In these later writers, the heroes do not return to recognise their place in society, or to dedicate their lives to "My people." They claim to have no people, turn their backs on politics, and eventually give up the struggle even for inner meaning. It is no surprise that St. Omer uses the dry disillusioned lines from Derek Walcott as epigraph to his first novel: "Only the gulls hunting the water's edge/Wheel like our lives, seeking something worth pity." Walcott, too, is caught up in this crisis that faces the sensitive West Indian, which involves the discovery of something in life and society worthy of one's emotion and commitment.

It may well be, too, that rootlessness and dry despair will remain a major dynamic in West Indian life. For the small-island blues which St. Omer sings, are simply a version of the general melancholy, an expression of the general anxiety. It would, however, be a welcome change to show the defeat and despair of one who has been seriously committed to society. This will of necessity involve the writer in a serious examination of the tragi-comedy of West Indian politics, which is what St. Omer and Patterson have so far neglected to do. Naipaul's success in *The Mimic Men* is a limited one. He, too, is showing the defeat of one who has never been committed to anything.

St. Omer's novels give evidence of considerable talent. He however needs to be careful lest the theme of disillusion leads him to a dead end.

This danger is clearly seen in *Nor Any Country*. Perhaps, too, he could strive to attain a more sustained symbolism, and to show his people in significant situations, rather than to talk about situations in which they have been. A tendency towards too pat intellectual analysis can be counterbalanced by a greater emphasis on bringing out the dramatic potential of the important moment. St. Omer's obvious dedication to technique ought to lead to a deepening of talent and achievement.

Note: page references are given first to the original Faber edition, then to the Peepal Tree edition.

RESPONSES: THE MAN

VELMA POLLARD

GARTH ST. OMER: THE MAN AT HOME

The sound of the telephone breaks my Sunday morning silence. The voice at the end of the line is unmistakeable. It is Garth St. Omer's voice. I have not heard it in more than ten years. It is a voice that immediately conjures up the Mona campus and a man, immaculately dressed in a casual sort of way. He is beginning his evening walk to anywhere on the 653 acres of the University campus at Mona. Coming from Taylor Hall, a man's hall then, he must pass Irvine, a woman's hall then, to get to the main exit from the residential area. He hails me by name as he passes happy and content, or so it seems, and smiling. His gait is graceful and precise, rather like his prose. You got the feeling he was going on a long walk and did not want to waste energy.

"Where are you?"

"I am here with my wife Lucy."

The year is 1969. I am living in New York City. St. Omer explains that he has come to do an MFA (Master of Fine Arts) at Columbia University where I myself am doing a part time MA in Teaching English while I lecture at Hunter College. And so began a remarkable three years interaction of my family, chiefly myself and three children and theirs with no children yet. They started out living in Columbia postgraduate flats convenient as a stopover station for me, an overworked body coming uptown to classes by bus or train or leaving classes or library, but always tired.

St. Omer had come directly from St. Lucia, but he had lived in France, Ghana, London since we parted at Mona in the late fifties. He had three novels on the market and had been peddling them in Castries. I was impressed. I was already beginning to be in awe of that island, St. Lucia. Derek Walcott had walked those streets with his books of poetry even before he came to University in Jamaica and he too had two recent books of poetry, in addition to the plays he had written and directed at Mona. My awe was to grow in the eighties when, back in Jamaica, I met the younger crew: Hippolyte and Lee for example. By 1992, there was also the matter of TWO Nobel Laureates from one island.

I wanted to know how St. Omer had managed to work and still write three novels. That seemed marvellous and almost impossible to me then. Of course I knew the talent had always been there. "Syrop" existed before he left the Mona campus. But these were novels, longer and requiring stretches of uninterrupted time and space. There would be many opportunities for him to give me details.

After a year in postgraduate housing Garth and Lucy moved to an apartment across the corridor from mine on the thirtieth floor of a building in the Lincoln Towers complex on the Upper West Side of Manhattan and life became even more wonderful. The man who liked to walk on the Mona campus knew how to enjoy Central Park and didn't mind taking children, especially my boys, on treats/feats I didn't dare while Lucy and I chatted about life and plants and animals – she from Biology me from Literature. How else would my sons get rowed in a boat on the Central Park lake or get hoisted up almost tree high by strong arms? Garth always treated them as if they were worthy of intense adult attention. For me there was the blessing of stopping at their door on my way from work and having a cup of tea and "Garth- made" bread and feeling as if I had a wife before I crossed the corridor and became a wife myself, and mother. On the weekend our families were a little slice of the Caribbean, high above the concrete of Manhattan

After Columbia, the St. Omers moved to Princeton and I moved to Guyana. That was the year *J-, Black Bam and the Masqueraders*, his fourth novel, was published. I visited them on the Princeton campus. I brought my Guyana-bought hard cover copy of *J-Bam* and took it up to be signed. People like me had begun having authors sign books by then. The visit was short and the break was to be long; another decade or more. But this time, we kept in touch with letters and telephone calls and when we met again they had two children and I was alone. Mine were grown and scattered. This time the telephone call was from me telling them I was in California.

UCLA/UCSB

It was 1986. I was at UC Los Angeles on a Fulbright Research Fellowship. Garth and Lucy were both employed at UC Santa Barbara where he taught *inter alia* a course on the novel. Very soon I found a workable plan. Every Thursday afternoon I got on the library bus that would take books from UCLA to UCSB and every Monday morning I got on it to return to UCLA to my graduate class and my office hours. How could I be so lucky? And my research did not suffer. I was introduced to an historian who was only too happy to lend me an office and his selection of Oral History tapes at UCSB. His data were a perfect match for the Oral History tapes I had used at Mona for conversation analysis courtesy of historian, Erna Brodber. So all day Friday I worked on that campus. Saturday and Sunday were my weekend in the St. Omer household enjoying family time with parents and son and daughter, now teenagers. It was like New York again, but better for I was freer. Now I was without children and they were parents involved in the school life and entertainment of teenaged son and daughter.

I was coming from Mona, indeed from the Caribbean with current news of so many people they knew! I was available for long hours of talk and walk with them and late hour conversations with Garth , a night owl like me (Lucy being an early sleeper). On one of my visits, Thanksgiving I think, I arrived accompanied by my daughter and my younger son, now grown and at Colombia, the same university where we had been years before. The excitement was palpable. Even the children were impressed with these big friends. The fifth novel was in progress then, suffering, I thought from a perfectionist's demands.

I was to note this same perfectionist feature in the supermarket choosing only the best vegetables and seasonings and in the kitchen, delivering perfect main courses to the evening table. I think of St. Omer when I include cilantro among my herbs (replacing the Caribbean shadon beni/ bhandhania/ spirit weed). I can still smell fish excellently seasoned and as attractive to the eye as the bunches of lemon in the garden visible through the window from my seat at the dining table. So many words of wisdom; so much to think about; so many new ways of seeing I remember from these talks at the dining table and those after meals. I remember, for example, that he did not know how to quarrel extensively with anybody, not having had much experience of it. Growing up with his mother and brother he had been spared the conjugal battles of words his friends had been heir to. This is a perspective I would never have had without his prompting. St. Lucia and his life there was never far away in these conversations. I got the impression that the sea was a constant and that much of the fun connected with growing up took place on the beach.

In a discussion on Caribbean Literature, St. Omer made a remark that sounds prophetic now and seemed then like something so obvious we all should have thought of it. He said that film is the way the Caribbean has to go. And I thought, indeed, how else could artists speak to non-literate masses? Plays yes, but the film has wider appeal and can easily go from place to place. I hope that is what he meant. And I feel gratified, as he must feel, that his daughter is a film maker. The last time I saw her she had come to Jamaica (her mother accompanying) to take part in a film festival where one of her short films was being presented and praised.

Afterwards

The hiatus in St. Omer's publishing history has resulted in some younger Caribbean readers not being aware of his work. I have been very saddened by that. He did read at the 1988 West Indian Literature conference at

Mona, Jamaica. Since then the world has been waiting for that fifth novel from which he read.

One can understand then how pleased I was when in March 2012, Peepal Tree Press republished *A Room on the Hill* and in 2013 *Shades of Grey* and *Nor Any Country* as part of its Caribbean Modern Classics Series. I thank Jeremy Poynting for his insight. Now I thank Dr. MacDonald, editor, and of course Peepal Tree Press for the idea of this collection and the execution of it.

The papers speak to the fact that this generation of young St. Lucians is aware of Garth St. Omer and his place in the history of their literature. Their papers underline the notion that he, as part of their extraordinary literary inheritance, has been an inspiration to them. There are poets and playwrights, but not many novelists in that history.

I was one of those downpressed with disappointment at the discovery that St. Omer was not to appear in the slot labelled " Plenary Conversation: Garth St. Omer and Jeremy Poynting", complementing an earlier "Plenary Conversation: Nobel Laureate Derek Walcott and Prof. Edward Baugh" at the ACLALS conference in St. Lucia in August. Without missing a beat however the committee quickly put together an evening not *with* but *about* St. Omer, showcasing St. Lucian graduate students talking about his work The session was very well received and truly informative.

I have been personally blessed to have continued to be in touch with Garth St. Omer and his family over the years. Chance has conspired to favour me so I have actually seen them from time to time. In the nineties, for example, it was Trinidad where Lucy was a Research Fellow and Garth a visiting husband. As an administrator at UWI, Mona, I had to attend University meetings scheduled on the St. Augustine campus. Most unlikely and distinctly memorable was time spent as well on the University of the Virgin Islands campus at a conference which both they and I attended. Prof. Gilbert Sprauve, one of my mentors there, and a friend of theirs from the Princeton years, was one of the organizers. I had the pleasure of playing tour guide as we did sightseeing on St. Thomas and went by ferry to St. John for an island tour and good food. Here were small beautiful islands, totally accessible and the ever-present sea. I really think that part of the seductive effect of Santa Barbara, California on the St. Omers is the nearness of the sea. I remember well a restaurant where we ate more than once, mid-morning brunch, (for me bagel with tomato, lox and cream cheese) on a boardwalk looking out on sea stones and extensive water.

I have been at the receiving end of exhilarating conversation, good humour, good food and sustained laughter. I have a sense that the over-worked lines " life is worth living/while friendship is true" are overworked with good reason. I still feel hopeful about that fifth novel. We will read it yet.

JANE KING

RE-READING ST OMER – SOME VERY PERSONAL THOUGHTS

I was so glad to see Garth St Omer's books in print once more. I read them when I was young, and when my father, a man of St Omer's generation, was around to point out how similar some of the characters were to some of the people they had known. When I was able to read them again through the Peepal Tree editions, I found that they raised for me the same questions as they had raised when I first read them. One day I will be able to write a more scholarly piece, but for now, here are some personal thoughts.

The books are said to deal with "the relatively privileged mulatto middle class" (Jeremy Poynting, from the introduction to *A Room on the Hill*) in Saint Lucia – or at least somewhere very like it – in the 1950s. We are told that St. Omer is sometimes criticized for, among other things, not being sufficiently political, for not being optimistic, and (is this one odd? Are they all odd criticisms?) for too frequently using death as a plot device. I would admit to being irritated by the characters who constantly chafe against what they see as the restrictions of island life – and also of the reaction of some of the men to the women who seem to embody those restrictions and who are available to be punished for it.

The mulatto class of whom, indeed, he often wrote were mostly the more or less "fair-skinned" grandchildren of an earlier generation of true mulattos. Fanon, in *Black Skin, White Masks,* suggested on this subject that if a black person in the Caribbean wanted to marry a white person, he had better find a "metropolitan" white, Caribbean white people being traditionally disinclined to marry black people. Many of St Omer's generation of brown men who studied in the United Kingdom married white girls while they were there. But their own brownness had come mostly from white grandfathers who came from the UK (mostly Scotland and Ireland) and married black women in the Caribbean. That is, the brownness of the bourgeois Castries Columbus Square crowd came from there. There were, in the countryside, in beautiful plantation houses on the big estates, white people who could trace their descent from aristocratic European families (presumably they were the not very important branches of them), and those families often allowed their aristocratic names to spread with their wild brown oats. The Castries group of whom Garth St Omer writes, however, were not so much a class as a group that inbred a bit for a couple of generations. Their white ancestors had had no pretensions to the aristocracy; they were colonial functionaries, typically policemen or civil servants of one sort or another, perhaps with a stronger sense of adventure than those who stayed home in "Great" Britain. Typically, the white policeman had married the black lady who had caught his fancy and they had raised a generation of townspeople who would work in the white-owned businesses in Castries. My own great grandfather (son of a Scottish policeman) was an accountant with Minvielle and Chastanet. That second generation raised children who started going into business for themselves, and the next generation educated their own clever boys (and, only very occasionally, their clever girls) sending them overseas if they could afford it, or if the children were clever enough to win scholarships. (Their less clever children stayed in Saint Lucia where they were able to take advantage of the attributes they had inherited, and the interconnectedness of their families – it's always who you know! – to get jobs which were more difficult for their darker cousins.) This last was the generation of which St Omer wrote. The boys of this generation, who were lucky enough to get away to study, went off to the United Kingdom at the very end of the second World War, or just after it. They knew they had to stay away until they got their qualifications; there were no planes to bring them home for expensive summer vacations. This group ended up marrying white women in Europe. Fanon had rightly pointed out that white women in the Caribbean would not have married them, even if they had played with them as children. (Britain was still the "mother land", few of them went to the United States, which was still in any case a deeply segregated society.)

They were acutely class conscious. The brown business people knew that they were infinitely socially inferior to the landowning aristocrats of the countryside who had been born with land and money. But just as they believed that money made through business was inferior to inherited money, they believed also that professional people were superior to business people – even when they had less money. They wanted their clever sons to be professional. They chose that these boys should be doctors or lawyers. Even engineering was not yet quite respectable enough.

They grew up in a society in which racism was deeply entrenched. One member of this generation, who was one of the few true mulattos of whom I am aware (in that his father was a white man who married a black women, rather than a brown person marrying another brown person), told me that his father would go off routinely to the "country club", leaving his mother behind, because, although they were married, "coloured" people were not allowed in the club. Neither his father nor his mother – nor it seemed any of their children, even when grown up – saw anything strange or reprehensible in that; it was just how it was. My mother, one of the British white girls brought back to the Caribbean by a returning young brown doctor, told me that in the early 1950s, the governor would have three different sets of parties: for whites married to whites, for whites married to "coloureds" (no-one was actually called black yet) and finally for coloureds married to coloureds. I have to say I have never tried to verify this. But there was no doubt about the depth of her feeling about the kinds of racial discrimination she found in Saint Lucia when she arrived here in the early 1950s. Many, perhaps most, of this generation born in the 1920s and 30s have now died. I spoke to one of the last of the old ladies a few years ago, and she told me stories about my family and other members of the Castries brown business class. She spoke of my father's dead sister, and of other children of this group who had died in the 1930s and 40s, when large families were common and parents did not really expect to be able to keep all of them alive. Seeming quite unconscious of what she was saying, she described each dead child as amazingly "fair", incredibly pretty, and possessed of lovely hair. It was as if the lost ones were the lightest ones, and as if their loss was felt as a greater burden because of it.

Apparently, some have accused St Omer of using death too often as a plot device. It is an interesting accusation, and thinking about it may help us to think about some of the differences between our small island societies and the metropolitan ones – because the way we deal with death is surely one very obvious difference, something that those of us who grow up in the Caribbean notice very soon after our arrival in the metropolis. In the small islands, death is something with which we are very familiar – with which we are on everyday terms, in fact. Cemeteries are generally active places, not interesting historical adjuncts to old Anglican churches. And because our societies are small, we are far more acutely aware of our connections to each other. We may not actually know each other directly, but we know of each other, we know each other's relatives and friends. When someone dies, we are able to explain who the person is to a fellow island dweller by saying something like: You remember the lady who used to sell tamarind balls outside such and such a shop? She was his auntie. He used to play with so-and-so's kids…" Even dead animals are more evident in the Caribbean, and even urban Caribbean children are familiar with the smell of death in a way that most metropolitan children are not. It would be hard, in the context of these societies, even today, to overuse death as a plot device and remain true to the realities of small island life. We watch the death announcements on television while we eat breakfast, we are always aware that someone we know has recently lost someone.

St Omer also writes of the love affairs that were supposed to be secret but that everyone knew about – and these are the realities of life and death in a small island. They extend beyond plot device into the deepest crevices of small island life, and these social realities as much as any more political or economic sorrows are probably among the reasons why our youngsters are so desperate to escape. There is no action that is unobserved. Whatever you do, someone will talk about it, and it will get back to people you know whether you like it or not. Wherever you walk, someone will say to you, as Walcott wrote: "Oh, so you is Walcott? Roddy brother? Teacher Alix son?" People will recognize you and ask how your mother is doing. To a lot of our children, that quickly becomes unbearable. And of course, the other side of that coin is that one cannot unburden oneself anywhere. The only way to keep a secret in the Caribbean is to keep it to yourself. In the metropolis, one can say something to a friend in one context and believe it will not get back to one's relatives; that can't happen here. Plots have to be different in such societies. Perhaps, if talk therapy and the theories behind it work, we could surmise that the people of whom St Omer writes become so conflicted and so desperate to escape, simply because there is absolutely nowhere they can unburden themselves.

St Omer's main politics are gender relations – is there anything more important? There are those who believe that your choice of life partner is the most important choice you will ever make. St Omer spends much time looking at how people make these choices. What did these discontented small island boys imagine people in metropolitan countries did, but get married, work, raise children, work more and die? Just that they did it without the sense of connectedness that St Omer's characters detest rather than celebrate. The ones who came back had a chance to build a society. Most of them would never have had that chance overseas. In "What the Twilight Says", Walcott argues that "if there was nothing, there was everything to be made". St Omer didn't see it like that – and one of our problems today is that we still have many young people who feel like St Omer, and are just waiting for those scholarships to get them far away so they can stay far away. I wonder how happy they are as they make their homes overseas, or if these are the same people who complain of racism and other forms of discrimination? If you can't be satisfied with Saint Lucia and all its beauty and the opportunities to be made in it – what kind of thing is going to satisfy you?

Of course, St Omer's male characters don't only complain about Saint Lucia, they complain bitterly about women. Maybe it's just because they are Saint Lucian women, it's hard to tell. Women in the novels obviously do function as traps, wanting to attach themselves to ambitious men and doom them to unfulfilled lives in the civil service. One character is refused a scholarship because he wouldn't marry a woman he had made pregnant. That is a strange piece of fiction, because in fact a married man would not have been eligible for the scholarship. The male characters are of their time, and very few can imagine that women might also have wanted to study or see a little more of the world. It has occurred to me more than once that it is an oddity in the human male that he will seek out a sexual partner whom he will then despise, precisely because and only because she agreed to become his sexual partner. Many of St Omer's characters suffer from this strange syndrome. I don't think I've ever met a real life woman who did. In St Omer's books, sex sometimes seems to become a mechanism for punishing women unwise enough to give in to the men who demand it.

St Omer's characters inhabit a dark and unhappy island. Full of drowning rats, garbage, and bloodstained bandages. One of the big questions the novels raise for me is: how many of our youngsters feel their world is still like that?

Reading this, a friend challenges me to say how I felt personally, growing up as a "coloured" child (that was the term used in my childhood) in this still tiny society. Was I eager to escape? Did I see my Island Scholarship, as some of St Omer's luckier characters saw theirs, as a means to escape? Did I always want to come back? And of course, the answer is that yes, at seventeen I was desperate to escape. Sick of the small island society that cannot mind its business and where, wherever I went, people I had never met felt it perfectly appropriate to point me out to their friends and discuss, without inhibition, my parentage and my pedigree and the deeds and misdeeds of my ancestors. And to report to my parents what I was wearing and with whom I was liming. I know that seventeen year olds today feel the same. And yes, my Island Scholarship provided a blessed opportunity for escape, and I do not know how I would have escaped without it. Did I always want to come back? Once the first desperate homesickness had worn off, I have to say that it took a number of years for me to want to return. There was no money for regular holiday visits, and one grows used to being away. But eventually, perhaps, most people begin to see the value of being in a place where they are connected? These questions are deeply relevant in our sixth forms today. I hope that St Omer's books provide an avenue for our young people to begin to analyse why they themselves still feel so desperately that they need to get out.

CONTEMPORARY CRITICISM

MALICA WILLIE

THE ESSENCE OF A PERIPHERAL EXISTENCE:
THE PHILOSOPHY OF PSYCHIC EXILE
IN *THE LIGHTS ON THE HILL*

Lots of times you can feel as an exile in a country you were born in.
— Azar Nafisi

Only the misfortune of exile can provide the in-depth understanding
and overview into the realities of the world. — Stefan Zwieg

But what I see is the millions of people, of whom I am just one, made
orphans: no motherland, no fatherland, no gods, no mounds of earth
for holy ground, no excess of love which might lead to the things that
an excess of love sometimes brings, and worst and most painful of all,
no tongue. — Jamaica Kincaid

John R. Lee, writing in the *St. Lucia Weekend Voice*, suggests that Garth
St. Omer is obsessed with writing about the "products of colonialism"
and that he chooses to examine the psyche of such people because he
has lived through that experience (Lee, 2). Born in 1931, at a time when
Saint Lucia was allowed only a small degree of self-governance, while
still being under British domination, St. Omer, in his young adult life,
experienced the full weight of a colonial society and its cultural oppression.
One guesses that he experienced the psychic break that puts one at
odds with oneself and imposes a sense of homelessness in one's own
place. It is evident that St. Omer found in works such as Albert Camus'
The Stranger, which draws on Camus' experience of colonialism in Algeria,
a way of seeing his experience of growing up in St. Lucia. In *The Lights
on the Hill*, St. Omer constructs a character who feels like an outsider
in his own society and retreats into a comatose state. He portrays the
experience of exile, the malaise and inferiority that ensue, and filters
this local condition through the philosophical lens of existentialism,
which he draws from both Camus and Sartre.

Both Camus and St. Omer are concerned with the outsider status of the
person who suffers mental and physical colonisation; their main characters
in some respects mirror each other, though St. Omer takes further the
exploration of the psychical impact of exile, whether external or internal.

Stephenson, the protagonist of *The Lights on the Hill*, might be termed a Creole version of Monsieur Meursault, whom Hebatollah M. Hegazy, in his essay, "The Stranger who Killed a Stranger: the Nihilistic Algerian Frenchman, Meursault and His Colonized Arab Counterpart in Camus' *The Stranger*", identifies as a victim of society's rigidity. Hegazy argues that Algerian society makes Meursault an outsider because it does not understand him and the manner in which he views life. For instance, the lawyer is "greatly perturbed" (51) when Meursault states that he has lost the habit of making note of his emotions and that he thinks that all normal people at one point or another recognise the need for the death of a loved one. When Meursault denounces God, both the magistrate and the priest, he states, were "truly sorry for me" (73). Later, when they become aware of his lack of emotion over his mother's passing and his activities afterwards, the court and the wider society accuse him of "callousness" (51). Hegazy sees Meursault as an outsider who has become particularly unfeeling, emotionless and individualistic because he has been made an exile in his own community – a status imposed upon him because he views human life and existence differently from society's supposed norms. Hegazy describes Meursault as amoral because he is not bound by any of his society's values, religious beliefs or mores, and because of his incomprehensible act of murder for which he feels no shame or remorse. Stephenson has also been pathologically damaged by colonialism in his Caribbean space. He, like Meursault, does not seem bound by social mores or values, though he clearly believes that his corrupt practices are common to his society. St. Omer writes that:

> Commodities unobtainable before were coming into the island now. Everybody wanted them. Contraband goods, especially wines and spirits, came regularly from Martinique. Fines were stiff. Bribes, therefore, correspondingly large. He sold cloth, rum, cigarettes, perfumes, everything. And he accepted bribes. Finally they caught him. He had bribed his way out before. He could not do so now. (98/96)

Stephenson's conscience is no battle ground; others do what he has done; he is just unlucky to be caught. Previously, he simply bribed his way out of jail with no qualms about breaking the law; this time around, he is caught and fired. He applies for other jobs and receives "unfavourable replies" (103/98). He is no longer trusted on his island. He has become a pariah. He also has to deal with his foster mother Meme's "uncomplaining" nagging (102/99), his "…half brother's quiet, imperturbable concern" (102/99) and other people's "pity" (102/99). The island begins to close in on him: "[h]is sins, as he had known, could not hide [there]. The island was too small" (105/101) and for that reason "[t]he present had become intolerable" (105/101). When he receives a job offer on another island, he welcomes the opportunity of escape from the suffocations of his society. St. Omer portrays this desire for escape as a common motivation for people who experience their island home as so small, so limiting that it provokes an acute sense of claustrophobia. Gordon Rohlehr avers in his essay, "Small Island Blues", that the characters depicted by St. Omer "are constantly dreaming of escape, but are incapable of the effort of will demanded and finally surrender to the tedious limbo around them" (24/111). However, Stephenson does not just dream of escape; he leaves his island home. Nonetheless, "the tedious limbo" that Rohlehr refers to seems inescapable. In exploring this need for escape, St. Omer departs from Camus's portrayal of Monsieur Meursault, who seems so desensitized that he does not even experience such feelings of claustrophobia as he journeys through life in Algeria. St. Omer is suggesting, perhaps, that the island smallness of the Caribbean creates a more emotional reaction. The Caribbean subject feels, in addition to his colonial "outsiderness", to be in a state of internal exile in a restricted space.

Even in his new space, Stephenson still feels like a stranger. Like Meursault, he uses swimming, cigarettes and sex to distract him from his lack of engagement with life. He states outrightly that "[h]e did not care. He was like a man on his annual holiday, in a strange land, unknown" (33/49). He is a spectator, watching things go by, not part of the action. He makes no plans for the future, but simply enjoys the present which "was perhaps in order to avoid having to look at his uncertainty and indirection…" (46/58). He is seemingly content with this lack of direction until "Ronald's insistence, not any desire of [his] … had made him agree, finally, to Ronald's suggestion" (43/56) to return to his abandoned plans for higher education. In acquiescing to this advice, Stephenson feels that he is not making an individual choice; that he is conforming to society's ideological norm requiring the individual to create goals and map out a future. In presenting himself as not having a responsibility for his actions, Stephenson is able to persist in and intensify his outsider status. On the island where he goes to work, no one, except for Marie, knows of his past shame, yet he still feels unable to become part of this "new" society. Later, when he moves on to the university, as one of the oldest students on campus, he does not feel part of the society of young students bursting with youth, enthusiasm and promise. (Here St. Omer touches on a more general Caribbean experience. A good many Caribbean students, especially Saint Lucians, have to delay university in order to work to save enough money. When they have earned enough to support themselves, they are among the oldest people in the classrooms.) Thus, Stephenson's sense of unbelonging/*unheimlich* is further reinforced; he is described as being "[a]lways restless, always dissatisfied, hovering on the fringe of things, avoiding the centre or the depths"

(21/40). Every experience situates him in a continuous state of exile and St. Omer suggests that people from other Caribbean islands experience the same feeling of unbelonging. Reading his books one can suspect that he sees this infection as passed on from generation to generation, that Caribbean people can be seen wandering the world trying to assert a "self or selves". This seems Dionne Brand's view in *At the Full and Change of the Moon,* where she explores how memory haunts the Caribbean individual and suggests that it is the memory of their past homeland, and its history of trauma, that keeps Caribbean people lost in a kind of psychical prison. This history, which began in the Caribbean as the experience of forcible removal from ancestral "homes" into perpetual exile in unfamiliar territory, has caused a division in their psyches. Kierkegaard uses the word "spirit" as tantamount to the self and so, in this regard, perhaps Caribbean people feel that in the process of being removed from one space to another, they have left their spirits behind and the memory of that lost "spirit" haunts them to the point of paralysis.

Although Sartre and Camus had different backgrounds and had philosophical disagreements, their discussion of the nature of choice points to the conclusion that the Caribbean person's acute paralysis must be regarded as self-imposed. It may be a coping mechanism, but is nonetheless a choice. Camus discusses the concept of choosing in his short story, "The Guest", where the main character, Daru, is faced with a dilemma: he has to choose whether to take an Arab prisoner, who has murdered his cousin, to prison, or whether he should allow the man to go free. Daru decides to allow the prisoner to choose for himself, so removing the burden from himself. The Arab chooses to go to prison and in doing so, according to Camus, he automatically chooses on behalf of Daru, because the choice was Daru's in the first place. Allowing somebody else to make the decision does not strip Daru of responsibility. Thus, he is still accountable for the prisoner's choice. This idea of choosing relates to Sartre's statement in *Existentialism is a Humanism:*

> The coward is responsible for his own cowardice. He is not the way he is because he has a cowardly heart, lung, or brain. He is not like that as the result of his physiological make-up; he is like that because he has made himself a coward through his actions. There is no such thing as a cowardly temperament... what produces cowardice is the act of giving up, or giving in. A temperament is not an action; a coward is defined by the action he has taken. What people are obscurely feeling, and what horrifies them, is that the coward, as we present him, is guilty of his cowardice. People would prefer to be born a coward or be born a hero. (34)

In other words, what an individual is – a coward or a hero – is because that person has chosen to act in that manner; he or she has chosen to become whatever it is he or she is in the present. This is why it is pertinent that Stephenson seems to think that life happens and things were merely accidents for him. As well as Ronald's role in making him apply to university, when he breaks things off with Thea, "[i]t seems a decision I stumbled on by accident only, not a decision I made" (108). This attempt to separate himself from blame makes Stephenson unstable as a character, for he cannot even acknowledge his own failings as a person. He describes his life as a tide where he does nothing except float in whatever direction the tide takes him, like "a rat on a piece of driftwood" (25). He has no connections and no sense of belonging. (Here, the reference to the 'rat' might allude to Camus' *The Plague*, suggesting that the rat is not only a symbol of Stephenson's personal inertia, but is representative of Caribbean stasis and the turmoil or trauma that plagues all psyches.) St. Omer presents Stephenson as a character who is suffering from anxiety and who attempts to remain in a state of apathy out of fear of really having to choose for himself and, by extension, for the entire world. St. Omer describes Stephenson as having been afraid

> even to dip his wet bedraggled muzzle in the water that swept him, relatively safe, along with it. If he had any feeling, it was not of excitement, but of terror, a vague terror that made him very unwilling to go back again into the water that surrounded him. (25/43)

He experiences the anguish that Sartre talks about, which is similar to Heidegger's idea of dread. Sartre explains anguish thus:

> A man who commits himself, and then realizes that he is not only the individual that he chooses to be, but also a legislator choosing at the same time what humanity as a whole should be, cannot help but be aware of his own full and profound responsibility. True, many people do not appear especially anguished, but we maintain that they are merely hiding their anguish or trying not to face it. (21)

Stephenson, as indicated, wants to shirk all responsibility and exist as a neutral, inert being. But as Camus explores in "The Guest", neutrality is absolutely impossible in life, and so, even in an individual's "not choosing", he or she is making the choice not to choose. Stephenson remains in this state for most of the narrative, though at the end there is some tentative moment of release when he realises that he has been suffering from what Sartre refers to as "*mauvaise foi*" (109) or "bad faith" (109). In *Being and Nothingness*, Sartre defines this state:

> We shall willingly grant that bad faith is a lie to oneself, on condition that we distinguish the lie to oneself from lying in general. Lying is a

negative attitude, we will agree to that. But this negation does not bear on consciousness itself; it aims only at the transcendent. The essence of the lie implies in fact that the liar actually is in complete possession, of the truth which he is hiding. A man does not lie about what he is ignorant of; he does not lie when he spreads an error of which he himself is the dupe; he does not lie when he is mistaken. The ideal description of the liar would be a cynical consciousness, affirming truth within himself, denying it in his words, and denying that negation as such. (109)

Stephenson suffers from this false consciousness because he has been purposefully deceiving himself, convincing himself that he is not responsible for any of his actions. However, he finally comes to the realisation that:

He had tried to persuade himself that perhaps he was not responsible. That he could not have denied or prevented that desire for achievement that had driven him nor the dissatisfaction that not having it caused him. He had told himself that he was merely that which, ever since his birth and without his having any say at all, he had been tending to become. Now, talking to himself as he walked, he wondered whether it was not too simple an explanation. (113/107)

St. Omer explores the existential view, found in both Camus' and Sartre's work, that people cannot function in a state of inactivity simply because of their profound fear of the responsibility that comes with choosing a life for themselves and for others. The novella exposes the false consciousness of the self-defined victim and by the end of the text Stephenson is portrayed as beginning to overcome his somnambulism and become a lucid, conscious being. As Camus states in *The Myth of Sisyphus*, to question oneself, to begin to think about one's state of being, is to begin to be undermined (5). It is this undermining, this "wonder[ing]" (113) which delivers St. Omer's character from the trap of further bad faith.

Camus argues in *The Myth of Sisyphus* that modern man feels "alien, a stranger" (6) when deprived of "home"; his sense of comfort. This is very much Stephenson's situation. He "did not know his father, had not lived with his mother, had nothing in common with his brother Carl. He did not know what his grandparents looked like…" (61/69). For me, here, St. Omer is portraying the exiled status of Caribbean subjects. Stephenson becomes representative of a Caribbean history of forced exile from "home", to the state of interminable physical or psychical wandering in search for what was lost, but which can no longer be recovered. This exile, Camus explains, is an exile "without remedy since [they are] deprived of a memory of a lost home" (6) and for that reason, there is always a sense of *unheimlich* which creates a "constipated" (20) state in which the profound fear of being or becoming keeps them locked in an apathetic condition and in possession of an acute "inferiority complex" (20). This view is presented in Sylvia Wynter's article "Unsettling the Coloniality of Being, Power, Truth, Freedom", where she argues that colonised people were constructed as "racially inferior" (266) and therefore became the "human other" (266). Wynter declares that colonial discourse reduced Caribbean "Others" to a state somewhere between human and animal, and in part convinced them that they were outside and beneath what was considered "human" and "normal". As such, they were rendered powerless and nameless, reduced to a state of nothingness or, as Aimé Césaire describes it in his *Discourse on Colonialism*, they have been "thingified" (11). Their identity, their selfhood has been stripped away. St. Omer portrays this state of unfeeling anomie quite clearly when an American soldier (ironically, a Negro) beats a policeman from the island. He describes it in this way:

> Once a group of American Negro sailors beat up a policeman with sticks until he fell. From behind the closed jalousies he and Meme watched... They beat the fallen policeman until he no longer moved. The street was empty. Everybody looked from behind closed windows. Nobody went to help. (95/94)

According to Wynter, even if the colonised think that they are in possession of a semblance of power, this is an illusion, because anyone who is of African descent is automatically classified as less than fully human; and membership of the developing/underdeveloped/third world lowers the Caribbean person's status even further; the colonisers see themselves as superior beings and the colonised ethnoclass as the "backward other" (266). St. Omer illustrates this kind of blatant contempt for Caribbean people when the poor blacks in town are given "free" rum that was set aside for animals that were going to be slaughtered (*Lights*, 96/94). Here, St. Omer gives us a searing portrait of powerlessness in a colonial Caribbean society, where people are exiled from their place and from themselves.

Derek Walcott, in his poem "Homecoming" (which was written for Garth St. Omer), claims that sometimes, "...there are homecomings without home" (line 41). St. Omer seems less optimistic, though there is much in Walcott's poem he would endorse, particularly Walcott's argument on the futility of looking back, that the wish to return to Africa or India or some other mythical homes leads to a state of somnambulism, because perpetuating the hope of repatriation leaves Caribbean people longing for an unreachable past and therefore eternally locked in a mental prison, a state of fantasy. As Camus argues, hope reduces one to a sleeping state because hoping, in itself, obstructs a clear view of reality. The hope of one day returning home to a lost originary ancestral space is a falsity that obscures the here and now, and St. Omer seems to echo Walcott's premise when Carlton tells Stephenson that there is no need to go back home, that if he does choose to do so, he will find absolutely nothing there.

William Tell Gifford, in "Garth St. Omer's Existential Parlance", asserts that Stephenson is a "spirit in exile" (98). This claim seems accurate as Stephenson has admitted to his state as being more about inner "feelings" than physical circumstance. Harav Ariel Bar Tzadok, a Jewish rabbi, explains in "The Nature of Exile" that there are levels of exile. He describes psychical exile as

> A state of mind… the individual become[s] disconnected from [his]… inner psyche, [and] loses contact with [his] purpose of being. When [he] can no longer see into the depths of [his] own being to understand [him]self, to know [him]self and to be [him]self, [he] goes into exile from [his] own self. (1)

St. Omer portrays Stephenson as being in such a state of mental exile when early in the novella he acknowledges that he "…was finished with thinking. The lid of his thinking mechanism had snapped shut…" (35/50). This is a man who feels he must avoid any kind of Socratic self-examination, because he fears it will expose a state of nothing-ness, the realisation that he belongs nowhere and that he is nothing except what he makes of himself. This depiction of Stephenson as mentally exiled, wherever he is, is perhaps St. Omer's agreeing with Walcott that "home" is not necessarily a physical space but a state of mind. If one is not "at home" in one's own mind, it is impossible to feel that one belongs anywhere. Stephenson's only recourse at the midpoint of the novella is essentially to "finish… with thinking" (35) which is a kind of purposeful unconsciousness. Kierkegaard in *The Sickness Unto Death* argues that "[a] human being is spirit. But what is spirit? Spirit is the self. But what is the self? The self is a relation that relates itself to itself or is the relation's relating itself to itself in the relation" (13). Kierkegaard sees spirit as synonymous with the self and there must always be some sort of dialogue within the self in order to truly know oneself. If Stephenson's "unconscious state" is representative of the situation of Caribbean people, St. Omer's text suggests the need to cease trying to find a physical home and, instead, attempt to be at home with/within ourselves. One must take an internal journey into memory, experiences and knowledge, examine what is within and be at peace with it. This is what Wilson Harris seems to be saying in "History, Fable and Myth", when he describes the effect of traumatic transplantation to the Caribbean as resulting in a state of (mental and physical) limbo. Similarly, Fanon has discussed the Negro's fragmented psyche as a battle within, where the "bright part" (140) is attempting to consistently repress the "black part" (140). St. Omer suggests that the only way to overcome this kind of trauma is through self-knowledge. According to Sartre in *Being and Nothingness*, because humans are beings-for-it-self (*pour soi*) they are automatically supposed to be conscious of their consciousness. Some people hide from self because of their fear of the possibility of what they may face, but it is only through self-knowledge that such fear, and the paralysis it incurs, can be overcome.

As suggested in his longest novel, *A Room on the Hill*, St. Omer holds an existential, humanist position with regards to religion, specifically Catholicism, which is portrayed as a kind of life raft which, while it prevents one from drowning in the overwhelming sea of consciousness, at the same time, according to Miriam in *A Room on the Hill*, crushes one "under the weight of it" (32/32). As Karl Marx states in *Critique of Hegel's Philosophy of Right*: "[religion] is the opium of the people" (1). In a humanistic existential perspective, religion is the opium that places us in a somnambulistic state – that keeps us from recognising the true nature of existence. St. Omer presents this idea in a conversation between Marie and Stephenson. They agree that "religion's like a lifebelt around [the] neck. Around [the] waist, too... And sometimes around [the] eyes like a band. It's like false teeth. Only an appearance. To eat with it is hell" (74/78). They agree that religion is restrictive and that it blinds us to the truth of existence. St. Omer's novel can be read to imply that since "[w]e need help to cope" (74/78) with the hopelessness and meaninglessness of life, we use religion to give us direction. However, for many of the characters in his novels, religion seems mostly to be about the nature of "appearance" (74). In a Catholic-dominated Caribbean space, like Saint Lucia, they seem to be living in a perpetual state of self-deception. They act a certain way in public and then privately act in opposition to what they present "on stage", and lie to themselves about the difference. St. Omer portrays Edith and Rosa in *The Lights on the Hill* as being representative of this kind of self-deception. They are always attending church, going to confession or to vespers and presenting the face of piety to the world, but behind closed doors, they are the opposite. When she refers to Moira, whose "eyes were without bitterness, her smile without harshness or ambition, her manner without secrecy or pretence" (35/50), Rosa would "curl... her lips which left no doubt about her disdain for girls who went to the beach on Sunday mornings with young men" (30/47). The irony is that she behaves much like Moira, but since Moira does not hide behind religion, or any such facade, the rest of the community view her as a sinful outsider. Rosa does not expose herself to the wider community but, like Moira, she also has extramarital sexual intercourse with men, married or not. The idea of self-deception is quite clear in this regard, because Rosa's attitude indicates that she is somehow a better person or – to be more direct – less of a strumpet than Moira. Stephenson notes that:

> Once or twice [Rosa] met him on the street. She smiled and passed on.
> He stopped once and she was compelled to stop too. He reflected that,
> on evenings, at the foot of the steps, it was very different. (31/47)

According to Patricia Ismond, Rosa's attitude is representative of the
wider community. In her essay, "West Indian literature as an expression
of national cultures: the literature of St. Lucia", Ismond describes St.
Lucian society as suffering from hypocrisy or rather a state of anomie.
She argues that "[o]ne thing becomes quite clear about the society St.
Omer recaptures: there were glaring gaps between its prescribed norms
and its actual practices. The system harboured [a] kind of hypocrisy…"
(7). She implies that the religion that the society is urged to abide by
has created a psychic break or a double identity that individuals cannot
escape, and St. Omer portrays Edith and Rosa as epitomising that sort
of psychopathology. Nietzsche argues in *The Birth of Tragedy* that
"Christianity was from the beginning, essentially and fundamentally,
life's nausea and disgust with life, merely concealed behind, masked
by, dressed up as, faith in 'another' or 'better life'" (23). According to
Nietzsche, it is disgust with the primitive self (perhaps one's sexual
self) that necessitated the creation of a religion to hide behind. Perhaps
this is one reason why Caribbean people cling to religion so closely.
They feel a sense of shame and disgust for self and cling to religion as
a life line. The outwardly religious Rosa and Edith possess so much
shame about their sexual appetites, shame as a result of society's
expectations of women, that they have to lie to themselves.

Like Meursault, Stephenson avoids the tentacles of religion, though his
outsider status is further exacerbated by his separation from a society that
is addicted to the prescriptions of religion. However, the fact that he does
not have religion to contend with is perhaps one of the reasons why he is
able to shake off his false consciousness by the end of the novel. The
Christian's two-facedness comes about because he feels shame at being one
thing as opposed to another, and although Stephenson has much to
contend with as an alienated person, he escapes the internal anomie that
religion creates. I think that, for St. Omer, clinging to religion results in a
state of *mauvaise foi,* that the only way Caribbean people can come to terms
with their world is to shun the religion that forces them to exist in a state
of perpetual false consciousness. However, whilst the reader might suspect
that St. Omer thinks this, he, as a non-directive novelist, does not go in for
this kind of preaching in his fiction.

Frantz Fanon, in *Black Skin, White Masks,* holds that the colonised person
suffers a psychopathological state. He explains this as a fragmentation of the
psyche where blackness is repressed in favour of a white identity. In
essence, the black man learns to walk, talk, and dress and perhaps even think
like the white man. In this respect, colonials become imitators, actors.

Further, according to Homi Bhabha in *The Location of Culture*, the colonial man sometimes portrays the act of whiteness so effectively that the actual white man may become disturbed. But mimicry necessitates repression of other parts of one's self. In his essay, "Psychopathic Characters on the Stage", Sigmund Freud suggests that when we view certain plays or acts that represent aspects of our repressed identity, or when a performance threatens to unearth it, "our repression… is shaken up…" (309). We want, however, to ensure that whatever it is we are repressing or hiding remains hidden. Thus, when Moira performs on the societal stage, she enacts what this particular society has repressed. Although they find her entertaining at times, she is a threat to the society's consistent self-deception. When she flaunts her sexuality, this is deeply troubling. This connects to Fanon's argument that the white man ill-treats the black man because he sees the black man as a symbol of his own inner darkness: "the uncivilised savage, the Negro that slumbers in every white man" (190). In effect, the white man projects his savagery onto a symbol, so he can claim the highest level of civility. This is why Moira has been made an outsider. By appearing to exist as a "primitive sexual being", she becomes a representative of the savagery (repressed sexuality) that slumbers within this specific community. In a society where persons are trying to achieve a degree of respectable "whiteness", Moira is othered, but rather than resist, she finds "anaesthesia in this lamb-like acceptance, this docility that opposed neither the anger of her parents nor the indifference of her friends" (37). Like both Stephenson and Meursault, Moira reacts to this outsider status by opting for a comatose state. Whilst, unlike Stephenson, she breaks no law that could get her incarcerated, according to her society's ideals, she *openly* breaks a biblical law and is reduced to the status of sinner. Like Stephenson, she collapses into herself, goes with the current, refuses attachment to anything or anyone; she, too, is a rat afloat on a piece of driftwood.

Stephenson's fascination with Moira is based on the fact that he thinks she is what he would have become had he remained on the island. The irony here is that Stephenson considers himself different because he is able to leave the society he feels is suffocating him. However, both he (at this point in the novella) and Moira are in a similar state of unconsciousness. It is the resulting paralysis that leads Mr. Jones, a minor character in the narrative, to say that "[t]here's nothing before for those who stay to build upon. They'll leave nothing behind for others to build on. And that's how it is. I'd want my children to go away too" (39/67). Whilst no one seems to have the desire to stay to build and improve the society, the society is, in a sense, blocking its own way forward. Those who leave and then return, do so with the sole purpose of increasing their personal wealth. At one point the island is described as a "stranglehold" (106/101) and the novel suggests that had Stephenson remained, he would have sunk into a life of redundancy, a life of habit.

> He could have been comfortably married at home, going everyday to work, drinking after it, at home with friends, at their homes, or in one of the clubs, waiting for his steady slow promotion if he were in the Service, based on seniority and therefore inevitable. (112/107)

For some, escaping the mechanical drone of island life means leaving to better appropriate the colonial master's culture and ideas in order to bring them back to their own countries. According to Césaire, the intent of the "master" is to colonise and decivilise his subjects (2). Thus, if every colonial subject returns to his country with the coloniser's mentality and forgets his own roots, nothing will improve. St. Omer's fiction suggests that returnees have to develop another kind of forgetting, a state of somnambulism that allows them to enact a more "whitened self". Stephenson recalls the magistrate who tried his case and who, though he has once known Stephenson, behaves as if he has no idea who he is. This is particularly poignant as an instance of a society deliberately existing in a sleeping state. Perhaps Mr. Jones must be seen as speaking for many in the region when he describes the Caribbean as doomed, impotent and unproductive, and as a result incapable or unwilling to create an authentic society in the space to which they were historically exiled. The inferiority complex that resulted from colonisation, according to Fanon, has forced Caribbean people into believing that they are incapable of creating themselves.

When it comes to discussing the treatment of sexuality in the novella, it is worth considering Albert Camus's exploration of the figure of Don Juan. Camus argues that although we may consider Don Juan either as particularly immoral or as a man searching for love, what is most pertinent is that Don Juan is a very conscious being, and the fact that he has coitus with a plethora of women, without making any specific attachment to any of them, means that he is lucidly attaining gratification from the present. Don Juan does not focus on the future, but on his present pleasures. Stephenson, on the foreign island where he works, seems to be St. Omer's Don Juan; he, too, has multiple sexual relations with no strings attached. Stephenson evidently does not care about his conquests. When he was on his island, he slept with the women who were willing, and when he moved to the other island, he slept with Rosa and Moira, but really "[he] did not care" (33) about them or their feelings. He openly acknowledges that he simply wants sexual pleasure: "It seemed also there were no limits to the pleasures he derived from his body nor in the increasing efficiency and strength which it performed what he asked of it" (33/49). But the difference between Camus' Don Juan and St. Omer's Stephenson is that Stephenson is not, at this stage, lucid. He is still stuck in the prison of false consciousness. In "Another Place, Another Time", Derek admits to trying to find himself in the depths of Berthe's legs. Similarly, I see Stephenson as using physical gratification as a self-centred and misogynist way of finding a "home" for himself. Linden Lewis, in "Man Talk, Masculinity and a Changing Social Environment", contends that the Caribbean man's conception of masculinity can be traced back to slavery. He argues that:

> In the context of the Caribbean, the weight of history and culture can never be overstated. Slavery and indenture[ship] have exerted tremendous pressures on the construction of masculinity, forcing adjustments and accommodation to circumstances over which men at times had no control. (7)

During slavery, black men could not pursue monogamous relationships because slave-owners required their property to procreate to replace aging resources. In such a setting, the male slave assimilated specific norms. It was acceptable to have multiple sexual partners, to be sexually violent and to objectify women. This slave mentality is seen in Stephenson as he discusses his brutality with Thea on the field, and when he describes his footprints on Rosa's sheets – an image of misogyny on his part and by extension on the part of many Caribbean men. Later, although Stephenson makes an attempt to have a relationship with Thea, his treatment of women is clearly critiqued. St. Omer portrays a Caribbean society that valorises males over females and marginalises women. Stephenson notes, for instance, that while all the females remained on the islands, the males went off to study. The fact that men are still adhering to what they were taught during slavery highlights their continuing unconscious state. Sartre avers, in his preface to Fanon's *The Wretched of the Earth*, that "… the decolonised world… is imaginable, or achievable, only in the process of resisting the peremptory and polarizing choices that the superpowers impose on us" (7). Caribbean people, as exiles, need to revolt to awaken from this somnambulist state. According to Camus, in *The Rebel*, they need to say no to whatever is infringing upon their right to be in this world (12). They need to say no to those who are forcing them to exist on the fringe of things. In turn, St. Omer is asking the Caribbean man to make a choice: between existing as exiled sleepwalker or existing in a lucid state that allows the creation of free and individual expression.

As an existentialist writer, St. Omer valorises an outsider or exiled status, but he recognises the psychical form of exile as a plague that eats away the self from the inside out; it eats away at the consciousness of man and puts him to sleep. For him, there is no going back to a collective ancestral history. Caribbean people must learn to live in the now, but rather than yield to the absurdity of unconsciousness, they should choose to live responsibly, and to be responsible for others. St. Omer echoes Sartre when his character Stephenson concludes "… that human effort, in the end, if it did not benefit

others, was futile" (114/108). St. Omer's work demonstrates that colonialism has infected Caribbean people with somnambulism and that such a
condition causes a rift between people as well as within the self. Such a state
results in a kind of psychopathology, a wilful paralysis or at most an aimless
psychic wandering. The "awakening" of Stephenson at the end of the novel
suggests that it is possible for the Caribbean to emerge from its sleeping
state. This injunction, in our current Caribbean, is as crucial as when it was
first articulated.

Note: page references to St. Omer's novels give the original Faber edition
first, followed by the Peepal Tree edition.

Bibliography

Ashcroft, Bill, Gareth Griffiths and Helen Tiffin. "Post Colonial Literatures
    and Counter-Discourse". *The Post-Colonial Studies Reader*. London:
    Routledge. 1995. 95-99.
Ashcroft, Bill, Gareth Griffiths, and Helen Tiffin. "The Limbo Gateway".
    The Post-Colonial Studies Reader. 378-382.
Bhabha, Homi K. *The Location of Culture*. London: Routledge. 1994.
Brand, Dionne. *At the Full and Change of the Moon*. New York: Grove
    Press. 1999.
Camus, Albert. *A Happy Death*. New York: Knopf. 1972.
———. *The Plague*. New York: Modern Library. 1948.
———. *The Rebel*. New York: Knopf. 1954.
———. *The Fall*. New York: A. A. Knopf. 1956.
———. *Exile and the Kingdom*. New York: Knopf. 1958.
———. *The Myth of Sisyphus*. Harmondsworth, Eng.: Penguin Books. 1975.
Césaire, Aimé. *Discourse on Colonialism*. New York: MR. 1972.
Césaire, Aimé, and Mireille Rosello. *Notebook of a return to my native
    land*. Newcastle upon Tyne, England: Bloodaxe Books. 1995.
Church, F. J. *The trial and death of Socrates: being the Euthyphron, Apology,
    Crito and Phaedo of Plato*. London: Macmillan. 1886.
Dance, Daryl. *Fifty Caribbean Writers: a Bio-bibliographic Critical Sourcebook*.
    New York: Greenwood Press. 1986.
Fanon, Frantz. *Black Skin, White Masks*. New York: Grove Press. 1967.
Fanon, Frantz. and Richard Philcox. *The Wretched of the Earth*. New York:
    Grove Press. 2004.
Freud, Sigmund. *The Psychopathology of Everyday Life*. New York: Norton.
    1966.
———. *The standard edition of the complete psychological works of Sigmund
    Freud*. London: Hogarth Press. 1953.

Gifford, William Tell. "Garth St. Omer's Existential Parlance." Diss: Sonoma State University. 1988.

Heady, Margaret. *Marvelous Journeys: Routes of Identity in the Caribbean Novel*. New York: Peter Lang Publishing Inc. 2008.

Hegazy, Hebatollah. "The Stranger Who Killed a Stranger: The Nihilist Algerian Frenchman Meursault and His Colonized Algerian Arab Counterpart in Camus's *The Stranger*". *Academia.edu - Share research*. N.p.. n.d. Web. 12 Sept. 2013.

Hegel, Georg Wilhelm Friedrich. *Dialectic of Desire and Recognition: texts and commentary*. New York: State University of New York Press. 1996.

Heidegger, Martin. *Being and Time*. New York: Harper. 1962.

Ismond, Patricia. "West Indian Literature as an Expression of National Cultures: The Literature of St. Lucia". *World Literature Written in English* 29.2 (1989): 104-115.

Kierkegaard, Soren. *The concept of Anxiety: A simple psychologically orienting deliberation of the dogmatic issue of hereditary sin*. Princeton: Princeton University Press, 1980.

———. *The sickness unto death*. Princeton: Princeton University Press. 1941.

Kincaid, Jamaica. *A Small Place*. New York: Farrar, Straus, Giroux, 1988.

Lee, John. "Garth St. Omer: An Introduction to his Novels". *The Weekend Voice* [Saint Lucia] 27 April 1985: 6.

Lewis, Linden. "Man Talk, Masculinity and a Changing Social Environment". *Caribbean Review of Gender Studies* 5.1 (2007): 1 - 20.

Marcel, Gabriel, *The Mystery of Being*. Chicago: H. Regnery. 1960.

Marx, Karl. *A Contribution to the Critique of Political Economy*. New York: International Publishers. 1970.

———. *Critique of Hegel's 'Philosophy of Right'*. Cambridge: Cambridge University Press. 1977.

McDonald, Audra (AudraEqualityMc). "Know thyself. Then get thy shit together". 13 Dec. 2010. 11:16 AM. Tweet.

Moore, Gerald. "Garth St. Omer". Contemporary Novelists. New York: St. Martin's Press. 1972. 1084 – 1086.

Nafisi, Azar. *Things I've been silent about*. New York: Random House. 2008.

Nietzsche, Friedrich Wilhelm. *The Anti-Christ, Ecce homo, Twilight of the idols and other writings*. New York: Cambridge University Press. 2005.

———. *Beyond Good and Evil*. Buffalo, N.Y.: Prometheus Books. 1989.

———. *The Birth of Tragedy*. Oxford: Oxford University Press. 2000.

——— and Thomas Common. *Thus Spake Zarathustra*. Pittsburgh, Penn.: English Dept., Carnegie Mellon University. 1994.

N'v'im, Yeshivat., "Online School for Advanced Biblical Studies". *HaRav*

Ariel Bar Tzadok Essays at Kosher Torah. N.p., 2 Oct. 1997. Web. 12 Sept. 2013.

Raskin, Richard. "Camus's Critiques of Existentialism". *An Internet Journal of Philosophy* 5 (2001): 156 - 165.

Rohlehr, Gordon. "Small Island Blues: A short review of the novels of Garth St. Omer". *Voices* (Port of Spain) 2 (1969): 22 – 28.

Sartre, Jean. *Being and nothingness: an essay on phenomenological ontology.* New York: Philosophical Library. 1956.

——. *Existentialism is a Humanism.* Brooklyn: Haskell House. 1977.

——. *Colonialism and Neocolonialism.* London: Routledge, 2001.

——. *Nausea.* New York: New Directions Publishing Corps. 1964.

——. *No Exit and three other plays.* New York: Vintage International. 1989.

——. *The philosophy of Jean-Paul Sartre.* New York: Random House, 1965.

Shah, Muhammad Maroof. "Vetoing Transcendence: Albert Camus as a Philosopher of Immanence". *The Criterion: An International Journal in English* 3.1 (2012): 17.

St. Omer, Garth. *Shades of Grey.* London: Faber. 1968.

——. *A Room on the Hill.* London: Faber. 1968.

——. *Nor any country.* London: Faber. 1969.

——. *J—, Black Bam and the Masqueraders.* London: Faber. 1972.

——. *The Lights on the Hill.* London: Heinemann. 1986.

——. "Syrop". *Introduction 2: stories by new writers.* London: Faber and Faber. 1964.

——. "The colonial novel: studies in the novels of Albert Camus, V.S. Naipaul and Alejo Carpentier". Diss: Princeton University. 1975.

The Holy Bible: King James Version, Peabody, Mass.: Hendrickson Publishers, 2004.

Thieme, John. "Double Identity in the Novels of Garth St. Omer". *Ariel* 8 (1977): 81 - 97.

Tzadok, Harav Ariel Bar. "The Nature of Exile". *KosherTorah.* 32.4 (2010): 1 – 3.

Walcott, Derek. *Selected Poems.* London: Heinemann. 1981.

Webber, Jonathan. *The Existentialism of Jean-Paul Sartre.* New York: Routledge. 2009.

——. *Reading Sartre: on phenomenology and existentialism.* London: Routledge, 2011.

Wynter, Sylvia. "Unsettling the Coloniality of Being/Power/Truth/Freedom: towards the Human, after Man, its Overrepresentation—an Argument". *Project Muse* 4 (2002): 257 - 337.

Zwieg, Stefan. *The World of Yesterday: An autobiography.* New York: Viking Press. 1943.

MILT MOISE

"BEYOND THE FLAMES": THE CASTRIES FIRE, TRAUMATIC DISCOURSE AND THE UTILITY OF FAITH IN DEREK WALCOTT'S "A CITY'S DEATH BY FIRE" AND GARTH ST. OMER'S "ANOTHER PLACE, ANOTHER TIME"

The most high Jah, deliver me.
Through my troubles and trials,
he comforts me." — Fantan Mojah

Ah love, let us be true
To one another! For the world, which seems,
To lie before us like a land of dreams,
So various, so beautiful, so new,
Have really neither joy, nor love, nor light,
Nor certitude, nor peace, nor help for pain;
And we are here, as on a darkling plain
Swept with confused alarms of struggle and flight
Where ignorant armies clash by night.
    "Dover Beach" — Matthew Arnold

Photo by Oliver Cadet

1948 Fire

In the morning hours of the 19th to the 20th of June in 1948, Castries, the capital of St. Lucia, was ravaged by fire. Much of the city was completely destroyed, with 809 families losing their homes and being displaced. The entire commercial district, most of the government buildings, the main library and the Voice publishing company, all perished in the blaze. A few places survived the onslaught, including St. Mary's College, St. Joseph's Convent, the Police headquarters and the Church of the Immaculate Conception. However, in the face of almost total destruction, the capital of this British colonial outpost lay in ashes, like a wasteland. Needless to say the effect on the populace was devastating, and for days many walked through the ruins of their beloved city in shock, with the memories of the conflagration etched firmly into their consciousness. Events such as a fire can render a population shattered, creating a sort of collective trauma that needs to be worked through. No one could have possibly imagined that a young man by the name of Derek Walcott would have traversed this desolation, and penned a poem entitled, "A City's Death by Fire" which would become the enduring representation of this traumatic event.[1] Although the poem was published a year after the fire, much of the city remained in ruins for a significant period of time, and so Walcott's poem would still have been found resonant by a majority of the populace.[2] In "A City's Death by Fire", the citizens of Castries would find the comfort, reassurance and hope required to press forward and rebuild the city. However, twenty years later in 1968, a contemporary of Walcott's, Garth St. Omer, would depict this catastrophic event in a much different light.

The protagonist of St. Omer's novella "Another Place, Another Time" (half of *Shades of Grey*) walks through the streets observing the fire with a very different perspective from the persona in Walcott's poem. While Walcott's observer ultimately decides to "rebuild a love I thought was dead as nails/ Blessing the death and baptism by fire" (lines 13-14), St. Omer's main character finds "himself calm, uninvolved" and passive, "exulting in its size, wanting it to go on for ever, the firemen and those who helped them to be ever more inefficient, the wind stronger and more capricious" (170). Two figures, two vastly different reactions to a disaster. One has been canonized, anthologized many times over, heralded as the coming-out party of one of the twentieth century's greatest poets, recited ad nauseam, and performed by schoolchildren across St. Lucia. The other has fallen into obscurity. Why has Walcott's rendition of this singular event in St. Lucian history achieved such a lofty position? Apart from its obvious literary merit, one has to consider how it addresses the issue of trauma. Both Walcott and St. Omer's texts function as literary spaces where a traumatic event is experienced, and ruminated upon. It seems obvious then, to turn to trauma theory in order to adequately grapple with the questions of representation and reception that surround these two literary works.

Since the American Psychological Association officially acknowledged Post Traumatic Stress Disorder as a disease in 1980, interest in trauma has grown exponentially. One outcome of this is the interdisciplinary field of trauma theory, which attempts to determine how writers negotiate and resolve their personal traumas, as well as interrogate their depiction of trauma on a larger scale. Trauma theorists propose that the sudden confrontation with violence or death creates a state of psychic shock, which writers attempt to alleviate through writing. By documenting or recreating their experience, authors seek to express voice and find meaning to such events via the act of testifying. The audience becomes an active sounding board, a "witness" that facilitates and participates in this act of mental healing, and defines how the event will be remembered. Speaking in *Trauma: Explorations in Memory* Cathy Caruth argues that:

> [i]f PTSD must be understood as a pathological symptom, then it is not so much a symptom of the unconscious, as it is a symptom of history. The traumatized, we might say, carry an impossible history within them, or they become themselves the symptom of a history that they cannot entirely possess. (5)

Caruth believes that because of the severity of traumatic shock, individuals who suffer from such experiences have a delayed reaction, whereby the experience is understood at a later date, in fragmented and overwhelming recollections. As a result, narratives of trauma exhibit what Freud described as *Nachträglichkeit*, which has been translated as 'deferred action or afterwardness' (Whitehead, 6). Such stories tend to be splintered and depart from traditional narrative structures, as they do not depict linear time frames. Michael Ondaatje's *The English Patient*, which deals with the lives of individuals in the crosshairs of the Second World War, is a novel of this type. It jumps from the consciousness of one character to another, with alternating time frames and various narrative perspectives. Caruth also agitates for trauma theory to serve as a space where cross-cultural engagement can take place, as catastrophes and our attempts to come to terms with them are ubiquitous across cultures, and solicit similar responses. However, the literary critic Stef Craps demurs, proposing that:

> the founding texts of the field (including Caruth's own work) largely fail to live up to this promise of cross cultural engagement. They fail on three counts: they marginalize or ignore traumatic experiences of non-Western or minority cultures: they tend to take for granted the universal

validity of definitions of trauma and recovery that have developed out
of the history of Western modernity: and they often favour or even prescribe
a modernist aesthetic of fragmentation and aporia as uniquely suited to
the task of bearing witness to trauma.

Since trauma theory was born out of the events of the Holocaust and
more recently 9/11, its methods of analysis have taken on a decidedly
Western tinge. Much attention has been paid to events and texts of the
Occident, at the expense of those from other parts of the world. In addition,
most of its practitioners have focused on more experimental texts, which
they believe, exhibit more accurately the conditions of trauma. However,
this is once again an example of what Sylvia Wynter has termed the
overrepresentation of Western man as the human, by which all other homo
sapiens should be judged and considered. People from the developing
world suffer from trauma as well, and the manner of its portrayal often
manifests itself in more established and recognizable forms of storytelling,
as exhibited in Walcott's sonnet and St. Omer's novella. This seemingly
traditional approach should not immediately exclude their depiction of the
Castries fire from the discourse, since they have much to say on how and
why particular representations of disaster take root and flourish, and others
do not. While "A City's Death by Fire" is a more uplifting work of literature,
I will argue that Garth St. Omer's brief mention of the Castries fire in
"Another Place, Another Time" is a more wholistic and terrifying dia-
chronic snapshot of a society, which merits consideration alongside
Walcott's. That St. Omer's version of events has been excluded from the St.
Lucian literary consciousness, and is virtually unknown when compared to
"A City's Death by Fire," is less of a reflection of his text's literary worth
than its frightening counter-discursive nature.

In his essay "What is an author?" Michel Foucault posits that every
culture has its own autochthonous discourses, and the author fulfils a
specific function within the community. The romantic notion of the
author, hermetically enclosed within his or her room is just that, romantic.
Foucault refers to what he calls "the author function", remarking that the
situation of the author having exclusive rights and being identified as the
originator of a work is a relatively new phenomenon in human history, and
fails to adequately describe how an author is created and sustained. The
acceptance and reception – even subsequent canonization – is determined
and regulated by the culture in which the work circulates (Foucault, 142).
Echoing the words of Bakhtin, Foucault argues that readers of a text
naturally find themselves engaging in hermeneutics that privilege a particular "tendency" or viewpoint concerning a literary work, which goes
beyond the text itself. In order to comprehend what is before them, they
must consider the social implications of the discourse which is embedded
within the work, and how and why the text, which is itself emblematic of

a particular set of discourses, has attained a particular status and reception. Discourse, while ubiquitous, constant and at times relentless, is potentially destabilizing and:

> ... in every society the production of discourse is at once controlled, selected, organized and redistributed according to a certain number of procedures, whose role is to avert its powers and dangers, to cope with chance events, to evade its ponderous, awesome materiality.
> (Foucault, 149)

He goes on to explain that there are three main systems that govern discourse. Firstly, prohibited words. Who gets to speak and what is this person allowed to say? Each culture has certain subjects that are taboo, and through the creation of disciplines, particular individuals are educated and granted dispensation to speak. Secondly, the division of madness. From the Middle Ages onwards, "a man was mad if his speech could not be said to form part of the discourse of men" (149). The ramblings of the declared insane are not considered cogent enough to be part of the general discourse, but writers have always used madness as a trope, positing the mad man or woman's words as revelatory and prophetic. The world itself is often portrayed as a crazy, chaotic place, which the "unstable" speaker ironically elucidates. Lastly, Foucault speaks of the "will to truth," that ever present human need to seek that which is *objectively* true, and can be proven. Exclusion is a vital function, as we fear the "uncontrollable aspect of discourse" and this logophobia of a mass of spoken things, is a fear of a violent irruption of words and their "weightedness," in terms of the worlds encased within them (158). Considering Walcott's "A City's Death by Fire" and St. Omer's "Another Place, Another Time" in the light of Foucault's theory of discourse, one thing becomes limpidly apparent: Walcott's more palatable evocation of the Castries fire fits into prevailing, acceptable discourse, while St. Omer's does not.[3]

Throughout literary history, fire has had many symbolic associations. In the story of Prometheus, it functions as a stand-in for knowledge, which the titan brings to humanity. In many instances of biblical exegesis it is associated with judgment. In the work of romantics such as Wordsworth and Keats, it often refers to the warmth of a hearth and home. Fire is also often employed as a symbol of sexual desire, as evidenced in Robert Frost's "Fire and Ice", as well as countless other poems and popular music. But more germane to this paper is the motif of fire as a transformative force. Surveying the landscape of a city that has been destroyed by flames, Walcott's persona exhibits a loss of faith in the octave of the sonnet:

After that hot gospeller had levelled all but the churched sky,

I wrote the tale by tallow of a city's death by fire;
Under a candle's eye, that smoked in tears, I
Wanted to tell, in more than wax, of faiths that were snapped like wire.
All day I walked abroad among the rubbled tales,
Shocked at each wall that stood on the street like a liar:
Loud was the bird-rocked sky, and all the clouds were bales
Torn open by looting, and white, in spite of the fire.

A questioning of one's religious belief is an understandable response to such an event. Adorno famously remarked that to write poetry after Auschwitz is barbaric, which speaks to the paralyzing effect disaster could have on poetic voice, and the inappropriateness of poetic language as a medium to depict such a tragedy. However, the young Walcott's precocious use of literary technique and imagery captures the desolation and anguish more than adequately. The setting is an animated, personified one, where the candle weeps over the destruction, and the walls, once safe and protective, are exposed as being unable to guard against the fire, leaving the persona to condemn them as liars. Edward Baugh, who is perhaps the preeminent scholar of Derek Walcott's corpus, maintains that his writing is deeply autobiographical and "[r]unning through his work is a continuously self-interrogative fictive persona in whose eyes a world takes shape" (Introduction. *Derek Walcott Selected Poems,* xv). But this process of self-knowledge does not occur at a remove from the community that he is a part of, as from early in his poetic career, he takes on the responsibility of being the voice and witness of his society. In lines 4-5 he articulates a longing to tell the story of those who had lost their faith, "in more than wax," expressing the desire to create a literary monument that will endure the test of time, unlike the walls of the city. There are resonances of Percy Bysshe Shelley's "Ozymandias", another sonnet where "[n]othing beside remains" (53), and in the organic creative process required of the sonnet, the poet reconstructs and captures for posterity the memory of what was witnessed. The poem becomes a repository of history, and the poet becomes its chronicler. In a later poem, "Mass Man," Walcott repeats this theme declaring that:

Upon your penitential morning
some skull must rub its memory with ashes,
some mind must squat down howling in your dust,
some hand must crawl and recollect your rubbish,
someone must write your poems. (*The Gulf and Other Poems,* 43)

The use of anaphora adds force to this declaration, underscoring the exigency of the need for someone to articulate the collective consciousness of the community. Walcott, in his self appointed role as poet laureate, accepted the task of documenting the trauma of his people. In "A City's Death by Fire" the persona ultimately returns to his faith, and offers placing trust in the spiritual, rather than the material "wooden world" (Walcott, *In A Green Night*, 10) as the solution to the existential crisis created by the devastation.

St. Lucia is a very Christian country. Roman Catholicism is the dominant denomination, but many strains of Christianity are found throughout the island, including the Methodism to which Walcott belonged. By using religious vocabulary, Walcott was speaking in a language that would have been received favourably. Having learned a lesson from his first foray into poetry at the age of 14, he employs a more ecumenical sentiment in "A City's Death by Fire", steering clear of theological and doctrinal minefields.[4] In the volta of the poem, he pivots from surveying the ruination, and asks "why/Should a man wax tears when his wooden world fails?" (9-10). From line 9 onwards his tone shifts and "expresses a need for a deeper meaning in existence beyond the physical and material facts of life" (D' Aguiar, 217). The fire, "that hot gospeller," is now seen as a transformational instead of a destructive force, whose levelling of "all but the churched sky" (Walcott, *In A Green Night*, 1) forces the persona into contemplation of the numinous. Walcott not only gives voice to the traumatic experience, but also offers a way to move past the state of psychic shock it engenders by focusing on spirituality. In a Christian nation, this sentiment would inevitably have been embraced, and would have provided the solace required by the majority of the people. In moments of national crisis, citizens turn to their leaders and influential figures for words of comfort and encouragement. Although not a well-known public persona at that point of his life, Walcott was preternaturally attuned to the soul of his fellow countrymen and women, and in "A City's Death by Fire" he created the perfect poem for the situation. Its considered, carefully crafted form firmly established him as St. Lucia's greatest poet.

By the time Garth St. Omer writes "Another Place, Another Time" in 1968, "A City's Death by Fire" had had twenty years as the definitive literary representation of the Castries fire. Quite a few St. Lucians, particularly the educated class to which St. Omer belonged, were familiar with the poem as it had been incredibly well received at home and abroad. Many poems were written about the fire from places such as St. Vincent, Barbados and Tobago, but in "A City's Death by Fire", according to Bruce King, "St. Lucia has its first [local] 'classic,' a literary work now taught in its schools, which defines an important moment in national history, symbolizing the end of an era" (53-54). A key aspect of postcolonial writing about trauma is the tendency to write back to classic European texts. The intertextual novelist, by relying on the familiarity of the source text, could attempt to speak for those who lie in the shadows of the original work, bringing the details of their material and spiritual exclusion to light (Whitehead, 90-91). Helen Tiffin describes this as "canonical counter discourse," citing *Wide Sargasso Sea* as the perfect exemplar of this technique (Tiffin, 92). In this novel, Jean Rhys takes up an already established set of characters and tells a different story, focusing on the marginalized individuals from the colonial space, highlighting issues of racial, national and cultural identity which would not have been present in the original work (Whitehead, 92). While much attention has been paid to how postcolonial writers employ intertextuality to critique canonical works such as *Robinson Crusoe* and *Wuthering Heights*, not enough consideration has been given to what I will term "intratextuality" in postcolonial, and specifically West Indian literature. Writers from all literary traditions engage with each other's work and the Caribbean is no exception. While it is clear that authors from the region continue to wrestle with the manner they have been described by their quondam masters and global powers, they are also involved in discussions amongst themselves. "A City's Death by Fire", because of its widespread dissemination and acceptance, can be viewed as a canonical source text, with which Garth St. Omer is engaging in critical dialogue.

That St. Omer sets his story in the same span of time as Walcott's poem, even choosing to name his protagonist Derek, is no coincidence. St. Omer is consciously responding to "A City's Death by Fire", and providing what he believes is much needed context. Walcott's portrayal evinces a widely held understanding of a traumatic event, which is defined by the American Psychiatric Association's diagnostic manual as a sudden and unexpected occurrence, which deals a devastating blow to the psyche. However, in St. Omer's depiction of how his protagonist Derek experiences the fire we see a different type of trauma, which attempts to move beyond the single event model that has so dominated the discourse. While Walcott's persona is concerned with the immediate aftermath and finding a way to cope with destruction on such a massive scale, St. Omer's protagonist revels in the fire, and remains detached from the suffering that surrounds him. His reactions are noticeably different from his mother's who was:

> [j]ust standing there watching the house begin to burn; just standing there too numb to speak, next to him still blowing hard, as if she heard no noise, felt no heat, saw no flame, no smoke, no flying sparks: as if she had not realized, standing next to the box of his books she had saved, that he had arrived too late to help her. (170)

Despite the apparent shock Derek's mother exhibits, she has displayed the presence of mind to rescue his books. Considerations of education bookend this section of the novella, as prior to the fire his mother had refused his offer to find a job in order to assist her, much to Derek's relief. Sylvia Plath, in her 1963 novel, *The Bell Jar*, remarks that "[w]hat a man is is an arrow into the future and what a woman is is the place the arrow shoots off from" (74). A recurring lietmotif of St. Omer's is the sacrifices made by women in order for their sons and lovers to be able to leave the island and attend university abroad, thus demonstrating how they function as the bow that launches the men off into the world, in the hope that they will return and be able to take care of them emotionally and financially. Despite the matrifocal nature of the society, women had little education and earning power, and depended on mates and offspring to contribute to the household (Blank, 4). Unfortunately, many of the men who were able to leave either settled abroad, or returned only to feel beholden and discontented with the life that awaited them.

In St. Omer's 1969 novella, *Nor Any Country*, Phyllis remains behind and suffers the loss of her twins alone, while her husband Peter gets to live overseas and work towards his doctorate. Upon returning to the island and finding her as faithful as Penelope, "[h]e resented the assurance with which, over eight years, Phyllis had waited for him" (38). After the fire, Derek sits staring at the sea, over which he will one day cross, and concludes that "[i]t had suddenly become absurd that she should have suffered and struggled merely that he should qualify for a clerkship in the Service and for the slow promotion within it over the years until he died" (172). Although he feels a burden of responsibility to render her efforts worthwhile, he rightly recognizes the opportunity his mother's hard work has afforded him. Derek's indifferent response to the fire is a luxury his mother simply does not have: while he will be able to eventually leave and start a new life in another place, because of her age and sex, she is bound to the environment in a way he is not. The destruction of the house she has taken years to make into a home can only render her numb with shock, and underscores her helplessness. Women in the West Indies have made tremendous strides, and from the mid 1980's onwards, they have consistently made up more than half the number of enrolled students at the University of the West Indies. (Lindsay, 61). While the glass ceiling persists, since women still do not make as much money as men and do not feature prominently enough in leadership positions relative to the population, things have changed for the better since the period in which "Another Place, Another Time" was set. St. Lucia (and the Caribbean) in 1948 was not a place where women had many options.

While Walcott's persona eventually views the fire as transformative, St. Omer's protagonist embraces its destructiveness. His indifference forces us to confront something that Walcott's poem, despite its acknowledged greatness, elides: the social and historical factors that underlie, and arguably precipitate, the trauma faced by the people for whom he is speaking. St. Lucia, in the period in which Garth St. Omer penned his account of the Castries fire, was a place where religion had a dominant stranglehold on the society. Patricia Ismond argues that in order to fully grasp the recurring topoi of Walcott's and St. Omer's work, one has to have an understanding of the "specific historical and sociological forces" that have shaped their consciousness. She outlines how, out of the transatlantic slave trade and the many battles between the French and the English for control of St. Lucia in the 19th century, Roman Catholicism emerged as the supreme force in the country, but by the time the British finally wrested control of it from the French, they inherited an island that was of little strategic importance and as a result, a form of inert colonial administration ensued. The "political absenteeism" that was Crown Colony rule meant that political life in St. Lucia was stagnant. In the place of a more vigorous and involved governmental presence, the church filled the void. Morality and codes of conduct became the province of the Catholic Church. Ismond sets out how both Walcott and St Omer respond to this stifling set of values from an alien culture which permeated through all spheres of the island's life, as well as its public and domestic affairs. The reach of the church was absolute, and its influence on the citizens was all encompassing. In "Another Place, Another Time", Derek is representative of many of St. Omer's anti-heroes, who attempt to escape from the Church's overwhelming and suffocating stranglehold by "maintain[ing] a defensive solipsism which is one of the symptoms of their traumatic route through unbelief" (Ismond, 33). By drawing into himself and becoming estranged from society and religion, Derek hopes not to succumb to the inertia and desolation of the social landscape, and seeks to keep it at bay. But for someone who has decided to extricate himself or herself from the restricting yet sustaining force of the church, the end result is alienation.

The "crash of structures" (169), which Derek views as mesmerizing and exulting, is a metaphor for the restrictive societal structures that were centred around religion and its ossifying influence, which he wishes to see come to an end. The fire is an agent of judgment, as in its purging potency "[h]e wanted every house to be gutted, everything in the houses destroyed" (170). The absoluteness of his calamitous vision speaks to the endemic hopelessness that pervades the society: in his eyes, not one household is exempt from degradation. In light of this, it is not surprising that St. Omer's depiction of the Castries fire would have been considered destabilizing and contrary to the ethos of social stability desired by the government, clergy and laity. In its celebration of destruction, retreat into individualism, and representation of sexuality, St. Omer's representation would have found itself a prime target for exclusion from the dominant discourse.

According to Foucault, "in every society the production of discourse is at once controlled, selected, organized and redistributed according to a certain number of procedures, whose role is to avert its powers and dangers" (148). Of particular importance is speech concerned with politics and sexuality, as it threatens to upset the often tenuous moral and civil consensus which has been achieved. In a deeply religious country like St. Lucia, the threat of potentially disruptive discourse would be even more fiercely guarded against. Derek's reaction to the fire would be viewed as a betrayal of his community and its Christian values. St. Omer presciently anticipates how the actions of his main character would have been perceived and through his narrator remarks that: "the fact of his betrayal had followed him, quietly too, lit up by the flames, as acute as the smell of Berthe on the middle finger of the hand he raised to his brow" (170). Berthe and Derek belong to the same social class, where poverty is commonplace and education is the only way of escape. But by cruelly dominating her sexually and risking a pregnancy that would limit her options, Derek proves to be selfish and betrays the trust she has placed in him (Ismond, 36). The manner in which he disregards her and revels in his fornication would have been anathema to a more conservative St. Lucian audience. His final declaration towards the end of the novella that "[h]e had no cause nor any country now other than himself" (190) is antithetical and contrary to that of the persona in "A City's Death by Fire", who took upon himself the responsibility of speaking for the collective. Perhaps if St. Omer's protagonist had acted callously, withdrawn into himself, resurfaced and reintegrated into the community, the story's reception would have been different. But ultimately St. Omer refuses to compromise his artistic vision. Jacqueline Cousins rejects the widely held view that because St. Omer does not offer any solutions to the trauma of religious oppression and the after-effects of colonialism, his writing is deficient, negative and cynical. Instead, she views him as a very moral writer:

> [w]hose subject matter is the social and psychic dislocation of individuals and whole communities who endure the colonial condition against the backdrop of an inimical universe. (20)

There is no place of spiritual retreat for St. Omer's characters and by extension, the people of St. Lucia and any similar colonial space: religion is a panacea, a sort of opium that maintains the status quo. Governments are ineffectual, indifferent and absent, and cannot be relied upon to effect any significant social change. The community is broken, devoid of impetus, role models, a genuine indigenous moral code, and cannot offer any real succour. His depiction may be brutal, but it is scrupulously honest and revelatory, and the only solution, he suggests, is a retreat into the self. Only then can one face the traumatic experience that is daily existence in a colonial society.

In Haruki Murakami's short story "The Mirror" a security guard in a high school late at night feels threatened by an unseen presence. In his

subsequent search, what he discovers, in a rather Lacanian epiphanic
moment, was his reflection in a mirror, leaving him to remark that:

> My reflection in the mirror wasn't me. It looked exactly like me on the
> outside, but it definitely wasn't me. No, that's not it. It *was* me, of course,
> but *another* me. Another me that never should have been. (56)

Subsequently the protagonist comes to a rather profound conclusion,
after not finding the mirror the following day: "I can never forget how
terrified I was that night, and whenever I remember it, this thought
springs to mind: that the most frightening thing in the world is our
own self" (59). Perhaps the reason Garth St. Omer's fiction remains
largely unread in his own country is the manner in which it reflects
aspects of the society which it would rather ignore, which it feels like
never should have been. As the security guard in the story rightly remarks,
the most terrifying thing in the world is to confront the dark inner
recesses of your own self. St. Omer is advocating for a confrontation
of this darkness, rather than the continued use of sex, religion and
alcohol as diversions. Only then, he argues, will the people be able to
arrive at a true sense of themselves, and adequately deal with the
longstanding issues they face. The worlds he limns does seem to "[h]ave
really neither joy, nor love, nor light, [n]or certitude, nor peace, nor
help for pain" (Arnold, 210), but if its inhabitants could be true to
themselves, the hope is eventually they would be able to be true to
one another and heal the society.

It would be wrong for one to conclude that Derek Walcott remained,
throughout his poetic career, wedded to the type of religious faith exemplified in "A City's Death by Fire". As Ismond articulates, he becomes more
critical of mainstream Christianity and its complicity in the perpetuation
of racial taxonomies, as demonstrated in the words of Afa, the fisherman in
his 1954 one act play, *The Sea of Dauphin*: "God is a white man. The sky is
his blue eye. His spit on Dauphin people is the sea" (61). But as an
octogenarian in the title poem of his 2011 collection *White Egrets* he states
that "Sometimes the hills themselves disappear/like friends, slowly, but I
am happier/that they have come back now, like memory, like prayer" (9).
Walcott's peripatetic existence mirrors that of his religious belief: despite
constant peregrination he always returns home to his native St. Lucia, and
in his faith, despite the remonstrations from the Catholic priest of his
childhood, he continues to find spiritual resonances in the natural landscapes he surveys. St. Omer, likewise, maintains his viewpoint of spirituality, dismissing it as an ineffectual coping strategy adopted by the down-
trodden postcolonial masses throughout his fiction. In "The Lights on the
Hill" one character describes it as "…false teeth. Only an appearance. To
eat with it is hell" (78). For St. Omer, religion and faith only provide a patina

of comfort that the reality of existence punctures. Ultimately, they are useless. It is to Walcott's credit that he presents a nuanced, evolving exploration of belief, which has allowed him to be embraced by those of both religious and secular persuasions. Perhaps the critics of St. Omer missed the mark when labelling his bleak depiction of St. Lucian society his greatest weakness: it seems obvious that his repudiation of the efficacy of religious belief ignores its potency and ability to serve as a force for good, even occasionally inspiring positive social change. Despite this limitation, the representation of the Castries fire in St. Omer's "Another Place, Another Time", if only for its elucidation of the social conditions of the period of Walcott's poem, which includes a contrasting and more complicated view of trauma, merits a reappraisal. Keats once said that "Beauty is truth," but the obverse is also true. A disconcerting ugliness can also contain verity.

Works Cited

Arnold, Matthew. "Dover Beach". *The Poetical Works of Matthew Arnold*. Ed. C. B. Tinker and H. F. Lowry. Oxford University Press, 1957. 210.

Baugh, Edward. Introduction. *Derek Walcott Selected Poems*. By Derek Walcott. New York: Farrar, Straus and Giroux, 2007. xv.

Blank, Sharla. "An Historical and Contemporary Overview of Gendered Caribbean Relations", *Journal of Arts and Humanities*. 2.4. (2013): 1-10. Web. 6 Feb. 2014.

Cadet, Oliver. *Fire in the City*. Photograph. Castries Fires. *Castriescitycouncil.org*. Web. 7 Jan. 2014.

Caruth, Cathy. Introduction. *Trauma: Explorations in Memory*. Ed. Cathy Caruth. The Johns Hopkins University Press, 1995.

Craps, Stef. "Beyond Eurocentricism: trauma theory in the global age". *The Future of Trauma Theory Contemporary Literary and Cultural Criticism*. Eds. Bert Guelens, Sam Durrant and Robert Eaglestone. New York: Routledge, 2013. Kindle File.

D' Aguiar, Fred. "'In God We Troust' Derek Walcott and God". *Callaloo*. 25.1 (2005): 216-223. Web. 4 Jan. 2014.

Fanton Mojah. "The Most High Jah". *Stronger*. Greensleeves, 2008. CD.

Foucault, Michel. "What is an author" and "The Discourse on Language". *Critical Theory Since 1965*. Eds. Hazard Adams and Leroy Searle. University of Florida Press, 1986. 138-162.

Frost, Robert. "Fire and Ice". *Selected Poems of Robert Frost*. Ed. Robert Graves. New York: Hope, Reinehart and Winston, 1963. 137.

Ismond, Patricia. "The St. Lucian Background in Garth St. Omer and

Derek Walcott". *Caribbean Quarterly*. 28.1. (1982): 32-43. Web. 4 Jan. 2014.

Keats, John. "Ode on a Grecian Urn". *The Poetical Works of John Keats*. Ed. H. W Garrod. Oxford University Press, 1956. 209-210.

King, Bruce, *Derek Walcott A Caribbean Life*. Oxford University Press, 2000.

Lindsay, Keisha. "Is the Caribbean Male an Endangered Species?" *Gendered Realities Essays in Caribbean Feminist Thought*. Ed. Patricia Mohammed. Kingston: University of the West Indies Press, 2002.

Murakami, Haruki. "The Mirror". *Blind Willow Sleeping Woman*. Trans. Philip Gabriel and Jay Rubin. New York: Knopf, 2006. 55-60.

Ondaatje, Michael. *The English Patient*. New York: Knopf, 1997.

Plath, Sylvia. *The Bell Jar*. London: Faber and Faber, 1963.

Rhys, Jean. *Wide Sargasso Sea*. New York: Norton, 1966.

Shelley, Percy Bysshe. "Ozymandias". *A Book of the Sonnet*. Eds. Martin Kallich, Jack C. Gray and Robert M. Rodney. New York: Twain Publishers, 1973. 53.

St. Omer, Garth. "Another Place, Another Time". *Shades of Grey*. Leeds: Peepal Tree Press, 2013. 113-191.

——. *A Room on the Hill*. Leeds: Peepal Tree Press, 2013.

——. "The Lights on the Hill". *Shades of Grey*. Leeds: Peepal Tree Press, 2013. 37-111.

——. *Nor Any Country*. London: Faber and Faber, 1963.

Tiffin, Helen. "Postcolonial Literatures and Counter Discourse." *The Postcolonial Studies Reader*. Eds. Bill Ashcroft, Gareth Griffiths and Helen Tiffin. New York: Routledge, 1995. 95-98.

Walcott, Derek. "A City's Death by Fire." *In A Green Night*. London: Jonathan Cape, 1962. 14.

——. *Another Life*. Boulder, Colorado: Lynne Reiner Publishers, 2004.

——. "Leaving School". *Critical Perspectives on Derek Walcott*. Ed. Robert D. Hamner. Boulder, Colorado: Lynne Reiner Publishers, 1997. 24-32.

——."The Sea at Dauphin". *Dream on Monkey Mountain and Other Plays*. New York: Farrar, Straus and Giroux, 1970. 41-80.

——. "White Egrets". *White Egrets*. New York: Farrar, Straus and Giroux, 2010. 6-10.

Whitehead, Anne. *Trauma Fiction*. Edinburgh University Press, 2004.

Wynter, Sylvia. "Unsettling the Coloniality of Being/Power/Truth/ Freedom: Towards the Human, After Man, Its Overrepresentation- An Argument." 257-337. *Project Muse*. Web. 5 Jan. 2014.

"1948 Fire". *Castriescitycouncil.org*. n.d. Web. 15 Jan. 2014.

Endnotes

1. Walcott would revisit the fire as a theme in his 1973 collection of poetry *Another Life* as well as in his 1965 essay "Leaving School." In both cases, undoubtedly due to his maturity as an individual and a poet, he exhibits a more complicated, almost existential view of the fire. However, I would argue that none of these depictions attained the iconic status of "A City's Death by Fire" due to factors I outline in this essay.

2. St. Omer also mentions the lengthy duration of the rebuilding project in *A Room on the Hill*, stating that "[a]fter eight years some portions [of the city] still had not been rebuilt. In the vacant lots the grass was high behind the concrete pavements and here and there a coconut – or a breadfruit-tree stood out of it" (36).

3. There was a flurry of critical interest in St. Omer's work that reached its apex in the 1980s which has since waned, leading to the bulk of his oeuvre going out of print until Peepal Tree Press decided to reissue his fiction in 2013. Currently, young St. Lucians are not exposed to St. Omer's work at secondary or tertiary level, and he has faded into obscurity on the island. This is in stark contrast to Walcott's corpus, which is taught, recited and performed at all levels of learning in St. Lucia.

4. In his first poem published in *The Voice of St. Lucia* as a teenager, the young Walcott was chastised in print by a Roman Catholic priest for advancing the romantic notion that one can learn about God from nature rather than the church.

JEREMY POYNTING

PRISNMS

Prisnms (Prisons/Prisms) is Garth St Omer's fifth, and hitherto unpublished novel. A first draft dates from the late 1970s and it went through a number of substantial structural revisions in the 1980s to take the form it is now published in; St Omer's continuing engagement with the novel is shown by the fact that he made a significant number of textual revisions after the novel was accepted by Peepal Tree in 2014.

Unlike his first four published novels (and his novella, *Syrop*), which are set in the Caribbean (in St Lucia and Jamaica, though unnamed in the novels) *Prisnms* is set in the USA. This change of setting, after St Omer had been away from the region for some years, is wholly consistent with his attachment to a scrupulous and intimate realism. Whilst the earlier novels were not necessarily written whilst St Omer was resident in the Caribbean, they all relate to periods when he was either a youth growing up in St Lucia, a resident on the Mona university campus in Jamaica or as a young man who had returned to St Lucia. *Prisnms*' main character and first person narrator, Eugene Coard,[1] is a St Lucian (though he reports that he arrived there as a youth from a flat, limestone island – no doubt Barbados), who is in contact with other expatriate St Lucians whose island, like his, is one of memory only.

As I hope this account will show, this is a novel that stands comparison in quality with St Omer's first four novels, all published by Faber, arguably the most distinguished literary publisher in the UK. Why *Prisnms* failed to find a publisher in the 1980s must be a matter of supposition, but I suspect that, on the one hand, it was seen as too embedded in its American location and, on the surface, too different from the four earlier novels to persuade Faber that they could market the novel in the UK. For American publishers *Prisnms* was perhaps not American enough, not falling into such recognised categories as the "African American" or the "immigrant" novel. *Prisnms* takes off in a more metafictional, symbolist direction, with an ancestry that includes Ralph Ellison's *The Invisible Man* (1952), but with a distinctively Caribbean angle of vision. It was also submitted for publication in a less risk-taking American publishing environment. Comparison can be made between *Prisnms* and the work of the African American writer, Percival Everett, whose *Erasure* (2001) satirises the propensity of American publishing houses to serve up only the crudest kinds of cultural stereotypes in African American writing. Everett's satire may well suggest one reason why the subtleties of *Prisnms* passed American publishers by.

In its structure, *Prisnms*, like several other St Omer novels, falls into three parts. It begins with a telephone call to the "I" narrator, Eugene Coard, from his St Lucian acquaintance, Selwyn, bringing him the news of the murder of "Red", formerly C.B, and once Eugene's closest friend. What follows is flashback into Eugene's memories of his island connections with Selwyn, Red/C.B. and their other mutual friend, the mostly absent Paul, now a globe-trotting concert pianist. Eugene reports on his sexual adventures as a medical student in London, his accident and temporary return to the island seven years after he left and his rapprochement with Beatrice, the first woman he has wronged, whose betrayal seems the one act he truly feels guilty about. Eugene confesses why he had to leave London and we learn of the different directions the lives of the four St Lucian men have taken in the USA. Here, St Omer, with characteristic economy, sums up the Caribbean novel of migration in a dozen or so pages, with a neat reference to Sam Selvon's Sir Galahad in *The Lonely Londoners*, when Eugene as the new arrivant meets up with Selwyn, who becomes his "surrogate, a modern knight errant in black face and a three-piece suit [...] His phallus was his lance, and I his fearful, repressed, and not always believing, yet not wholly unadmiring squire" (p. 20). But mostly we share Eugene's confessions of his complicated and duplicitous dealings with women both in London and after he settles in the USA.

The second part of the novel begins on the morning after the phone call, and ends with the funeral of Red/C.B., at which a fifth St Lucian character appears – Frederick Olsen, known to the others on the island, but never as an intimate because of his lower-class origins, as Red Bam. In this part of the novel we witness the mounting deviousness of the narrator in his practice as a psychiatrist, where he inverts the supposed clinician/patient relationship to manipulate his clients to meet his own needs.

A coda, the last part of the novel, takes place on the day after Red's funeral, on All Hallows or "trick or treat" day, when Eugene's Japanese-American girlfriend, Peggy, a writer who has been working with Paul on his biography, returns from travel. They attend a masked party and then, in a bizarre, and chilling episode, are attacked on their way home by a group of masked skaters. The last scene takes place in hospital where Eugene is just beginning to recover from life-threatening injuries, and becoming conscious that Peggy has told him that she can't marry him (why is not explained, though there is a hint that she has been raped during the attack) and that Frederick Olsen is dead, killed in one of those random incursions of violence by which St Omer is wont to remind the reader of human fragility and the occasional malignity of chance.

If readers of St Omer's earlier novels have begun to pick up some echoes in this brief resumé, they would be right. Although there is a sizeable gap between the writing of *Prisnms* and the earlier novels, and there are no common characters (though there is a reference to the dying Black Bam from *J—, Black Bam and the Masqueraders* (1971)), St Omer continues to invite the reading of his individual novels as part of a collected work. In the first part of the novel, the account of Eugene's misogynist, dysfunctional relationships with women has overt similarities with episodes and characters in the earlier novels. The close friendship between Eugene and C.B./Red ends violently when Eugene is caught by C.B. as he is "angrily, inexpertly" doing to his sister, Beatrice, dress up, backed up against a wall, what he has heard she has done with "every other man on the island". C.B. tries to kill Eugene but manages only to break his arm, held back by Paul and Selwyn. It is an episode that echoes the sexual violence of Derek Charles's relationship with Berthe (also, like Beatrice, raped by others) in "Another Place, Another Time" (*Shades of Grey*), or the sexual contempt Paul Breville expresses towards his first girlfriend, Patsy, in *J—, Black Bam and the Masqueraders*, or Stephenson towards Moira (a girl with a similar reputation to Beatrice) in "The Lights on the Hill" (also in *Shades of Grey*).

When Eugene is in London as a student (like Peter Breville in *Nor Any Country*) he is involved in double-dealing but self-defeating relationships; in his case with an upper-class white woman, Sarah, whom he betrays through his exploitative relationship with Ekua, a West African nurse, whom he casually makes pregnant, then allows her to think they will marry before going to Africa. Meantime he has deliberately impregnated Sarah (using a sabotaged condom) so she will have to marry him. It is the women's discovery of each other and his expulsion from Sarah's comfortable house that makes Eugene reinvent himself as an immigrant to the USA. Eugene's relationship with the two women inverts the class/ethnic dimensions of Peter Breville's relationships with Anna (upper-class Black) and Daphne (lower middle-class White) in *Nor Any Country* but exhibits the same traits of male hypocrisy and confused identity.

What makes *Prisnms* different from the four St Lucian novels, is the monstrous character and narrative role of Eugene Coard, though even here a closer look shows how it extends earlier themes and, indeed, suggests ways in which we should reread elements of the earlier novels. Eugene Coard is, indeed, perhaps the most unreliable first person narrator in any Caribbean novel, a Dostoyevskian/Sartrean anti-hero who exhibits a deviousness of psychopathic, almost mythic proportions.

That element of myth is suggested in a curious fragment in the narrative when Eugene tells us that he returned to St Lucia "while my breast healed", after suffering an automobile accident in London, a "rent in my sternum" that nearly killed him. It is curious because the detail has no direct narrative function, but recalls the beginning of *Nor Any Country* where the novel references the Homeric *nostos* (homecoming) in a playful way. At one level, the accident provides Eugene with a justification for his manipulation of others: "I knew accident. I had recovered from one. I wanted to avoid accident. I wanted my children to be safer than I had been" (p. 13), but perhaps the rent in his breast also signals the passage through which his metaphorical heart has escaped. It makes ironic the scene when Eugene is going through the calculated step of becoming an American citizen and he describes himself with his "hand over my heart" making his pledge of loyalty.

Eugene admits to inventing so much (one of his repeated confessions is, "I lied") that one should perhaps put his name in quotation marks; can we be sure even of his name? The novel reinforces this point by introducing other St Lucian characters whose migration to the USA has involved a change of name as well as of persona. Middle-class C.B. becomes the disreputable Red, whilst Red Bam becomes the respectable businessman, Frederick Olsen. These reversals open into one of the social contexts in which the novel is grounded – the institution of race in the USA as it may be experienced by someone from the Caribbean middle class. It appears that both C.B. and Red Bam have the kind of "mixed" appearance that in St Lucia invites the epithet "red" (as in Walcott's "red nigger" Shabine in "The Schooner *Flight*"), though mainly as a signifier of lower classness, whilst C.B.'s initials are the signifier of his middle-classness, signalling the kind of school he has attended. However, their inverted fortunes in the USA seem shaped by just where they lie on the spectrum of shade. C.B., from a respectable Protestant family becomes the karate champion, killer of an unarmed man in a fight, jailbird and denizen of the ghetto ("Red's Kingdom") that Eugene regards as alien, dangerous territory although its people "were like people I had grown up with". St Omer would undoubt-edly have known *The Autobiography of Malcolm X* (1973), where the former Malcolm Little (whose mother was Grenadian) became the hustler "De-troit Red". Red Bam, on the other hand, is the "illegitimate" child of a part Indian prostitute and a white seaman, a "wharf rat" whom the children of respectable St Lucians are commanded to avoid, but who in the USA, because no one knows his origins, and no doubt aided by his paleness of shade and the Europeanness of his features, is able to take on the seaman's imagined name and reinvent himself as a prosperous shipping agent.

The self-transformations that Eugene makes are similarly ones that could only be made in a society such as the USA, and he is throughout the novel located at a point of contradiction in American society between the opportunities that people from the Third World can only dream of, and the racism deeply embedded in its culture. Eugene, indeed, finds particularly inventive ways of exploiting both the presence of the luxury industries (such as the well-rewarded practice of psychoanalysis) supported by the country's material wealth, and the opportunities – though at great cost to others and ultimately to himself – for making a profitable profession of race. The occupation of professional black man is naturally not one that was well rewarded in the St Lucia from which Eugene comes. But Eugene is more than just a portrait of a man grown monstrous in a particular social context; he is also an extension and deepening of what St Omer had been exploring in characters such as Peter and Paul Breville in *Nor Any Country* and *J—, Black Bam and the Masqueraders*. In those two novels, St Omer draws ironic contrasts: Peter is the brother who is regarded as sane, Paul as deranged. What St Omer shows us is really the opposite: that Peter Breville, though apparently managing his successful career as a university lecturer (admittedly living in an environment where casual infidelity, drunkenness, violent misogyny and political and social hypocrisy appear to be quite easily countenanced), is, in fact, divided in ways that indicate that, in comparison, it is really his brother Paul, the family failure, who has fallen into derelic- tion, who is sane with his painful and self-critical honesty – if sanity is defined as a truthful relationship to reality.

Peter Breville proclaims his blackness as a man of the people, but is actually deeply glamoured by whiteness and class privilege; he spouts radical slogans about decolonization and social equality whilst having an affair with Jeannine, a white French Caribbean woman of the upper classes with patrician views; he has seized on the social advantages of marriage to a woman of mulatto brownness, but is snobbishly contemptuous of her lack of education. At the end of *J—, Black Bam and the Masqueraders*, Peter Breville is portrayed as trapped in stasis,[2] on the edge of collapse, no longer able to hold together a profoundly divided self.

At the end of his period in London, Eugene is in much the same position, and what *Prisnms* does is to explore the trajectory of what comes next. The difference is that whilst Eugene Coard evades the kind of collapse that Peter Breville may be headed towards, he does this by projecting his divisions outwards, in a much more hazardously public way, dramatising the conflicts within his divided psyche by manipulating the minds of others, treating them as if they were characters in a play he is writing.

Thus, in the USA, Eugene's dealings with women are even more devious than his affairs in London. They begin with an account of his telephone relationship with a woman called Janice, a bank-worker who finds his voice "So English […] so cultured". In all his conversations with her, Eugene has employed the upper-class English accent (no trace of island) that his ex-wife Sarah has taught him to use. As he must know (in the racial context of America), Janice assumes that he is English and white, and he doesn't disabuse her. When they finally set up a meeting in a café, Janice fails to recognise him. As Eugene narrates the episode, it concerns his humiliation that Janice can't connect his voice and his appearance, and his (pretended) surprise that things should be this way. However, read with the hindsight of Eugene's later behaviour, the episode also becomes the first revelation of his unreliability as a narrator and his aptitude for learning. It is in this respect that Eugene surpasses Peter Breville. While Peter becomes ever more trapped in his contradictions, Eugene takes something from each episode of deception that furthers his skills in manipulation. His discovery here is that his ability to mimic various accents allows him to disturb the racial gaze ("a peculiar look of recognition, which I found insolent in its familiarity" (p. 21)) and this signals the beginning of his much more ambitious career of psychological deceptions.

The "rejection" by Janice initiates the next episode of manipulation and revenge. Eugene spots an African American woman outside the café with her young son. He imposes himself on her by addressing her as "Sister", as if by their shared blackness she owes him some special consideration (something he rejects angrily in his relationship with his African American student colleague, Reginald). Thereafter he stalks the woman, Carol, in a predatory way, looking for a "weapon to use against her", which he finds in her emotional vulnerability. When Carol makes it plain she doesn't want to have anything to do with another foreigner (she has just been abandoned by her South African husband, supposedly a freedom fighter), Eugene transforms himself into an American, taking citizenship classes and learning to speak with an American accent (though not at first successfully, because he horrifies Carol by speaking like a white American). Eventually, Carol gives in to Eugene's persistence, but the marriage lasts only twelve weeks, because he expresses such jealousy towards the ex-husband that Carol begins to suspect (rightly, though she only knows the half of it) that she is dealing with a very disturbed character. The ending of the marriage suggests that Eugene has seized on Carol as an act of displaced racial and sexual revenge over the injustice he thinks he suffered at the hands of Sarah and Ekua in England, because they have denied him access to his sons. As Eugene confesses when he first catches up with Carol and her son: "I would make him my ally in my campaign against his mother. I would pretend that I was to him the father I could not be to my sons" (p. 31). At the point where he tells us he has worked through his feelings of jealousy (if they really existed), and has found more sexual satisfaction in masturbation than sex with Carol, he confesses: "I decided that she was no longer necessary to me, it was easy one night to rape her and rid myself of her and her South African ex-husband once and for all."

Now whether Eugene is just coldly calculating, or in the grip of the compunctions he claims, is left unclear, but what is evident is the lesson he learns from his engagement with Carol. He knows that to win her he needs to construct a life she can admire and this must exclude the actual history of why he had to leave London. Given that Carol has no means of investigating his claims, what he constructs is telling. In his invented story, the reason for his divorce was his white wife, Sarah's "promiscuity", and he even invents letters purporting to describe the child that he knows nothing about. What he learns from the success of this narrative, which feeds into his next project as a psychiatrist, is the usefulness of inverted or slightly transformed versions of the actual as sources of plausibility, precisely because such details have the ring of the truth. But St Omer also has Eugene reveal a level of wish-fulfilment in his inventions that hint at his vulnerabilities. He admits: "And I was forced to create, for her admiration, my own version of the life I would have liked truthfully to claim I had so far lived, a life that would reveal that I, too, like her ex-husband, was a good man, a good husband and father" (p. 37). However, whilst Eugene's habits of self-reflection enable him to learn new levels of deceit, his acute self-consciousness also begins to undermine his ease in playing particular roles. He imagines, for instance, that if he resumes speaking as an educated (West Indian) foreigner he might recover the privileged position of anomaly he has enjoyed with his three postgraduate student colleagues, but he also discovers that his engagement in manipulative role play has undermined any guiding sense of authenticity. Even to speak as a West Indian would be an act of calculating projection designed to "escape the presumptions of my listeners", and there comes a point when Eugene realises that he can no longer perform this since he had "given up the lilting accent of the Caribbean in order to acquire Sarah's aristocratic English accent". He recognises that there has been something self-enslaving in his acts of imitation, and that, referencing Robert Louis Stevenson, he has played "the sedulous ape". All this makes him feel "bitterly, more than ever appropriated by them [i.e., the roles he performs]" (p. 44). However, this self-contempt leads him to engage in ever more outrageous acts of deception.

There are a couple of occasions when, for instance, Eugene makes a mistake with his accent (when he speaks to the waitress in the café and tries to disguise his accent ("sound like an American") so as not to reveal himself to Janice and his voice comes out "raised, not pleasantly"; and when he learns the wrong kind of American accent to impress Carol. Here, he counsels himself to have patience, reminding himself that when he was in London "Sarah had not allowed me to try my new English accent until she was sure I spoke it like one who had always used it" (p. 25). What is not said, but implied, is that this creates a gap between the thinking mind and the speaking voice, the creation of a persona who is always involved in translating himself into someone else. It is his mastery of this gap that makes Eugene so dangerous for others, and dangerous to himself because he progressively loses touch with any grasp of reality. Later in the novel this is something he admits when he recognises that using the African American accent that Carol demands of him not only has given him a persona that offers him no protection in the USA, but that also "I was becoming, indeed that I had already become, someone else, someone other than myself, whom I did not know" (p. 43). He recognises, too, that "I could not feel safe for long. My private sense of myself could not withstand the constant public assaults upon it" (p. 43). It is in the mistakes that Eugene makes and his revelation of uncertainty at such moments that create the tension necessary to put his character into motion, beyond the flatness of a case history, and provide the novel's narrative dynamics.

Indeed, it is the tension between Eugene's persuasive analysis of the pathologies of American social life and his very evident unreliability as an observer that makes *Prisnms* so rewarding. It satirises the compartmentalisation of American life through race and class, but also undermines the bonafides of its narrator's attempts to deal with that social sickness. We see this in Eugene's relationship with his three study companions when he begins his university course in psychiatry, when he discovers that though he gets separate invitations of hospitality from each of them (from white upperclass Porter to the family estate in the hills, to Jewish Jonathan's Reform temple and parents' apartment, and African American Reginald's invitation to his mother's home in the ghetto and request that he join him in teaching supplementary classes in his old high school), none of them has ever invited the other two to their homes. Eugene realises that he enjoys the privileges of the educated foreigner whose cultural difference and apparent lack of history in America's race wars outweighs his visible racial identity, though he recognises that his colleagues' approaches are shaped by their own particular ideologies of race and class and not as a response to his individual character.

Significantly, it is with privileged Porter that he feels most affinity; Eugene's social position in St Lucia has, after all, been one of relative privilege. He records that, on the island, "I had always been made to feel whole", even if that has involved amnesia about his slave antecedents. With Jonathan and Reginald, on the contrary, he is anxious not to be implicated "in their sense of themselves as victims or victim-missionaries" (p. 59). St Omer leaves ambivalent Eugene's dismissive response. Is he genuinely affronted by his colleagues' polite racial profiling? Is he someone who has swallowed the American dream of "unrestricted personal fulfilment" and wants no distractions? Or is he just a sociopathic loner in flight from the mess he has made for himself in London?

The novel is full of sharp, economically written cameos that appear to show how that social order works: there's a scene where a white woman tries to give Eugene a spare cinema ticket and she refuses to accept the money he offers, "Especially from you"; another when Eugene is waiting at a bus stop and is engaged in what may or may not be sly racist banter by a white man in front of a group of observing white boys. Eugene's response is as old as slavery: he plays a Sambo deaf-mute routine, but the episode is then complicated by the arrival of a white tramp, the kind of derelict Eugene knows he would have abused and mocked as a child in St Lucia, but who here insults him as a nigger. But as we read each of these episodes, and ponder their presentation, we are invited to wonder whether they, like so much else, are also Eugene's inventions.

It is at this point that the novel slides away from a precarious kind of realism to a metafictional inventiveness that is both playful and deadly serious. Eugene finally completes his studies as a psychiatrist and launches a career that can only be described as a calculated means of working out his own contradictions by tormenting the minds of his patients. It begins quite literally in invention, when Eugene publishes some case studies as academic papers and confesses: "I claimed they were actual case histories; but those studies of alienation were based on my experiences which I concocted and attributed to patients I invented." The examples he quotes are slyly funny, describing behaviour that was "always outrageous and often inexplicable." There is the "Janice Syndrome" suffered by a young bank clerk who after meeting the man with whom she has been flirting on the phone, suddenly becomes deaf and blind, but with no medical explanation for her condition; or the patient who suffers from the Ellisonian illusion of invisibility.

Then in one of the neat comic ironies that characterise the novel, Eugene, the fictionaliser, is offered the psychiatric practise that his Jewish colleague Jonathan wishes to give up in order to pursue a serious career as a novelist. What this gives Eugene is a clientele of wealthy Euro-American patients. He begins a search in books, museums and art galleries for the cultural shaping of his new patients "not simply as people formed and shaped in America, but as Americans influenced by the traditions of Europe they or their ancestors had fled from" (p. 67). This research into ancestry inevitable leads Eugene to "examine my own condition as an American". There are new publications which, behind the "neutral, academic tone", express his despairing recognition that "as my fellow countryman had fled Europe and come to America to be powerful and white, so I had come to be powerless and black" (p. 68). He knows that the logical path would be to flee America as the ancestors of his clients fled Europe, but he can't imagine himself as "important, influential or relevant" in any other country. The history he goes back to is as much Caribbean as American, when he studies the psychology of the slave driver who is himself a slave, or the colonial administrator who is one of the colonised. He becomes "an expert in the psychology of the collaborationist in all his guises and disguises", though in his book the word collaborationist does not appear: "I used words like shrewd, practical and pragmatic". Throughout his narrative, Eugene describes his actions with a peculiar honesty, but the self-contempt he describes (real or pretended) again only serves to sanction the next episode of revenge. This is his project to deprive his clients of their "comforting hybrid sense of themselves as belonging still to another country", so that they see themselves merely as white, "in opposition to those of us who were not." His goal is to make racist those who are not, and more racist those who already are. As he admits, "The idea was to mangle them psychologically, confuse them about who they were […] I wanted to debase them and to make them come willingly to be debased by me" (p. 70). It is a narrative that functions at many levels: as a potent analysis of the way racism in America structures social interactions; as an analogical referencing of the psychological processes that converted enslaved Africans into Blacks; as a satire on the ideology of Afro-centric separatism; as a Sartrean exploration of the imposition of inauthenticity through the "gaze" of the powerful in conditions of colonial inequality, and as a fictive portrayal of the transformation of a disturbingly fascinating character.

Of course, the question arises, do we read Eugene's account of his dealings with his patients as "fictively true" or as fantasies, like his published case studies? There is the woman of mixed ancestry who looks white, whom Eugene has made totally dependent by persuading her that she can claim no single hyphenated European-American identity, and so can only be white if there are blacks like him around. Then there is Fiona, a white woman of Scottish ancestry, who comes complaining of a bullying white neighbour who appears to be of Anglo-origins. At first, Eugene sees some mileage in her because he is writing a book about the dangers to white Americans of replaying old European ethnic and religious antagonisms in the USA. But when she tells him she is married to a black West Indian, and that the neighbour abuses her as a "nigger-lover", Eugene is disgusted to be offered a story of victimhood that no longer interests him. When he cannot get rid of Fiona, he first plays on what he thinks may be elements of racial guilt (expressed in her resentment of the difficulties of being in a mixed marriage), but when this doesn't work, he persuades her that as a sovereign, free individual she has the moral right and duty to do whatever she thinks is just. His assiduous encouragement leads her to kill the neighbour and come to him to confess. However, when Fiona narrates the circumstances leading to the murder (which includes a cock-and-bull story about how she acquires a gun), St Omer plants clues that the narrative is Eugene's invention. What telling the story really means for him is suggested in his confession that he was not finished with his revenge on her. He provokes her (by calling her every racially offensive name for a white person he can think of) into calling him a nigger, coon, nap, sachel-mouth and many more – to her great shame. St Omer's point, (beyond creating horrified delight in his character's monstrous effrontery) is, I think, to suggest that despite denials, both white and black remain trapped in racial perceptions of themselves and that in American society, the idea of any kind of objectivity on the matter of race is chimerical.

It is in the second part of the novel that St Omer foregrounds what has been present throughout: the character of Eugene as the fictive inventor of a narrative that is wholly unreliable. Here the metafictional elements in *Prisnms* work at multiple levels and connect a number of themes: how people may take ownership of themselves through ownership of their stories; how confessional narratives may redeem, but are quite capable of doing the opposite; and how the truth quotient of other kinds of narratives that are presented as true (autobiographies, case studies, academic studies of, say, race in America) need to be questioned. This metafictional element also contribute to the pleasures of the text in its serious playfulness.

There is a linkage, too, to themes St Omer explored in the earlier novels, connecting the power of gaze to shape the perceived person as the "other" (one of the existential themes St Omer extends in a more politicised context in this novel), and the metaphor of writing/being written. The opinion of others has been crucial in the making of the two Breville brothers – Peter through seeking admiration in the eyes of the lower-class black people he leads in a steelband; Paul in the approbation of the church and the island's white elite. In *Prisnms*, Eugene comments on his meeting with the mature and contented Beatrice: "I felt she had a new sense of herself, her independence, her freedom from the opinion of others" (p. 8), but then, as we have seen, he is also shown exploiting the idea of gaze in manipulating his clients.

This connects to the trope of the difference between being written by others, and writing one's own authentic narrative. In *J—, Black Bam and the Masqueraders*, for instance, Paul Breville regains himself through scrupulous self-examination in his letters – by becoming a character in his own narrative, just as Stephenson in "The Lights on the Hill" begins to grow from the point when he realises he actually has a story of his own to tell. When he meets Beatrice, Eugene notes how her new equanimity is signalled in the way "She spoke of herself as a character in a book which we had both read" (p. 10). However, if Paul Breville works through the confessions in his letters to a redemptive honesty, Eugene's confessions lead in quite a different direction. They are made with an attitude of amused dissociation, as if Eugene Coard is a character he has invented, with no relationship to actual life.

If at the heart of *Prisnms* there is the metafictional joke that Eugene, the psychiatrist, behaves as if he was a novelist, whilst his earnest colleague Jonathan gives up psychiatry in order to write fiction, *Prisnms* is also built around several playful but purposeful intertextual references. In addition to St Omer's own novels and Selvon's *The Lonely Londoners*, there's also Saul Bellow's *Sammler's Planet* and Ralph Ellison's *The Invisible Man*),

St Omer uses these references to point to the porous divisions between different kinds of storytelling: how we impose a narrative on experience to make it meaningful (as Beatrice does); how we invent self-narratives as a means of objectifying a fugitive sense of self (sometimes with the deliberate intention of deceiving others); and how sometimes we "borrow" from other narratives, whether from history, fable or myth (as Eugene's patient, Walker does). What is clear, though, is that if in the earlier novels the idea of self-narration is predominantly a positive one, here in *Prisnms* it becomes an altogether more slippery idea: it may be as much about lying as discovering a truth.

The metafictionality becomes most explicit when St Omer introduces the character of Walker into the narrative. Walker is one of Eugene's very few black clients and what characterises him is that the stories he brings to Eugene are appropriations of "public information for private purposes". He brings stories of masked men in white robes, burning crosses, bombs thrown through windows. But the narrative also hints that Walker is Eugene's fiction since he "was the only patient left from the early days of my practice when I was obsessively inventing fictional patients" (p. 89). Walker is clearly an alter-ego since he comes to the office wearing clothes like Eugene's, so he has "the slightly unnerving impression that I was looking at a reflection of my own self." Flagging up the metafictionality, perhaps a little too obviously, though wittily, Walker comes into the office expressing such urgent need for support that he takes the appointment of a white client, a Mr. S. Bellow, who later becomes the source of one of Walker's fantasy narratives.

This is his story of a run-in on a bus with a white, Jewish photographer who accuses him of being a pickpocket. This, of course, Eugene recognises as a careful inversion of the scene in Bellow's *Sammler's Planet* where the black pickpocket frightens off Sammler with his display of his "large tan-and-purple uncircumcised thing". Walker insists that he actually has a small, circumcised dick, but is moved to admit that he wishes the racist stereotype of black sexuality was true: "All my life I've dreamed of owning a prick like that." In this hall of reflecting mirrors, the Walker narrative ends when he tells Eugene, his head swathed in bandages, that he fell off the bus while fighting with the photographer, but that whilst hospitalised, he was visited by this man who has come to apologise for what has been a case of mistaken identity. Then Walker gives Eugene a look of mock suspicion and asks him whether he might be in the habit of travelling that bus and says, "Don't you need a doctor's touch to be a good pickpocket?" (pp. 127-129)

What is St Omer doing with this hall of mirrors? At one level there's a joke about infinite fictivity: a novel about a character who uses fiction to express aspects of himself, who invents characters but pretends they are real, one of whom turns round to accuse him of being responsible for a case of mistaken identity! In this respect, *Prisnms* is indeed a novel that constantly takes the ground from under the readers' feet, and it does so, I think, because Garth St Omer wants the reader to resist accepting any ready-made sermon on the nature of race in American society. But it is also about the power of essentialisms of race in a society that has several racial orders: one that resembles the subtleties and exceptionalisms in the interplay between graduations of skin colour and aspects of class and culture that characterises race in the Caribbean, distinctions that operate *within* African American communities; and an absolute of race that divides black and white. Eugene's narrative has little to say about the former, much about the latter. In this respect, however unreliable Eugene is as a witness, his derangement does operate as a critique of American society where for the white majority race is an absolute. This is why, I think, St Omer introduces the character of Red Bam/Frederick Olsen, the "wharf rat" who becomes the model of the successful immigrant in the USA (until he is murdered) because he can marry his energy with apparent whiteness. But the hall of mirrors also reflects on the perils of essentialist Black racial ideologies that treat race as an absolute. The image in *Sammler's Planet* is a racist one but, as Walker admits, it is an image that has found fertile ground in the black imaginary. This is also what Percival Everett's *Erasure* argues, and countless images from gangsta rap would appear to endorse.

Perhaps the deepest level of social critique in *Prisnms* is of a society where individuals cannot connect as authentic individuals, but must define themselves and interact with others behind the masks they wear. The irony, of course, is that masks are worn to protect the wearer; *Prisnms* suggests that it is the wearer who is most damaged by the mask.

It is here, in its coda, that *Prisnms* also connects to the earlier novels, to the scenes of carnival and masquerade that close, most obviously, *A Room on the Hill* and particularly *J—, Black Bam and the Masqueraders*. In *Prisnms* it is the trick and treat ritual of Halloween that provides the public occasion for the wearing of masks. Here, too, there are both continuities and significant differences in the treatment of the theme between the earlier novels and this one.

In the St Lucian novels, masquerade is a deeply ambivalent public performance. The street theatre that J—, Black Bam and the masqueraders perform, and Paul Breville reports on, is an enactment that has a variety of meanings. One is of the fragility of the restraints that protect polite society from the turbulent energies that seethe below it. Black Bam plays the role of the vicious cow that has to be restrained by the ropes held by the other masqueraders. This is an enactment that reminds the middle and upper classes that the subservience of the lower orders is always conditional. Masquerading is also about the act of hiding the true self beneath disguises, referencing the masquerade's origins in slavery, and signifying the potentiality of the slave behind the various masks of obedience that he or she put on. It references, too, the hiding of Africa (where the act of masking was most often about social authority rather than social powerlessness) behind apparent forms of Creole play. And on the street it is a commercialised ritual in which the performers demand money from the onlookers to encourage the masked Black Bam to reveal himself, to let the cat out of the bag as the masqueraders chant "Chat-a-founga".

In *Prisnms* the ritual is less open to such multiple readings, but is similarly ambivalent. It is, on the one hand, the harmless fun of the middle-class masked party which Eugene and Peggy attend, where everyone speaks in a disguised voice and tries to be as unself-revealing in gesture as possible until identities are guessed. On the other hand, it connects to the darker rituals of the trick and treaters at Halloween, where the assembled costumed devils, imps, goblins and hobgoblins are described as fortunate if they have not yet "bitten on a razor blade embedded in an apple, or to have chewed on finely ground glass mixed in with powdered candy" (p. 122) – the last an image resonant with the history of slave poisonings in the Caribbean. The party ends when everyone is discovered, Eugene – predictably – last. "I took off the mask then", he reports and he and Peggy set off through the now empty streets.

The closing scene, where Eugene and Peggy are mesmerized by the performance of a group of masked skaters, who are dressed like clowns, is a poetic realisation of the ironies that ripple through the novel. Who more than Eugene should be alert to the potential of harmful deceptions under the guise of masks? Indeed, at first, he feels "uneasy" over the performance, but then comes to the mistaken conclusion that the skaters are "serenading us", and even after the first hint of malice (he suffers a mild electric shock when he is invited to shake hands with one of the skaters), reports finding the game "pleasantly confusing". He lowers his guard and he and Peggy become victims of the malign energies that lurk beneath the surface of American society. The biter is bit.

In the creation of Eugene Coard, St Omer poses very squarely the issues of how societies shape and give particular kinds of space to the most damaging kinds of human behaviour, whilst never ducking the question of individual moral responsibility. Eugene lives in racist social order, but at all points he has moral choice. His articulate self-consciousness neither allows us to see him as a victim nor a free agent, but to see that he has always had other choices: not to fuck Beatrice, not to accept becoming Sarah's privileged pet, not to betray Ekua, not to have sought revenge on Carol, not to have lied about his case studies, not to have used his clients as playthings.

But what St Omer shows us is Eugene turning a deaf ear to the critical voices of "those ghosts from the past", in particular his betrayal of Beatrice, which are allowed to emerge only in a nightmare dream-trial (a homage, perhaps, to the hallucinatory Circe episode of *Ulysses* where Leopold Bloom is tried for his sexual transgressions) where a prosecutor lays Eugene's misdeeds before a dream court.

One can see the novel's origins in the experience of a writer who has come from the Caribbean to find a society that is both vaster and less constricting in its material and social opportunities than the one from which he has come, but also vastly more humanly constricting because of the racialisation of its institutions. One can also see, in the novel, St Omer's response to his own earlier fiction, particularly, his portrayal of Peter and Paul Breville. In the case of Peter he extends his alarm over a particular species of male hypocrisy and misogyny and the failure to recognise their consequences. In the case of Paul, he has to admit that confession and the self-ownership of a narrative does not necessarily lead to redemption.

Prisnms was mostly written more than thirty years ago, but as the terrible roll-call of the deaths of young black men at the hands of white policemen continues (and as I write, the slaying by a police officer of a black child in a playground who was holding a toy gun), it is sadly evident that the insights that *Prisnms* offers on the nature of race as an institution in America are far from redundant. Perhaps it was also this vision, coming from a black immigrant to the USA, that the publishers of the time did not feel their readers were ready to hear.

Endnotes

1. I wonder about St Omer's choice of name. Bernard Coard was the Grenadian revolutionary leader widely seen as responsible for the murder of the popular Maurice Bishop in 1983. Coard was arrested following the American invasion, sentenced to death, reprieved but only freed from prison in 2009. St Omer must have been aware that this connection would be made. Can he have imagined that many years later several of the "Grenada 17" would have engaged in writing confessional narratives about their role in the events of 1979-1983.
2. I am inclined to agree slightly more with Michael Gilkes than Antonia MacDonald (see note 10, p. 156) that with his new child St Omer at least offers the possibility that Peter Breville may find his way back to some accommodation with his marriage and his life, though I think Michael Gilkes understates the fatal hypocrisy of the gap between Peter's personal life and his public pronouncements.

EDWARD BAUGH

ST OMER'S WORD CRAFT

A defining feature of Garth St Omer's novels is his narrative style, which poses a nice challenge for analysis. Its distinctiveness is immediately appreciable as being quite other than that of, say, Samuel Selvon, Earl Lovelace, Austin Clarke or George Lamming. To the extent that it is more akin to the style of others that calls less attention to itself than does the style of the four just named, it remains distinctive, enjoying in its own way a synergy with the subject-matter and meaning of the novels. It may recall somewhat the styles of Vidia Naipaul and John Hearne, in stance and effect, but there are appreciable differences. In any event, the overall impact of St Omer's novels is inseparable from the quality of the prose style. It is a style that is studiedly undemonstrative, pointedly avoiding verbal display, yet in a way that demands attention and constitutes craft and craftiness.

It may seem at first easy enough to define the style, but one may still feel that there is some factor left unidentified, some elusive nuance. It is a style that puts a premium on clarity, cleanness, directness, on simplicity in the best sense of the word. It generally avoids emotive colouring and verbal irony. A few reviewers have called attention to it. Robert Lee, reviewing *J—, Black Bam and the Masqueraders*, writes: "There is compactness. St Omer wastes no words as he sketches directly, and without fuss, his particular portraits of these wretched of the earth."[1] Christopher Wordsworth says of *Shades of Grey*, "The writing is quiet and controlled, with *patois* put to taut not exuberant purpose…"[2] Also with reference to *Shades*, Wallace Hildick writes of St Omer's "vivid, subtly rhythmic intensity." He points to other levels of subtlety when he observes that "it becomes increasingly clear as one reads on that the initial colourlessness, insipidity and weary banality have been intentional.[3] This impression of "colourlessness, insipidity and weary banality" is a risk that the style seems knowingly to take.

One might say that the style aims at transparency and neutrality, a not-calling-attention-to-itself, at objectivity, a looking unflinchingly at the truth by way of a precise, meticulous correctness of English that cultivates a tone of the impersonal, a quality of distance. In cultivating these effects, the style may at times seem mannered, postured, studiedly serious. These qualities work together, not just to mark a style that distinguishes the novelist and to that extent to be an end in itself. It is also more particularly functional, effectively embodying and projecting by parallel the St Omer protagonist and his way of seeing, his way of moving through circumstance.

The sense of distancing is also suggested in St Omer's penchant for not naming places. Even places that are obviously actual and familiar to the novelist, and to many of his readers, are usually not named, not even fictitiously, so as to give them some aura of "locatedness" and familiarity – the kind of procedure to which we are accustomed in prose fiction. So, the island that is obviously St Lucia is simply, always "the island". The town that is obviously Castries is simply "the town". London is simply "the metropolis."

The mannered touch appears in different forms. Here, for instance, in "Syrop", we are in the mind of Emilienne as she reflects on her futile effort to conceive: "She was remembering the long, hopeful period of waiting afterwards until, her cycle having passed, there was again, like a malignant periodic growth, the little appearance that made her feel that everything was so hopeless."[4] The "little appearance" is a precious, distancing abstraction, especially when one remembers St Omer's skill at meticulous, definitive recording of physical detail. Somewhat similar to "the little appearance" is the awkward, seemingly unnecessary coinage "progresslessly," in the following sentence from *A Room on the Hill*: "It heaved and moved, progresslessly, with the milling activity of worms in a pit latrine."[5] The "*milling activity* [my emphasis] of worms" may also be worth notice.

There is also the matter of sentence structure, in the way in which qualifying phrases are sometimes positioned to hold back a sentence, again for a distancing effect. An example is "very tiredly" in this sentence: "He was already beginning to climb, very tiredly, the hill, when the lights of the town went out."[6] One might more naturally have written: "He was already beginning to climb the hill very tiredly when the lights of the town went out." Of course, the tiredness is underscored by St Omer's placing of the phrase.

The functionality of the style as reflecting the personality of the protagonist is complemented by the way in which the style highlights the personality by ironic counterpoint. The objectivity and stance of impersonality which style and protagonist cultivate are the obverse of, and a response to an intense subjectivity and self-regarding, intense feelings of anger, pride, embarrassment, fear and guilt. The practised looking-unflinchingly-at-the-truth is the other side of, even a mask for, the protagonist's escapism, his shutting himself away from the implications of the truth that he thinks he has found, a withdrawal from involvement with other people, from commitment to any individual or cause.

A typical scenario is one in which the protagonist goes for a walk, alone, in response to a disconcerting situation, such as a confrontation with someone with whom he has a close but conflicted relationship. He takes this walk ostensibly as a way of dealing with, coming to grips with the situation, with his feelings about it. Interestingly, though, this way of dealing with the issue is also an escape, a walking away from the issue.

As he walks, we are given a description of his surroundings, detail after exact detail. But this is not the kind of description of surroundings that is commonly provided by novelists primarily to set the scene, so to speak, to evoke a localizing sense of place and to enhance the "reality" of the action such as it is. It may, with St Omer, fulfil this function, but it does more as well. We come to realize that the description is really an acting-out of the personality of the protagonist, of the way his mind works. The precise, graphic, unadorned record of the surroundings is really a record-ing of what his gaze is registering as he moves along, however unrelated it may be to the emotional-psychological issue with which he is wrestling. It represents his compulsion to see and record circumstance with a clear, cold eye, and thereby to acknowledge and confront the reality of the world he convinces himself he cannot change. So the description of his surroundings as he walks is ultimately functional, reflecting his essential nature.

An illustration as good as any other occurs in the last chapter of *The Lights on the Hill*. Eddie, Stephenson's fellow undergraduate, close friend and confidante, dies. His sudden, untimely death is a crushing blow to Stephenson, not least because Eddie's approach to life had kept flickeringly alive in Stephenson the possibility of bright promise and achievement, an ambition which circumstance and his nature had made him afraid to undertake, a fear which preferred to protect itself under a profession of the futility of life.

So when Eddie's parents, whom Stephenson knows, come to the hall of residence on the day after their son's death, to retrieve his belongings, Stephenson, instead of commiserating with them, sharing his grief with them and assisting them, as anyone else would, avoids them, cultivating a stoic indifference. He walks away. He goes for a walk. "He had not wished to think of Eddie any more than he had wished to hear bits of his father's conversation with the warden or to say that he was sorry."[7]

As he walks, his mind registers his surroundings, the sights and sounds. It is raining.

> He walked out of the campus gates and turned left along the main road. The rain fell. Under the trees whose branches almost covered the little-used road the pattern of its fall was disturbed. Drops of water, accumulated,

fell from the many leaves heavily, irregularly. Only occasionally, between their fall, he heard the light, dripping rain.[8]

He is hunched under his raincoat. This situation images his mood, his inward turning. As he walks, he looks into himself, reviewing his life, conflating present, past and future into what he wishes to see as his stance on life. The style of recording both areas of subject-matter is as much Stephenson's as the novelist's. The style in which the surroundings are registered underscores how Stephenson seeks to present his persona. On the other hand, the unproblematic "thereness" of the surroundings highlights by contrast his conflicted self-searching. The precise assurance of the style counterpoints the unease of his self-scrutiny: "Stephenson thought of his own pursuit of achievement which had pushed him to dishonesty and which all along, had been the principal cause of his fear and of his dissatisfaction."[9] When we read, "He was committed to his pursuit of futility"[10], the ostensible decisiveness of the statement carries, nonetheless, the sense of a willed, uneasy posture.

In contrast,

> He turned again and walked now along the road between the playing fields and the river. He could hear it out of sight below the road. Away in front of him white mist hung around the hill on which, at nights, the cluster of lights showed. The rain fell here in thin lines. There were no trees to interfere with its fall.[11]

The clarity, economy and certainty of the narration suggest indirectly a self-confidence and certainty of purpose in the person.

The St Omer style was fully realized in his first work to achieve metropolitan publication, the short story/novella "Syrop". At the end of the story, the style is trenchantly effective when it narrates how Syrop is chopped to death by the propeller of the ship alongside which he is diving for coins tossed by persons on board. His tragedy, just at the moment when he thinks he is about to achieve a kind of success, is all the more telling because of the restraint and unflinching objectivity of the narrative:

> His hands moved in the accustomed levered action against the body of water but he did not move where he wished to. Instead he felt himself slowly being drawn, head first, towards the threshing, gurgling, foaming patch of water to his left. Now he used all his strength of his legs and the power in his desperate arms, the coin in his mouth, driving, twisting, straining, panicking; opening his mouth to cry and letting the coin drop for ever to the bottom; knowing that he was about to die and fearing death…[12]

Even so, the "for ever" may be a bit of unnecessary reaching for emotional response.

We may all the more appreciate the St Omer style when we know what it replaced, and the latter is well evidenced in the first piece of his prose fiction that appeared in *Bim*, "The Meeting (Extract from Work in Progress)". This brief paragraph is typical of the entire piece:

> Their parents were inside. They were alone in the yard. Oh, how pretty, how very pretty she was! An almost irresistible longing overwhelmed him; he wanted to feel her to touch her clothes to stroke her long black hair to caress her slender brown legs as brown as doves. How shapely they were, what silky smoothness they possessed! His soul subsided sibilant with him in a gentle sussuration of longing.[13]

Readers acquainted with St Omer's mature style would never guess that this paragraph, except for the first two sentences, is from the same pen. Here is "true romance" subject-matter, style and tone at their most sentimentally blatant: the cliché-type images ("long black hair", "slender brown legs", "as brown as doves", "silky smoothness"). The "they possessed" is "stagily" superfluous, and the last sentence, with its self-indulgence of alliteration, is the proverbial last straw.

As it happens, in appreciating St. Omer's style and its formation, we have the benefit of comments made by V.S. Naipaul on certain early pieces by St Omer, comments which are also germane to appreciating Naipaul's own fiction. In the 1950s, when St. Omer's work was read on the BBC's *Caribbean Voices* programme, Naipaul was an editor-presenter for the programme. On the broadcast for May 24, 1955, two short stories were read, one of them being St Omer's "La Revendeuse", which also appeared in *Bim*, no. 22 (June 1955). Naipaul introduced the stories with a favourable comment:

> They both deal with the poor and both are well-written. But what matters here, I feel, is not so much what the author describes as his own attitude. Both writers approach their squalid subjects with a quiet, sometimes savage, bitterness; but this bitterness is really the other side of a too sensitive humanitarianism. It is in this that lie the appeal of the writing and the hope for social improvement in the Caribbean.[14]

Curiously, though, one year later (June 19, 1956), Naipaul is highly critical of St Omer's style, as exemplified in the short story "It Will Last Forever," which was read by Ulric Cross. Having said that he will leave the audience to judge how effective the story is, Naipaul says that he cannot but comment on the style, which is "imitative:"[15] "It derives too obviously from Hemingway." However, he finds that, almost paradoxically,

> so many of the very many imitators of Hemingway side-step economy. [...] [St Omer] seems to run on and on in the best style of typewriter

prose. Every story he has sent us has had to be cut; and this has never
been an exacting job. The Hemingway virtues of terseness, clarity, we
do not find in St Omer.[16]

In the 1950's, adulation of Hemingway was in vogue among the student
literati on the Mona campus of the University College of the West Indies,
although Hemingway was still far from having a place in the English
syllabus. St Omer was one of those students during the late 1950s.

Unfortunately, we do not have the original MS of "It Will Last Forever",
and so are unable to compare it with the broadcast version in order to
appreciate the cuts. However, we may compare the broadcast version of
"The Departure", transmitted on 23 October 1955, with the version that
appeared in *Bim*, No. 23 (Dec. 1955). For example, the first two sentences
of the *Bim* version are omitted from the "Caribbean Voices" version.
However, assuming that the *Bim* version was the one submitted to "Caribbean Voices", there is not much cutting and editing overall in the case of
this story, one of St Omer's best.

Naipaul gives a brief lesson on Hemingway, using the first two sentences of the story "A Simple Enquiry" as example of Hemingway's model
terseness, concreteness of images and avoidance of adjectives. He goes on
to criticize St Omer's dialogue, suggesting that it is another example of his
failed attempt to copy Hemingway. Naipaul finds the dialogue stilted and
bland, too "proper", failing to distinguish the characters' voices from the
narrator's. Such validity as there is in this observation may accord with what
I have deemed the cultivating of a tone of distance and the impersonal, a
manoeuvre in which the life-attitude of protagonist and narrator are
pointedly conflated.

Still, there is some distinguishing of characters by way of dialogue in the
later work, as, for example, when, in *J—, Black Bam and the Masqueraders*,
Patsy's mother, a domestic servant, confronts Paul Breville. As Paul
reports:

> She spoke in English. Nothing could have achieved less the seriousness
> she intended than those patois expressions which she transliterated for
> most of that meeting. I cannot blame her [...] for reaching for what
> she believed was dignity, by talking to me in English.[17]

Interestingly, this statement suggests a factor which may have had some
bearing on the language of St Omer's protagonists, its tone and register
in their direct speech, which are the same as in the narrative style.

"There is," says Naipaul, "always a good story buried in St Omer's
essays; but in none of them have I yet heard St Omer talking in anything
but a borrowed voice. He ought to be past that now."[18] St Omer did find
his own voice, and if one feels that Hemingway was an influence on it, that

feeling would in no way be a detraction. And could it be that Naipaul played some part in the evolution of the St Omer voice and style?

Endnotes

1. Robert Lee, "Peter Plays for Paul," *Tapia*, 3 Feb. 1974, p.7.
2. Christopher Wordsworth, "Caribbean Contrasts," *The Guardian*, 12 Dec. 1968.
3. Wallace Hildick, "A Brilliant Grey," in *The Listener*, 12 Dec. 1968.
4. *Introduction 2: Stories by New Writers* (London: Faber & Faber, 1964), p.55.
5. *A Room on the Hill* (London: Faber & Faber, 1968), p.175.
6. *Ibid.*, p. 113.
7. *The Lights on the Hill* (London: Heinemann, 1986), p.112.
8. *Ibid.*, p.118.
9. *Ibid.*, p.112.
10. *Ibid.*, p.115.
11. *Ibid.*, p.118.
12. *Ibid.*, p.181.
13. *Bim*, No. 15 [Dec. 1951], p.176.
14. BBC "Caribbean Voices" transcripts, University of the West Indies Library, Jamaica.
15. *Ibid.*
16. *Ibid.*
17. *J—, Black Bam and the Masqueraders* (London: Faber & Faber, 1972), p. 80
18. *Ibid.*

ANTONIA MACDONALD

'NO NATION, ONLY ME, MYSELF AND I.' PORTRAITS
OF THE EDUCATED MAN IN GARTH ST. OMER'S
QUINTET[1] OF STORIES.

"Give your people a chance... and they forget the rest of you. They
think only of themselves" (66).

In *Mirror, Mirror: Identity, Race and Protest in Jamaica*, Rex Nettleford
advocates that one of the virtues of education is "...the preparation of
a citizenry ready for participation in the political, social and economic
processes of its country" (229). The universal truth of this statement
is self-evident and data provided by international organizations such
as UNESCO will attest to the correlation between development and
education. It is through education (whether it is taking place in schools,
in the home or through social institutions) that young people are prepared
for participation in the civic life of their country. Moreover, education
not only trains for economic, social and political participation but it
also helps to create a sense of community, be it the social cohesion
that is gained through the sharing of a body of knowledge and/ or the
networking that emerges out of the experience of learning. In the colonial
twentieth century, because of its cost and restricted accessibility, education
was not readily available to a large section of the Caribbean population.
Those who received a secondary and tertiary education became positioned
to be leaders in their society and, by extension, active agents of national
development.[2] In a post-independent Caribbean context, the increase
in the accessibility of education to the majority of the population has
seen the reduction of poverty and the development of a skilled labour
force. It has also allowed for the emergence of a black middle class
unfettered by what Rohlehr in "Small Island Blues..." has described
as "the links that connect them in blood, history and psychology to
the blacks at the bottom of the social greasy-pole" (22).

Modern Caribbean history is replete with examples of how formal
education prepared Caribbean citizens for leadership and how seriously
these leaders took on the responsibility of becoming active participants in

the anti-colonial struggle and the drama of nationalism. Significantly, education offered the working-class Afro-Caribbean man the chance to seize the reins of political leadership at a time when power was narrowly located within an elite brown and white upper class. For example, in Barbados, Grantley Adams, a black man born in poverty, through his secondary education at a prestigious boys' school, his academic excellence therein and then an excellent Oxfordian education, became a political giant both locally and regionally. His seminal contribution to trade union legislation in Barbados allowed for the formation of the Barbados Workers Union, thus heralding the improvement of the material conditions of working class Barbadians.[3] Similarly, Eric Williams, because of his sound secondary and tertiary education, rose beyond his humble origins to become Prime Minister of Trinidad. In his book, *Inward Hunger: The Education of a Prime Minister*, Williams establishes the weight of expectations on those who had the benefit of high school and university training. Undoubtedly, it was this education, notwithstanding the colonial character of its curriculum, which gave leaders such as Grantley Adams in Barbados, Norman Manley in Jamaica and Eric Williams in Trinidad a deep knowl-edge of British politics, culture and economics. But at the same time, that same education produced a cadre of thinkers who saw themselves as builders of a new Caribbean social order.[4] The educated would also become the Caribbean's intelligentsia, committed to shaping creatively, discursively and politically a Caribbean post-colonial society.

   This education was functioning both personally and politically. On the individual level, education was intimately connected to a search for selfhood, albeit black male self-fashioning, and the escape from poverty. Collectively, in its creation of a hopeful future for a rising black middle class, education became a vehicle for social and political change. In an interview with David Scott, George Lamming talks about his perception of the role the intellectual plays in the shaping of postcolonial society and his belief that there is always a dialectic between productive hope and debilitating despair:

> I see that complexity; that seed of negation is always there. But let us put it this way about these journeys of expectation, there is a period when (I see it now as almost an innocence in a way) I believed – and I think this was shared by certain people of my generation – that the writers, the artists, were actually creating something new. The creation of that something new, the exercise involved in creating that, could not but have impact. I think that although we are very different, that sense of the importance of something you are doing is to be found in [Derek] Walcott (162).

Similarly, the responsibility of the educated to become creators of a new world is extended in Eric Williams' 'University of Woodford Square

Lectures'. Here Williams was moving education beyond institutional walls and in this informal setting was popularizing access to information and ideas. Caribbean citizens were being both formally and informally prepared to take an active role in the shaping of their social and political future. Political advocacy was one such route. So too was identification with the working class, if only because it was understood that this cause would allow political traction in an environment where the educated colonial was struggling for viability and visibility.

Much of Caribbean literature has articulated the enduring struggle and triumphant hope that characterized the journey to selfhood and nationhood.[5] In the instance of the St. Lucian novelist Garth St. Omer, his quintet of novels, set in a small Caribbean island during the 1940s and 50s, very carefully delineates the forces that assist and impede this journey. In *A Room on The Hill*; *The Lights on the Hill*; *Another Place, Another Time*; *Nor Any Country* and *J—, Black Bam and the Masqueraders*, St. Omer creates black male protagonists who are constantly reacting to a sense of entrapment.[6] While the reasons for entrapment may differ – race, class/family structure and poverty – education is consistently presented as the means to escape their entrapment. However, what remains distinctive about St. Omer's novellas/ novels is that education is themed as producing men who, in their search for selfhood, fail to take responsibility for anything other than themselves and are narrowly focused on self-advancement with little or no regard for the community from which they sprang.

Unlike some of their real world counterparts, these fictional characters do not use the benefits of higher education to become agents of social or political change in the emerging nation but remain what Patricia Ismond, in "The St Lucian Background in Garth St. Omer and Derek Walcott", describes as "permutations of one essential crisis, an alienated consciousness turned inwardly on itself"(33). I want to specifically highlight this notion of isolation and passivity, given that in the real world in which St. Omer was operating there were many local and regional examples of educated men who were active agents of social change and whose vision of a future expanded outward to include the community from which they came. For example, labour leader George F.L Charles, West Indies Federation deputy Prime Minister Carl La Corbiniere, historian Roy Augier,[7] and economist Arthur Lewis belong to a confraternity of St. Lucian gamechangers. These men left their mark on the political and intellectual life of St. Lucia and the Caribbean, just as St. Omer and his contemporary Derek Walcott would shape St. Lucia's *belles lettres*.

St. Omer's presentation of education not only relates to formal education, but also to social education – the development of reasoning and judgment acquired through cultural interactions or through the religious socialization being wrought by the Catholic Church and by the urban community within which these protagonists are located. There is circulating in his quintet the notion of a changing guard, of a black cadre of professionals returning to St. Lucia preoccupied with personal advancement as a reward for the long years of study and sacrifice. Their sense of responsibility is primarily to self: that is, self in society rather than self as part of community. For the St. Omerian protagonists, the newly-minted privilege of belonging to an educated minority provokes in its recipients an overwhelming desire to fit into social circles from which they had formerly been denied access. Anxious to overcome the race barriers that preclude entry into the bourgeois community with which their education now naturally aligns them, his protagonists separate themselves from their former lower-middle class communities, forsaking in this process those who had facilitated their social mobility. The sacrifice of the poor is unacknowledged and the amelioration of the socio-economic conditions of these communities never becomes a priority. Ultimately, the responsibility of building a new postcolonial society, one that replaces a fragmented social order, is subsumed in the desire for personal advancement.

Many Caribbean writers/artists of St. Omer's time saw themselves as part of and responsible for the process of social and political change, participating in what Martin Carter in his 1974 graduation address at the University of Guyana so aptly described as "the building of a free community of valid persons" (32). The work of the St. Lucia Arts Guild[8] is one such example. While St. Omer's works pay scant attention to the cultural fermentation generated by the writers and guild members (and where there is mention of a nascent artistic community this is configured as a mimicry that lacks sustainability), the St. Lucia Arts Guild provided much of the context for Derek Walcott's artistic production. It would be interesting here to consider both St. Omer and Walcott as offering a representation of the social history of an island which, when viewed side by side, can provide a multi-textured portrait of the island. While it is primarily through his autobiographical essays and interviews that Walcott sketches out the social history of the island, St. Omer is providing it through his creative prose. Ismond has argued that while both St. Lucian writers demonstrate a private orientation, the essential difference between St. Omer and Walcott resides in one being brought up in a Catholic family and the latter Methodist. Growing up in a society that was rigidly Catholic, St. Omer would have experienced a restrictiveness that the Methodist outsider, though always aware of, would not have been similarly affected by. It is this sense of a strangled society that St. Omer is constantly reacting to and seeking to discursively represent.

Many critics have used an existential lens to read his work, citing the various influences to which St. Omer's education would have exposed him.[9] I am proposing that the pessimism of his representation springs from the alienation that is bred by the colonial society within which he operates – despair that in his case, art does not manage to dissolve. This malaise is similar to what is so eloquently articulated by Walcott in his essay, "What the Twilight Says". "… [A] black French island somnolent in its Catholicism and black magic, blind faith and blinder overbreeding, a society which triangulated itself mediaevally into land-baron, serf and cleric, with a vapid brown bourgeoisie" (11). But where in his creative writing Walcott chooses to focus on the beauty of his society, St. Omer deliberately and methodically brings his society into close focus, directing the reader's gaze to magnified images of pettiness, cruelty and narrow individualism.

Part 1
Education as Salvation from Poverty and its Anonymity

> "Is education I talking about, yes. The only thing to save us poor people" (*Another Place, Another Time*, 122).

> "You go away and you come back qualified… and all you think of is money, money, money… and your place in the island's warm social sun, mass-produced in your education, mass-produced in your intentions afterwards; empty, empty, empty" (*A Room on the Hill*, 117).

St. Omer's quintet painstakingly demonstrates the socio-historical reality that, in developing societies, poverty was and continues to be a barrier to schooling. The cost of tuition – the price of textbooks and uniforms, added to the opportunity cost of what a child's labour would have contributed to the family's finances – has meant that many young people are denied access to education and in some instances have dropped out of school for early entry into the labour market. In *Another Place, Another Time*, the novel that most intimately explores education as salvation from poverty, St. Omer uses Miss Elaine as the mouthpiece to voice this ambition for education and the social perception of its value as self-advancement: "Education…" she said. "I always telling Berthe that. Or is sweetie she'll have to sell. Like me" (122). Discussing the value of education with the teenage protagonist, Derek, Miss Elaine contrasts her social status with that of the educated doctor who had once been a poor child in the same class as her during primary school. This conversation signals to the reader not only the difference in access available to males and females, but more particularly, the immense economic and social leap that education affords its recipients.

In mid-twentieth century Caribbean societies where there was no government-supported free education, the children of poor parents advanced through the education system (from elementary through secondary and potentially to university) because of scholarships and the sacrifice of parents. These parents were mostly single mothers, who sacrificed every-thing so that their sons could be educated, mothers who believed that the advancements to be gained through their child's education would pay long-term dividends that would benefit the entire family. In *Another Place, Another Time*, Derek is repeatedly reminded by friends and family members who have been denied access, or who have benefited from their own limited education, that he is lucky to be attending secondary school.

> 'If even I had finish school, is not here I'd be now. I can tell you that.'
> Derek knew the expression well. He had heard his mother use it. His uncle, Beaurire, particularly when he was drunk, which was often, talked about the virtues of education and especially about the virtues of his own. (121)

While it may be easy to ignore the nostalgic yearning of these older people, Derek has in his consumptive cousin Cecil a glaring and guilty reminder of the privilege of continuing on to further education. Cecil is an example of someone whom poverty denied ongoing access to education. Upon his father's death, Cecil prematurely left elementary school to become a tailor apprentice and thus, in spite of his deep desire to continue on to secondary school, forfeited that opportunity. His death from consumption can be read as the symbolic choking of that dream, his being robbed of the chance for another life.

Towards the end of the novel, after the Castries fire has left his family indigent, Derek knows that his leaving school would ease the financial pressure on his mother. But while he offers to leave school, Derek is certain that his mother will refuse this offer and will continue to make the sacrifice necessary to keep him in school. His award of a scholarship to continue higher education overseas becomes the fulfilment of his mother's dream for him and the means to lift himself (and by extension, her) out of poverty. Similarly, in *The Room on the Hill*, we are shown the extent of maternal sacrifice when the mother of protagonist, John Lestrade, chooses to go barefoot so that her son can wear her shoes to school. In *The Lights on the Hill*, Stephenson is lucky to be the ward of Mémé, the childless seamstress who is happy to devote her meagre earnings to feeding and clothing him. At the same time, his mother, who has married a farmer and moved to the country, supports her son by ensuring that there is a regular food supply going to him and Mémé. However, St. Omer is scrupulous in his demon-stration that this awareness of parental sacrifice never reconfigures the narrow individualism that defines these two male characters. Future male advancement, made possible by mothers and other mothers who have been denied the opportunity to go beyond secondary school, never changes the material conditions of these women. Education, in fact, moves these protagonists beyond the 'race' of their poor, black mothers – a reality the women accept as a natural progression.

St. Omer presents the pathos of the mothers' easy acceptance that these children for whom they labour, will, because of education, no longer belong to them. For these women, their sons represent escape from the linearity that defines the lives of the poor: the continual eking out of a miserable living from birth to death. Dotted through these novellas/novels are examples of men (Alphonse, Black Bam, Choux Macaque, J—, Lindbergh, and Skeete) for whom this linearity meshes into an entrapping cobweb of nihilism. Thus, while these mothers may not escape poverty, they hold fast to the hope that through education their children will have a better life than theirs, that their children will not succumb to the fate of social dereliction. Accordingly, they spend their lives in pious churchgoing so that their sons can be rewarded for their devoutness. St. Omer, however, shows the irony of this maternal devotion. It is primarily against mothers that his protagonists are insistent on asserting themselves, mothers who are so deeply interpellated by Catholicism that they preach adherence to the status quo, mothers who most acutely represent the social family that these sons conjure up as the force that seeks to hold them back. The denial of the mother is tantamount to the denial/dismissal of community. In her essay, "The West Indian Male Sensibility in Search of itself…" Pamela Mordecai describes the consequence of this disconnection: "…[I]n a West Indian situation the impossibility of receiving the woman-as-self and the related re-entry into community may well be the predicament" facing the West Indian male who does not accept his mother both "as a person who is part of his history and part of his place" (641).

Another recurring theme in St. Omer's quintet is the social status held by young men who attend the sole secondary school for boys. Jacqueline Kaye, in "Anonymity and Subjectivism in the Novels of Garth St. Omer", outlines the limited and negative choices facing the black educated St. Omerian characters: nihilism, isolation, feigned madness and moral collapse. She argues that in response to such debilitating options, they "reject both ideas and actions in favour of a fixed anonymity, like a cloak of neutrality and indifference" (47) and concludes that these protagonists all display "anonymous egotism" (52). While I agree with her that these protagonists are driven by egotism, I am arguing that this self-absorption is a consequence of the privilege of receiving education that is denied to so many. In *Another Place, Another Time,* the school uniform is portrayed as the most visible marker of this difference:

> And over the years he had behaved as if he really had belonged to that race apart he had moved with, with the blue blazers and brass buttons, the white shirt and trousers, the white cork helmet with the piece of tricolour band, the special blue tie and grey flannel trousers. (171)

Held up by their community as exceptional, these young men are not being offered an alternative view of themselves because the educational curriculum to which they are being exposed reinforces this elitism. Moreover, I take issue with Kaye's theorizing of anonymity in St. Omer's novels. Where she sees the protagonists as deliberating trying to be no one – persons who deliberately shed their history and who resort to "fixed anonymity" (47), I see these men as overwhelmingly self-conscious; rather than being a present absence, they are deeply aware of their growing social value. For even while these educated black men forsake community participation in favour of narrow self-advancement, and even as they eschew a collective race-based identity in favour of a personal identity, they are by no means anonymous in so far as they remain almost pathologically aware of the elite position that their education has given them in society.

In his quintet, St. Omer portrays the social structures that ensure the visibility of the educated schoolboy, the social arrangements that encourage him to see himself as an exceptional individual in his community – as someone who is always on display. Mention is made of the special uniforms worn to high mass on Sundays, the assigned seating in church for college boys, the newspaper coverage of their sporting events, the salutation 'Mr.', no matter how tongue-in-cheek some may use it, and constantly circulating gossip about their academic progress. St. Omer presents those who receive a university education as even more distinctive. In *Nor Any Country*, the protagonist, Peter Breville, is happy to end his eight-year long anonymity in the metropolis. Qualified with a doctoral degree, he returns to his island home for a brief visit before taking a teaching position at the regional university where he studied as an undergraduate. His arrival home is greeted with smiles and gestures of surprise, where the taxi driver is someone "he did not know but who recognized him, not like the woman in the metropolitan supermarket, as part of a generality, but as a person, the footballer he had been" (18); where "out of a passing car, an astonished hand waved at him" (20) and where he is kept busy by visitors because the news of his unexpected arrival has spread in the small town and has made the newspaper (45). On day two of his return home he misses the excitement of the previous day: "the people he went past did not know him" (47).

In *Nor Any Country* and its sequel, *J—, Black Bam and the Masqueraders*, university education is portrayed as the ultimate means to gain economic independence and social advancement. Given that this higher education is not available locally, the island naturally becomes a place where one waits to escape from, where one dreams of scholarships to the regional university, or to Canada or to England as salvation, the start of a real life. Until this is achieved, life lacks solidity and these protagonists remain in stasis, marking time through ephemeral and transitory relationships. This notion circulates throughout the novellas/novels and St. Omer is careful to show how it manifests itself in various permutations. *A Room on the Hill* depicts John's best friend, Stephen, as resorting to suicide because of the repeated thwarting of that dream to escape. Stephen cannot imagine life on the island without his acquisition of a higher degree. Juxtaposed against Stephen's suicide is the living death experienced by those who remain on the island, fated to be slowly suffocated by its poisonous air of narrow-mindedness, and by the daily rounds of too much alcohol, meaningless conversations, and sterile sexual relationships.

St. Omer is careful to juxtapose the misfortune of those who remain against the fortunes of those who manage to escape. Derek Charles, to whom the reader will again be introduced in the novella, *Another Place, Another Time*, is John's doppelganger. He gets a coveted scholarship and is able to leave the island for studies abroad. The reader is presented with Derek's prosperous return: a trained barrister with a white wife, the dream life of every black aspirant. Backdropped against Derek's success are the lives of men who are fated to remain on the island post-secondary school, either as teachers or in the Civil Service. St. Omer depicts these men as being educated into a social world of drinking and womanizing, one that transforms them into automatons with keys in their backs, slowly being programmed to inhabit a world circumscribed by class prejudice and colourism.

In his characterization of Derek Charles, St. Omer suggests that it is because of the scarcity of educational opportunities that the young men, upon acquiring access, choose to do law. A career in law offers the most immediate socio-economic returns: barristers are able to re-enter their island society not beholden to others for employment. With what Gordon Rohlehr has dubbed "scrupulous meanness",[10] St. Omer seems to be suggesting that even though they may not be very successful at their *métier*, or honest in professional conduct, these young lawyers, with their "faint smell of dishonesty and the unattractive aura of opportunism and exploitation" (*Room*, 119) are visible symbols of triumph over anonymity. Encouraged by their social elevation, they cultivate an image of themselves as superior. St. Omer balances this presentation of success with a contrapuntal portraiture of those who, like the painter Dennys, refuse to play by the rules. In choosing to be a painter rather than what the society deems to be a more orthodox profession, Dennys is doomed to be a social misfit and the object of benign pity. In spite of his proclaimed defiant nonconformity, Dennys views himself as being on the constant brink of social dereliction – as a potential Old Alphonse who is the object of laughter for the town's urchins.

Where Dennys – a minor character – is an example of deliberate nonconformity, major characters like Stephenson in *The Lights on the Hills* and Paul Breville in *Nor Any Country* are presented by St. Omer as

admonitory examples of what happens when one breaks away from conformity. Stephenson, like Derek Charles, maps out for himself a successful
future. Stephenson's secondary school education lands him the opportunity to work as a customs officer – a job he considers temporary, a means
of saving enough so that he can continue on to a university in the metropolis
to study law. Sidetracked by greed and corruption, he finds himself taking
bribes and selling contraband goods. Caught, and convicted, Stephenson
has to use the money he has been amassing over the past five years to pay
the heavy fine. Saved from jail, he now loses the future education that
would have given his life meaning. As the illegitimate half-white boy with
no father, university education would have given him a chance to create a
new self, a professional self, the means to start his own personal history.
Significantly, the magistrate who has fined Stephenson is the example of
what Stephenson had dreamt of becoming. He is a former schoolmate –
one with whom Stephenson has played cricket, but now a man who, by
virtue of having been able to go directly to university, is socially (and
morally) superior to Stephenson.

After his conviction, Stephenson's descent into existential despair and
his identification with the various derelicts that populate the town's
streets confirm for us that in the world depicted by St. Omer, the fall to
social opprobrium is an easy one. We see Stephenson actively considering
how to break into the safes of business houses, dreaming that these ill-
gotten gains will allow him to escape the island. Although employment
on another island, and later a bonded scholarship to study at a regional
university gives him a reprieve from criminal thoughts and a sense of
entrapment, Stephenson is portrayed as unable to recover from his
thwarted dreams to study law in the metropolis. His disengaged restlessness continues in spite of this second chance to remake himself as
university graduate rather than as lawyer. The damage wrought by his
earlier deferred dream is so significant that Stephenson is unable to settle
into this new university life. Instead he finds himself unenthralled by his
studies and remains at university only because he is too scared to seek
other options. Moreover, St. Omer is careful to offer up Carlton as a foil
to Stephenson. When Stephenson considers giving up university, it is the
vision of Carlton, a man who never made it to university, which prevents
Stephenson from abandoning his studies. Carlton is a supposedly well-
paid journalist working in a southern Caribbean island. Inflated by false
bravado, he does not quite manage to mask his envy of Stephenson and
his regret that he did not have the opportunity to study at university. Nor
can Carlton deny the reality that, in spite of his improved economic
standing, should he return to his home island he will never enjoy the
social privileges that attend his professional friends. It is this realization
of anonymity that pushes Carlton into voluntary exile to a larger society

where he can remake himself as someone of merit. Stephenson reads Carlton's fate as a cautionary tale and chooses to remain at university because any degree is better than no degree at all:

> After his walk in the rain and the grey light suffused with heat, he would go back to the books he had read which did not interest him… His sense of loss would dull, his anger too as well as the feeling of impotence (110).

The degree in English which Stephenson is doing will prepare him to be a teacher. This provides a useful segue into St. Omer's representation of the black teaching professional in Caribbean colonial society. In *Nor Any Country*, Dr. Peter Breville admits: "Yes I think I can remember teachers were a very important thing. Not many of us could hope to go beyond being a teacher" (94-5). The importance of educators is reiterated in *J—, Black Bam and the Masqueraders*, when Peter again declares: "…responsibility was what education must be about"(13). However, through the irresponsibility of Peter's subsequent behaviour on campus and his publicized domestic 'bacchanal', St. Omer succeeds in representing teachers and educators in a less than positive light. Peter, in spite of his advanced education, lacks moral probity. He never takes responsibility for his role in the impregnation of Phyllis. Rather, St. Omer portrays him as wallowing in self-pity and enacting systematic cruelty against the wife whom he blames for trapping him in an early marriage. Peter laments the fact that the uneducated Phyllis is not a fit mother for the child she is about to bear. However, he is not portrayed as enabling his wife in her mission to educate herself. His efforts to support her are half-hearted, and he comes to dismiss her efforts as an elaborate show that is designed merely to impress him.

Nonetheless, through his use of the omniscient narrator, St. Omer deconstructs this narrative of scorn. The reader is presented with frequent references to Phyllis's attempts to continue the education to which her father's death and the consequent lack of financial privilege deprived her. Moreover, in allowing the reader access to Phyllis's thoughts on her social position and her vision for her advancement, St. Omer throws into further relief Peter's failure as an educator. In spite of the advantage of higher education, Peter is unable to move beyond his narrow prejudices so as to become what Father Thomas describes as a bridge joining the present to the future, the known to the unknown (101). Significantly, the unnamed and ungendered child that Phyllis bears does not represent a hopeful future[11]. Referred to for the most part as 'it', the child is a casualty of the ongoing fight between the parents. This representation is in keeping with the portrayal of small children in St. Omer's novellas/novels – they are sometimes used by women as pawns in the marriage game, and sometimes are resented by fathers who on occasion advocate abortions in order to escape the burden of parenting.

Ironically, it is the Catholic priest, Father Thomas, who functions as an educator and in him St. Omer presents his readers with the lone example of a figure of social change. Father Thomas is presented as a foil to the St. Omerian protagonist. He does not view access to education as a personal triumph, or a reward that is not to be shared with the masses. Like many of the St. Omerian protagonists, this minor character is portrayed as being glad for his chance at higher education. However, unlike Derek, Stephenson or Peter, Father Thomas is concerned with sharing the benefits of this education with his community and worries that his choice of vocation will not allow this to happen. Believing that his decision to be a priest, one that he made only because it gave him access to higher education, is not good for the economic betterment of his family, Father Thomas nonetheless is an activist for a new social order. As the young island-born, black priest in a society where priests are typically white foreigners, Father Thomas is well aware of the need to free his society from the stifling grip of Catholic rituals and dogma. Mindful that change is a gradual process, Father Thomas makes small inroads into the prejudices propagated by the Catholic Church by re-socializing the black community to an alternative reality. Not only does he attempt to get rid of the tolling funeral/requiem bells that mark out social status[12] but he also speaks out against Fr. Mouret's instigating of the firing of the Seventh Day Adventist doctor. The characterization of Father Thomas not only serves to highlight the inadequacies of Peter Breville, but it also throws into relief the deep egotism of his brother, Paul.

Paul Breville is the most self-absorbed of St. Omer's protagonists. Like the other protagonists, he is depicted as intimately understanding the privileges of his education and, because of it, is constantly crafting an imagined future – one that will give authenticity to his wilfully-alienated self. Unlike the other protagonists, Paul is an outstanding student who takes confidence in his exceptional sporting talent. He cashes in on his status as *victor ludorum*[13] and as a cricketer representing his school and his island; he fraternizes with the elite, both at home and abroad. Momentarily, he is part of the inner circle to which his skin colour and socio-economic position has disbarred him. St. Omer describes Paul's cricketing prowess as an individualized performance – one to which Paul devotes many hours to finesse. In the description of the overseas matches at which Paul represents his school, there is seldom mention of the team and how it performed, only of how well Paul believed he did. These matches are presented as Paul's opportunity to show off, and to escape anonymity. His self-aggrandizement is manifested in the over-elaborateness with which he plays cricket and football and in his desire to stand out as the exceptional black. St. Omer goes on to show how Paul's ambitious social aspirations are fed by his sporting success. Paul's trips to other islands allow him a close-up view of life among the upper-class brown coterie – fuelling his ambition to have membership in its clubhouse, to dine on a diet that is not the diurnal bread and fried fish that his mother provides. This taste of another life imbues Paul with a sense of a future promise of excellence – one that starts with sports and the public acclaim it is already bestowing upon him. This future will be buttressed by a sound university education. Together, sporting and academic success will galvanize him into certain social *milieus* and will provide him with opportunities for social advancement and the display of power.

The incident where Paul sneaks into the prestigious social club is a significant moment in St. Omer's narration. Having successfully made it through the front door, Paul resents the carnival revellers who also gain temporary access. He is not looking for a wider social liberation, just to advance personally, to be exceptional because of the socio-economic opportunities promised through his secondary school education. Crucial to his notion of exceptionalism is the desire to stand out and over his family, his peers and other young black men. He has no desire to disrupt the status quo, or to dismantle the hegemony of brownness and whiteness. Instead, he is preparing himself for a life where his exceptionalism will compensate for and ultimately erase his blackness. After leaving secondary school, while he is awaiting an expected scholarship, Paul commissions a wooden desk and bookshelf to be made: these are to be props in his drama of academic self-development. Higher education is the means of escape from his blackness, from his poverty – and he has no doubt that he will be given the opportunity to gain, through a university education, the authenticity he had so long rehearsed. Paul imagines his return as a fêted professional, one with automatic entrance into an envied social class.

Like John Lestrade, Paul is depicted as a man who is fated to be denied the dream of educational advancement. Their circumstances, however, are different. Believing in the power of his popularity, his academic success and his sporting prowess, Paul refuses to marry Patricia, the girl he has impregnated. He justifies his decision because he views a union with her as the irrevocable denial of access to that longed-for social world. St. Omer crafts Paul's choices with scrupulous care. In marrying Patricia, Paul would be yoked to an unwanted wife. However, this socially-sanctioned act would have the compensatory benefit of allowing him to continue in his teaching job. Having received a First in the external examinations, Paul is depicted as confident enough to believe that he can gain a university education without having to surrender to the marriage trap. The egotism that so richly characterises Paul, blinds him to the need for compromise, to adhere to the socio-cultural convention that dictates that up-and-coming black men conform, that they "accept that a marriage afterwards could nullify the sin of fornication that had preceded it" (118). Reduced to the status of a social pariah, Paul is unable to secure a job commensurate with his qualifications and with his self-definition as socially remarkable. Scorned by those who had once entertained him, Paul is unable to cope with his public disintegration into a spectre of ridicule.

Paul's resultant social death is set up in contradistinction to Peter's hopeful future. When faced with similar options, Peter submits to a shotgun wedding to Phyllis. In a society governed by "sin, guilt and punishment", St. Omer presents Peter as being rewarded with a scholarship to a regional university – the means of escaping from a pregnant wife, a chance to remake himself as a successful professional. In *J—, Black Bam and the Masqueraders* St. Omer, in ensuring that Paul's voice interlaces the narrative, offers his readers an image of what Peter himself is escaping from yet remains entrapped by: race, class, social acceptability. In the long run, the tertiary education and its passport to the professional class denied to Paul, because of his rejection of the *status quo*, does not serve Peter in any good stead. Peter is never able to move beyond his personal history – entrapment in an unhappy marriage, and the guilt and resentment that characterizes it. Peter's hand is forced by a puritanical society whose motto seems to be social compliance at whatever cost, or at least the veneer of compliance, because once Peter marries Phyllis he is not required to be a good husband. He can have as many mistresses as he wants and is complimented on it by men who paradoxically condemn Paul for his refusal to marry Patricia. Ultimately, in St. Omer's quintet, formal education does not operate independent of social education. The Catholic Church, in controlling both, ensures that access to formal education, in bringing the black man out of anonymity, also develops in him an appreciation for social compliance that comes with this new visibility.

Part 2: The Absence of Mentoring into Social Responsibility

In a 2012 interview with Catherine John, Erna Brodber, the Jamaican novelist, describes the world into which she was socialized, one which was somewhat different to what St. Omer portrays in St. Lucia:

> Well, I went to Excelsior High School, which at the time was a school for lower-middle-class country people… We saw people there who went out of their way to effect change and who tried to make us into change agents. You had teachers… who had more or less gone and done their degrees; they had worked very hard to get their degrees and to get the money to do degrees. But when they returned, they were probably not going to be chosen to teach at…[elite high schools in Kingston] and so they themselves knew what it meant to be black and what it meant to be trying black people. (77)

While this is also the world delineated in St. Omer's oeuvre, he presents protagonists who are differently motivated. Restricted by their narrow individualism, uncommitted to the collective, they are not concerned with ensuring that there is a future black intelligentsia to replace the dying gentry. In St. Omer's novellas/novels, the strategic absence of Afro-Caribbean mentors on whom the male protagonists could model themselves might well account for the narrow self-interest of these protagonists. I am proposing that because they are the first of their generation to experience higher learning, they have not yet acquired the sensibility that will direct them to leverage that education for public good rather than private gain. I read them as being unable to use what Pierre Bourdieu defines as cultural capital – the language competencies, the disposition, attitudes to knowledge and cultural awareness passed on through family from one generation to another. Bourdieu in his essay "Cultural Reproduction and Social Reproduction" argues that the more cultural capital a student possesses, the better the student will perform in school. Establishing his thesis that school systems operate on the presumption of possession of such capital, Bourdieu asserts that children from lower-class families have less cultural capital than those from upper-class families, and accordingly do not perform as well in the education system.

Following from Bourdieu's thesis, in the world of St. Omer's novellas/ novels his protagonists are all lower-class boys with limited cultural capital. Emerging from households with a dominant French Creole vernacular, these young men have reduced language competence and have to work hard to master that limitation. In these single-parent and/or low economic status households, reading is not part of their everyday routine, nor are they able to get help with their homework or discuss with their parents the information learnt at school because they have already exceeded the educational reach of their parents. In *J—, Black Bam and the Masqueraders*, Paul puts it well:

> Your father had no experience of his own to measure ours against. He could not assess ability since he had no conception of what constituted it or how it could be measured. ... And out of his experience alone he could find little or no advice to pass on to us. (50)

What neither Paul acknowledges, nor Bourdieu's theory accommodates, however, is the intangible path-clearing support that ambitious parents are providing. While they may not be able to help with homework, what these poor black men and women were offering was sacrifice as in the instance of Derek's mother who sentences herself to the daily struggle of providing for herself and for her son, so that he can complete secondary school. We see too the pride Mr. Breville takes when Paul gets a first: "[Y]our father was laughing and talking. I had never seen him like that before. It was clear that this was the achievement that he had been working and waiting for and had all along seen clearly. I was on the threshold of his success" (59).[13] As a reward for their sacrifice, parents are able to cash in on their children's cultural capital and in some instances are vicariously participating in the privilege attendant on their sons' access to the social milieu of the island.

Moreover, whilst Bourdieu's theory of cultural competence is useful in explaining the high number of upper and middle-class mulatto boys being awarded scholarships to pursue university education abroad, it does not take into sufficient consideration the way boys from lower classes are gaining cultural capital through association and imitation of the social habits of their middle-class schoolmates. In St. Omer's works, sporting success can be read as the opportunity to extend one's cultural capital. We are provided with countless instances of the Breville brothers involved in athletics, football and cricket. They are making a name for themselves; their reputation as cricketers ensures that they are publicly known. Where sporting prowess is matched with academic excellence, this increase in cultural capital can be leveraged in the alliances they form with boys from higher social classes – Du Coteau for example – so as to transcend the restrictions of their working class roots and join the ranks of the profes- sional class. Paul's fraternizing with the school team during away matches, eating in fancy restaurants and being hosted in upper-middle-class homes, encourages him to display what Bordieu describes as 'habitus'. Outside of his island home, he firmly adopts the social manners of the upper class:

> Among us, on that island, the distinguishing marks I knew at home were absent. We existed for the islanders without antecedents to characterize us. No one on the island knew where I lived on mine. We went to the same parties, had lunches with the Governor, were entertained in homes the equivalent of which I had never entered on our island (46).

Coveting a lifestyle that he has no desire to share with his disenfranchised black brethren, Paul is intent on building his cultural capital so as to convert it into social capital. This capital will be manifested as living in a house close to Columbus Square; marrying a woman who is nothing like Patricia; with children – a son who is not Michael, "the very badly cracked image of son" (51), but instead one with whom he would share 'habitus', one with whom he would have a common experience of secondary school. "I would show him clippings, photographs and certificates. I would refer him to standards I had known and had myself tested. We would communicate" (51). It can be argued that Paul's social consciousness has not been sufficiently radicalized through the tertiary education afforded to his brother. Unlike Peter, Paul has not travelled outside of his island home and therefore his imagination has not expanded to apprehend a large colonial world where his naive ideology of exceptionalism will be tested and rendered inadequate in the face of social marginalization and injustice.

Historically, while sporting prowess did in fact give weight to the notion of the exceptional West Indian, it also developed in him self-discipline, reciprocity and a sense of allegiance – characteristics that the St. Omerian protagonists are not fully educated into. In *Beyond a Boundary* C.L.R. James discusses the colonial experience of cricket in terms of the restraint that is at the core the Puritanism that characterized his experience of the sport. This self-control not only manifests itself in the playing of the game but also in one's daily existence:

> [I]n the West Indies, the cricket ethic has shaped not only the cricketers but also social life as a whole: along with restraint, not so much externally as in internal inhibitions, we learnt loyalty. It is good to be loyal to what you believe in… (50).

James' emphasis on the fellowship and loyalty gained through sports networking allows for an interesting comparison of the way St. Omer presents the student protagonist as a sportsman. Although sports provide visibility, popularity and the opportunity for young black men to interact with brown boys of a higher social class, this interaction is by no means sustained, nor does it extend outside of the sporting arenas. St. Omer is careful to depict the absence of an enduring team spirit. There is no sense of a team. Instead, less than competent brown boys use their social status and financial sponsorship to stay on the team. Meanwhile for black boys, this temporary popularity generates self-aggrandizement, the chance to see oneself as more important than one actually is. Moreover, the restraint that James references as a by-product of sports education is not part of these protagonists' code of behaviour. Instead popularity, married to a sense of privilege, produces sexual aggressiveness, the *droit de seigneur* that boys like Peter, Paul, Stephenson and Derek exercise against lower-class girls. These young women are honoured to attract the gaze of these schoolboys. Although they are pragmatic enough to understand that these boys, by virtue of their education, will not see them as marriage candidates, these lower-class girls are not beyond using pregnancy to force their hands.

Like sports, culture is another avenue for acquiring social capital. The Methodist Arts Society – the antithesis of the steelpan players – is preoccupied with the veneration of European culture. Populated by civil servants and teachers, this group defines its artistic sensibility and by extension its respectability, through piano recitals, operatic singing, and dramatic renditions of English plays. However, St. Omer presents them as aspirants: they are not professionals (doctors and lawyers), nor are they white. They too are struggling to belong, to make a social mark. Paul has no desire to join their ranks, although by virtue of his high school education that world is now available to him. Instead, he has aspirations beyond it. To join them is to settle for an inferior social location, even though it is a step above what he currently occupies. "And, daily, I walked the streets and measured my potential distance above, and my growing superiority to them" (34). He is anxious to become visible, and he can only do so by distancing himself from the working poor, from the carnival-loving blacks and from non-professional aspirants. Paul's dark skin and his reduced economic situation will make this a difficult quest, but he is confident that he can capitalise on the power of his educational success. The fact that some blacks now occupy positions of social privilege is an encouragement, the proof that Paul's aspirations are attainable, because already these black professionals have, through marriage to white or brown women, breached the colour/class barrier.

Ultimately, in St. Omer's quintet, education (social and formal) does not instil compassion, and the ability to love and care for others – values which in turn allow one to develop into an agent of change who is committed to helping elevate his community. It is no coincidence that St. Omer's novellas/novels are brutal in their depiction of male/female relationships, and in so doing the theme of a doomed future is reinforced. Women in these novellas/novels are never fully developed, and are reduced to sites on which male protagonists play out their sexual aggression. We are witness to Derek's rape of Berthe when he discovers that she is not a virgin; Stephenson's sexual escapades with Moira and Rosa; Paul's exploitative use of Patricia to ease his libidinal excess; and Peter's callous jockeying of mistresses. St. Omer is no less pessimistic in his exploration of situations where love overlays sexual behaviour. In *The Lights on the Hill*, St. Omer creates in Stephenson a man who does not trust the happiness he finds in Thea. Stephenson, suspicious of love and convinced of his unworthiness, orchestrates their break-up. This is similar to what John Lestrade does in *A Room on the Hill* when, after he has manoeuvred Rose into having sex with him, after he has led her to believe there is a future for them, tells her that there is no point to their relationship. "The memory of his so recent happiness ... receding rapidly" (49), John chooses to terminate their liaison because he wants to go to Canada and does not believe that the relationship can survive seven years of separation. These two men are unwilling to take a chance on the happiness of today because they envision a future elsewhere, one that is better than whatever happiness they are experiencing in the present. This sense of the inadequacy of the now, of the present as a deferral of the future, is part of what their socialization has created.

Part 3: The Physical and Social Cartography of a Small Place

In his exploration of education, St. Omer strategically links the cartography
of the place, its mores and its social customs to the themes of entrapment
and escape. The physical landscape works in support of the social education
to which the protagonists are reacting. Religious and urban landscapes
are the two most significant tropes used to illustrate this. The Catholic
Church, "that squat edifice crouching in the centre of the town" has a
paternalistic grip on the people and is educating them into social
compliance. Class operates in church. It determines who sits in what
pews. Whites and mulattoes have assigned seating. So, too, do secondary
schools boys and girls. In this depiction of social stratification, St. Omer
offers his readers a social history of St. Lucia in the nineteen-fifties.
In the Catholic Church, pews were designated to certain persons (who
most likely purchased them) and church wardens were assigned to remove
interlopers from those pews. St. Omer portrays Catholic priests – the
most obvious symbols of whiteness – as highly respected men who
have garnered deep social privilege. Those who dare to challenge the
authority of these priests are not viewed as rebels instigating social
change, but instead they label them as *'vieux negres'*, upstarts, show-
offs – people who do not know their place, and who wish to abrogate
an accepted social hierarchy.

Interestingly, in the world of St. Omer's novellas/novels, the Church,
although it is the public guardian of morality, is unable to instill good moral
conduct in its parishioners. Extramarital affairs, pregnancies outside of
wedlock and abortions circulate virulently in this society. Going to church,
following the dictates of the priests, regularly attending mass, sitting in
assigned pews, and publicly performing obeisance to the status quo are part
of a daily routine into which one is socialized. Peter breaks away from all
of this when he migrates. Having absolved himself through his performance of his large act of marrying the girl he impregnates, his tertiary
education puts him even further away from censure for his noncompliant
social conduct. His wife-beating, his indiscreet womanizing and his constant drunkenness, while socially commented on, are not censured – it is
as if this is expected of the academic. While St. Omer does not depict Peter
reflecting on the repugnance of his social action, the reader is nonetheless
critically aware of how deeply he is interpellated by Catholicism. It is
significant that his public ill-treatment of Phyllis occurs outside of his
island, in another larger, more impersonal island far from the censuring
gaze of the priests and other guardians of social conduct. His growing
descent into self-aberration and his resultant psychosis suggests his awareness of sin, his unadmitted guilt and his punishment of self and of others
because of his inability to confess his deeds. We note that he has no

confidante to whom he opens up or who brings him absolution. On the other hand, Paul's abrogation of the status quo brings him first to public acts of penitence and the unvoiced plea for absolution, which when they prove unattainable, lead him to an almost theatrical performance of madness. Peter, by virtue of separating himself from church, fully interiorizes his psychosis because there is no public stage on which it can be deflected. The final image at the end of *J—, Black Bam and the Masqueraders*, where we are told of Peter's laughing reflection, "…he laughed. His eyes in the mirror were grave. A vein stood out on the neck in front of him" (109), confirms that his psychosis is now exteriorized.

It is important to note that in St. Omer's works there is no evocation of the beauty of the island's tropical landscape which frames the main town. Instead, we are given a social picture of an urban space before and after the Castries fire of 1948. Significantly, this is the same space that Derek Walcott evokes in his "A City's Death by Fire". But where for Walcott, the green hills backdropping the towns are seen as a testimony of faith, in St. Omer's portraiture, the focus never enlarges to accommodate the panorama of the surrounding hills; instead it remains narrowly on the streets crisscrossing the town, the CDCs (concrete structures built to provide mass housing after the fire), and the harbour. Core to this environment is noise: the constant hum of the power station, the chorus of vendors, the relentless tolling of church bells, the cacophony of masqueraders, the buzzing voices of people living in cramped, dilapidated houses, the honking of oversized American cars in crowded streets. And it is this noise from which the St. Omerian protagonist wishes to escape.

Social class is meticulously depicted through the geography of the town – the wealthy live in buildings furthest away from the noise of poverty and squalor. Their houses are close to the Catholic Church, hidden behind high walls from the vulgar view of the common man. The "quiet, not as an absence of noise, but as the unnatural intensification of the most ordinary sound… and… the smell of the food was always richer than the smell of food at home. The stretch of houses and the intervening closed gates were orderly and private" (30). The members-only club where they are entertained is in public view, yet private in its exclusivity. St. Omer depicts Paul Breville as yearning for that world. He has been quietly socialized into this desire by his father's admiration for the old white man who passes the house in his chauffeur-driven car, inaccessible and enviable. The father's imitation of this pipe-smoking man morphs into his children's role-playing and fuels Paul's growing sense of superiority. Whereas the father believes that separation from his poor rural roots will bring him within spectator-distance of the lives of the well-to-do, Paul in his treatment of his father, externalizes this contempt for origins. He is confident that his determination, his education, and his sporting prowess will provide him with the access that is denied to his father – a man fated to imitate the privileges of that world without ever being a part of it. Paul, by virtue of his success at sports, has already received a taste of it. In his letter to Peter, he claims "Your father wanted to impress; I, to overwhelm" (32). Meanwhile, St. Omer's strategic authorial intrusion allows us to recognize that the Breville's household finances are so dire that they cannot afford to pay Doux Doux, the servant woman in their hire. Moreover, to make ends meet, Mrs. Breville, to the deep chagrin of her family, has to resort to selling vegetables and ground provisions on a tray outside the house.

In St. Omer's quintet, the sea is a constant presence. Beaches, harbours, wharves – all these feature prominently. Wharves in St. Omer's opus are sites of death – literally, socially and symbolically. The town's harbour is where Mr. Breville forbids his children from swimming and from being in the company of boys that he labels "wharf-rats". These boys, unschooled and poor, are not fitting company for his sons whose high school education destines them for a respectable future. Ironically, while the wharf is perceived as the place where the detritus of society congregate, it is at this same site that the college boys are holding their school competitions and, by virtue of it being used as such, it gains legitimacy in the father's eyes. Ultimately, it is not the wharf *per se* that the father is reacting to but the company who frequent the wharf. Symbolically, it is this harbour that St. Omer uses as the site of Patricia's suicide. Like the wharf-rats, she has been deemed unsuitable for a college boy who believes that he deserves "more than that pink umbrella and the too-oiled hair" (59).

The beach is also presented in a myriad of negative ways. It is the site for pseudo-romantic liaisons – where some of the male protagonists come of sexual age. In *A Room on The Hill*, John Lestrade seduces Rose in "the clear shallow water that scarcely rippled" (48). Yet the feeling of exhilaration generated by their lovemaking is presented as a dream that he wishes to wake up free from. Under the almond and sea grape trees which line the beach, Paul Breville spends his frustrations out in a meaningless sexual encounter with a passive Patricia, who mistakes his sexual advances for a passport to middle-class propriety and marriage to an up-and-coming young man. In the instance of Stephenson In *The Lights on the Hill* and Peter in *J—, Black Bam and The Masqueraders*, the sea represents escape into nothingness. Death-seeking, Stephenson is depicted as drifting aimlessly on the beach, a willing sexual victim to a mysterious woman, "with the figure of a bag of charcoal on sticks" (95) who emerges from the sea. Peter is also drawn to the nothingness of the ocean. "And on the beach, discarding [Jeanine] near the shore, he swam far out, returning, much later, to dive again and again… " (36). His long swims seem to suggest a desire to be absorbed into this liquid world, freed from the responsibilities and cares that weigh him down.

Conclusion

In their failure to act, St. Omerian protagonists appear to be puppets orchestrated by the indifferent hand of fate, called on to perform without ever internalizing the reasons for their actions. Even while they claim interiority and dedicate their energies to self-questioning, they lack the wherewithal to move beyond self-indulgence and self-pity. The education they have received has not given them these particular skill-sets. In his essay "Double Identity in the Novels of Garth St. Omer", John Thieme suggests that there is no escape for St. Omer's protagonists, "only the anguished emancipation which comes from inner awareness" (96). John, Derek, Stephenson, Peter and Paul are indeed anguished characters. The level of self-awareness each attains is somewhat dubious. Their education, while it may be for some of them a means of economic upliftment, is not a source of mental emancipation nor does it bring them to self-reflectivity. David Williams, in his essay "Mixing Memory and Desire: St. Omer's *Nor Any Country*", posits that "the interweaving and the juxtaposition of memory and the actuality of the present" constitute the major device used by St. Omer to trace Peter Breville's "growth into the truth of human responsibility" (37). The quality and degree of that growth towards truth remains debatable. While these men are portrayed as having an inner life, diseased though it may be, it does not come from the critical thinking that is typically part of education. Instead, their interiority is narcissistic in its intensity, its focus concentrated on escape through the education they have been privileged to receive.

Thieme, in his articulation of doubleness in the novels of Garth St. Omer, sees the educated protagonist as being both part of and alien to his society. The socio-cultural consequence of this disassociation notwithstanding, consideration must also be given to the psychological import of this doubleness. In *The Lights on The Hill*, the link between education and madness can be seen in the geographical proximity of the university to the mental asylum. Even while education offers asylum – protection from myopia and small island blues – it makes it difficult for the intellectual to be reintegrated into society. Where professionals seem to be easily absorbed into high society, it is harder for the academician to find his place. In *Nor Any Country*, Peter Breville, returning to his island home with his doctorate in Economics, does not quite fit into the upper class, although he is drinking whiskey and having lobster dinners with them. At the dinner party held in his honour, the alacrity with which Peter's nickname, *pine boeuf* (penis like a bull's) is remembered and invoked is noteworthy. Not only is the nickname derogatory and reductive, but it also inevitably plays into the stereotype of the well-endowed Afro-Caribbean man. Thus, in spite of his outstanding academic qualifications, Dr. Peter Breville is reduced to a man whose claim to fame is the large size of his penis. Moreover, his womanizing in England is seamlessly woven into this discourse of anatomical generosity. The dinner conversation between Peter and his old schoolmates reinforces how little they have in common and how much of an outsider he is: "And they talked again about their school days. Apart from their religion and the fact that they had been born on the island, it was the only common ground between their separate and disparate existence" (76). Although he has managed to distance himself from the working poor, Peter does not succeed in being elevated into the ranks of the educated browns to whom whites are gradually demitting control of the commanding heights of his island's economic and social life. It can be argued that St. Omer uses this scene to critique the restrictiveness of a small-island Caribbean society that fails to make a place for the black intellectual. However, in the real world it may have been in part the failure to fit into that elitist corps of Caribbean society that led many educated blacks to identify with a nationalist agenda, to become vigorous advocates for parliamentary reform and champions of the labour rights of the poor. St. Omer's fictional world offers his protagonists no such hopeful solution.

The social realism of St. Omer's novellas/ novels, and the unflinching candour with which he creates his protagonists, the death of anticipation to which they all eventually succumb, prompts a reading of the Caribbean intelligentsia of that period as desperate to belong to a bourgeois social order. The colonial education to which they have been exposed, their social history, and the lack of a cohesive support group with commonly-shared ideals and values doom these protagonists to an inherently nihilistic psychological adaptation. Revolt against the colonial status quo is not yet an option. In these novellas/novels we are not presented with emerging black leaders, nor is there a progressive middle-class lobbying for the rights of the working poor. In conclusion, all of St. Omer's novellas/novels written between 1968 and 1972 deal with the contradictions and complexities of formal and social education in a colonial society. Each story is an iteration that expands and finesses this preoccupation. Unkind though it may seem in its brutal honesty, he does present, with "intelligence and understanding" (*Room*, 113) a truthful portrait of St. Lucian society. But there are other truths, ones that will be written by those with kinder eyes.

> . . . you will observe
> butterflies
> how they fly higher
> and higher before their hope dries
> with endeavour
> and they fall among flies (*Arrivants*, 104)

Works Cited

Bourdieu, Pierre. " Cultural Reproduction and Social Reproduction". Web, May 2015. edu301s2011.files.wordpress.com/2011/02/cultural-reproduction-and-social-reproduction.pdf

Brathwaite, Edward. *Arrivants*. Oxford: Oxford University Press, 1981.

Cobley, Alan G. "The Historical Development of Higher Education in the Anglophone Caribbean". In Glenford Howe, Ed. *Higher Education in the Caribbean, Past, Present, Future*. Jamaica: UWI Press, 2000.

Carter, Martin. "A Free Community of Valid persons". In "A Martin Carter Prose Sampler", *Kyk-Over-Al*, Vol. 44 (May 1993). pp. 30- 32.

Cousins, Jacqueline. "Symbol and Metaphor in the Early Novels of Garth St. Omer". *Journal of West Indian Literature*, Vol. 3, (September 1989). Pp. 20-38.

Gifford, William Tell. "Garth St. Omer's Existential parlance". A thesis submitted to Sonoma State University in partial fulfilment of the degree of Masters of Arts, 1988.

Gilkes, Michael. *The West Indian Novel*, Boston: G.K. Hall, 1981.

Ismond, Patricia. "The St. Lucian Background in Garth St. Omer and Derek Walcott", *Caribbean Quarterly*. Volume 28, Numbers 1&2, (March – June 1982). Pp 32-43

James, C. L. R. *Beyond a Boundary*. London: Hutchinson & Co., 1963.

John, Catherine. "Caribbean Organic Intellectual: The Legacy and Challenge of Erna Brodber's Life work". *Small Axe: A Caribbean Journal of Criticism*, Volume 16, Number 39, (2012). pp. 72-88.

Kaye Jacqueline. "Anonymity and Subjectivism in the Novels of Garth St. Omer", *Journal of Commonwealth Literature* 10 (August, 1975). pp. 45-52.

Lee, John, Robert, and Kendel Hippolyte. Eds. *St. Lucian Literature and Theatre: An Anthology*. Castries: Cultural Development Foundation, 2007.

Moore, Gerald. "Garth St. Omer". In *Contemporary Novelists*. Ed. James Vinson. New York: St Martin's Press, 1972. pp. 1084-1086.

Mordecai, Pamela C. "The West Indian Male Sensibility in Search of Itself: Some Comments on *Nor Any Country, The Mimic Men*, and *The Secret Ladder*". *World Literature Written in English* 21 (Autumn 1982): pp. 629-644.

Nettleford, Rex. *Mirror, Mirror: Identity, Race and Protest in Jamaica*. Jamaica: William Collins and Sangster, Ltd., 1970.

Rohlehr, Gordon. "Small Island Blues: A short review of the novels of Garth St. Omer", In *St. Lucian Literature and Theatre: An Anthology of Reviews*, eds. John Robert Lee and Kendel Hippolyte, Castries: Cultural Development Foundation, pp.15-19.

Scott, David. "The Sovereignty of the Imagination: An Interview with George Lamming". *Small Axe: A Caribbean Journal of Criticism*, Number 12, September, 2002. pp. 77-200.

St. Omer, Garth. "Syrop." In *Introduction Two: Stories by New Writers*. London: Faber, 1964.

———. *A Room on the Hill*. London: Faber and Faber, 1968.

———. *Shades of Grey*. London: Faber and Faber, 1968.

———. *Nor Any Country*. London: Faber and Faber, 1969.

———. *J—, Black Bam and The Masqueraders*. London: Faber and Faber, 1972.

Thieme, John. "Double Identity in the Novels of Garth St. Omer". *Ariel*, Volume 8, (July 1977). Pp. 81-97.

Walcott, Derek. *What the Twilight Says: Essays*. New York: Farrar, Straus and Giroux. 1999.

Williams, David. "Mixing Memory and Desire: St Omer's *Nor Any Country*" *Journal of West Indian Literature* 2.2 (1988): pp. 36-41. Web.

Williams, Eric. *Inward Hunger: The Education of a Prime Minister*. London: Deutsch, 1969.

Endnotes

1. I refer to them as a quintet because their publication dates (1968-9) suggest that they were being written together. Additionally, the characters in one novella or novel often reappear in another, thus prompting a reading of the five novellas/ novels as part of a whole. (Although three years apart, the 1972 publication is the sequel of the 1969 book).

2. Alan Cobley in "The Historical development to Higher Education in the Anglophone Caribbean" has established that higher education in the Caribbean was sanctioned by colonial authorities as an effective means of ensuring that Caribbean islands remained intellectually and ideologically tied to Britain (10).

3. For a more in-depth exploration of Sir Grantley Adam's contribution to trade union legislation, see F.A. Hoyos, *Grantley Adams and the Social Revolution: The Story of the Movement that Changed the Pattern of West Indian Society* (London: MacMillan, 1974).

4. Whereas public school education in Britain was geared towards the development of leadership, in the Anglo-Caribbean context, colonial education was directed at training of civil servants to support expatriate leaders.

5. See for example Samuel Selvon's *A Brighter Sun*, George Lamming's In *The Castle of My Skin*, or V. S. Naipaul's *A House for Mr. Biswas*.

6. The characters to which this essay make mention are: Derek Charles in *Another Place, Another Time*, Stephenson in *The Lights on the Hill* (together these two books make up *Shades of Grey*), John Lestrade in *A Room on The Hill*, and Peter and Paul Breville in *Nor Any Country* and *J—, Black Bam and The Masqueraders*.

7. Professor Emeritus at the University of the West Indies (UWI, Mona), Sir Roy Augier has the distinction of being a key figure in the introduction of West Indian History on the Caribbean Secondary school curriculum. He has also made a pivotal contribution to the Caribbean Examinations Council (CXC).

8. Founded in 1950 by the poet/playwright Derek Walcott, his twin brother playwright Roderick, and Maurice Mason, The St. Lucia Arts Guild provided the enabling space for the Walcott brothers to write, direct and produce their plays. It also facilitated budding actors and directors in the development of their artistic talents.

9. See for example the following: William Tell Gifford, John Thieme's "Garth St. Omer's Existential Parlance," or Gerald Moore's, "Garth St. Omer."

10. Rohlehr borrows this term from James Joyce who used it as a descriptor of the style of his collection of short stories, *Dubliners*. See Rohlehr's "Small Island Blues: A short review of the novels of Garth St. Omer"; in *St. Lucian Literature and Theatre: An Anthology of Reviews*, eds. John Robert Lee and Kendel Hippolyte, Castries: Cultural Development Foundation, pp.15-19; and in this *Casebook*, pp. 89-94.

11. I disagree with Michael Gilkes's reading in *The West Indian Novel* of the child as sounding a note of hope in the novel (114). There are too many images of the child being restricted by Peter, not so much because he wants to keep the child safe but because he sees it as Phyllis's way of forcing him into the role of the caring, responsible father and accordingly measures out his interaction with the child.

12. In colonial St. Lucian society the number of bells tolled and the frequency with which they were tolled depending on the amount of money paid to the priest for the funeral service. For example, first class funerals – the privilege of the well-to-do – had all three church bells tolled, twice daily leading up to the funeral. The very poor could not afford to pay for tolling bells. Similarly, at requiem masses, the number of bells and the length of time for which they were rung, was a function of social class and economics. (Telephone conversation with Monsignor Cyril LaMontagne, Grenada May 14, 2015.)

13. The Latin phrase, *Victor Ludorum* means winner of the games.

14. This is reminiscent of the episode in *Inward Hunger* where Eric Williams' father beams indulgently as he listens to his son conjugating the Latin verb *'amo'*.

INDEX

CONTRIBUTORS

Edward Baugh is the Emeritus Professor at UWI Mona. He is a major Caribbean poet and critic whose distinguished academic career has been devoted to the region's literature. He is the author of the poetry collections *A Tale from the Rain Forest*, *It Was the Singing* and *Black Sand: New and Selected Poems* (2013). His recent academic books include *Derek Walcott: Cambridge Studies in African and Caribbean Literature* (2013) and *Frank Collymore: A Biography* (2009)

Kamau Brathwaite is the internationally celebrated poet and author of *The Arrivants* (1973), *Ancestors* (2001), *Born to Slow Horses* (2005), *Elegguas* (2010), *Strange Fruit* (2016) and many more collections. His *The Development of Creole Society in Jamaica* (1971), *Contradictory Omens* (1974), *History of the Voice* (1979), *MR* (2002), *Golokwati* (2002) are seminal documents of Caribbean thought. His awards include The Griffin Prize, the Neustadt International Prize, the Frost medal from the Poetry Society of America.

Maurice Capitanchik (d. 1985) was a British author who wrote two novels about gay and bisexual men: *Joseph* (1968) and *Friends and Lovers* (1971).

Jacqueline Cousins. At the time of writing the essay included in this *Casebook*, Jacqueline Cousins was a postgraduate student in the Department of English, UWI Mona, working on her M. Phil on St. Omer.

John Hemmings (Professor F.W.J. 1920-1993) was a scholar of 19th century French and Russian literature; he taught at the University of Leicester for many years and reviewed regularly for the *New Statesman* and *The Listener* in the 1960s.

Pat Ismond (1944-2006). Dr Ismond was born in St. Lucia, taught in the USA and UWI St. Augustine. She was the author of numerous articles and published *Abandoning Dead Metaphors: The Caribbean Phase of Derek Walcott's Poetry* (2001).

Jane King is a St Lucian poet and critic. She worked as a senior lecturer at the Sir Arthur Lewis Community College in St Lucia, and was a founding director of the Lighthouse Theatre Company. She was awarded the James Rodway Memorial Prize, awarded by Derek Walcott for *Fellow Traveller* in 1994. Her other publications include *In to the Centre* (1993) and *Performance Anxiety* (2013).

Cliff Lashley was a senior lecturer at UWI Mona who, tragically, was murdered in 1993. He was a critic who wrote his PhD thesis on V.S. Reid and published articles on Caribbean aesthetics and dramatic comedy.

John Robert Lee is a widely anthologised St Lucian poet, editor, reviewer, newspaper columnist and radio and TV presenter. His books include *Saint Lucian* (1988), *Artefacts* (2000), *Canticles* (2007), *Elemental* (2008), and *Collected Poems 1975-2015* (2017). He is the compiler of a *Bibliography of St. Lucian Writing 1948-2013* (2013).

Antonia MacDonald was born and grew up in St. Lucia. She now lives in Grenada where she is a professor in the Department of Humanities and Social Sciences, School of Arts and Sciences, and Associate Dean in the School of Graduate Studies at St. George's University. She is author of *Making Homes in the West/Indies: Constructions of Subjectivity in the Writings of Michelle Cliff and Jamaica Kincaid.*

Milt (Milton A.P.) Moise studied literature and psychology at UWI Cave Hill. He has an M.Phil in Postcolonial Literatures in English and is currently working for a doctorate at the University of Florida, writing on images of bipolar disorder in contemporary American fiction.

Jeremy Poynting is the founding and managing editor of Peepal Tree Press. His doctoral thesis was on the East Indian presence in Caribbean Writing (1985). His *Kwame Dawes' Prophets: A Readers Guide* comes out in 2018.

Velma Pollard is a poet, short-story writer, linguist and educationist. When she retired it was as Dean of the Faculty of Education at UWI, Mona in Jamaica. Her publications include (poetry): *Crown Point, Shame Trees Don't Grow Here, Leaving Traces, And Caret Bay Again: New and Selected Poems.* Her fiction includes *Homestretch, Karl and Other Stories,* and *Considering Woman 1 & 2.* Her *Dread Talk: The Language of Rastafari* is widely referenced.

Kenneth Ramchand is Emeritus Professor at UWI St Augustine and Colgate University (USA). He is the author of numerous articles and the defining critical books, *West Indian Narrative: an Introductory Anthology* (editor, 1966); *West Indian Poetry: An Anthology for Schools* (editor, 1989), *An Introduction to the Study of West Indian Literature* (1976), and *The West Indian Novel and its Background* (1970).

Gordon Rohlehr is Emeritus Professor at UWI St. Augustine, Trinidad, the author of *Pathfinder: Black Awakening in "The Arrivants" of Edward Kamau Brathwaite* (1981); *Calypso and Society in Pre-Independence Trinidad* (1989); *My Strangled City and Other Essays* (1992); *The Shape of That*

Hurt and Other Essays (1992); *A Scuffling of Islands: Essays on Calypso* (2004); Transgression, Transition, Transformation: *Essays in Caribbean Culture* (2007); and *Ancestories: Readings of Kamau Brathwaite's "Ancestors"* (Trinidad: Lexicon, 2010) and *My Whole Life is Calypso: Essays on Sparrow* (2015).

John Wickham is the Barbadian author of *Casuarina Row* (1975), *World Without* End (1983), and *Discoveries* (1993). He was one-time editor of *Bim*.

Malica S. Willie is a Saint Lucian who was awarded a PhD at the University of the West Indies, Cave Hill for her thesis on the writing of Garth St. Omer. She was awarded an Erasmus Mundus scholarship, which allowed her to attend the University of Liege as a guest scholar, and as a visiting fellow at Linnaeus University in Sweden.

ALSO FROM PEEPAL TREE PRESS

GARTH ST. OMER IN CARIBBEAN MODERN CLASSICS
All with introductions by Jeremy Poynting

Room on the Hill
ISBN: 9781845230937; pp. 162; pub. 2012 [1968]; price £8.99

John Lestrade is attempting to come to terms with the suicide of his friend Stephen and his guilt that he did nothing to prevent it. In an island society suffocating in its smallness and deeply in the grip of a reactionary Roman Catholic church, Lestrade feels like a sleepwalker, almost a zombie. His escape to a room on the hill is an act of internal exile, an attempt to find in isolation the space to cut away, through honest self-reflection, the inauthentic, automaton-like quality of his life. But, equally unsparing of himself and his acquaintances, Lestrade's self-loathing and despair poison any hope of relationship with others. It is only when his friend Derek's abandoned girlfriend is killed in a reckless, even suicidal car crash, and is then refused a proper church burial by the Catholic church, that Lestrade is induced to action. Yet even when he and his friends attempt to hold an unofficial ceremony, the circumscribed nature of their protest is put into perspective by the two parades that interrupt it, one of masqueraders, the other of Old Alphonse, recently released from the lunatic asylum, who is leading a raucous procession of children. In the energy of the latter in particular, and in its clear rejection of the colonial straightjacket that locks in the middle-class intellectuals in the novel, there is an image of some possibility, an escape from the inauthentic.

Shades of Grey
ISBN: 9781845230920; pp. 192; pub. 2013 [1968]; price £8.99

Shades of Grey brings together two separate but interconnected novellas, *The Lights on the Hill* and *Another Place, Another Time*. Both deal with young men, cut adrift from their roots by education, trying to find themselves.
  In *The Lights on the Hill*, when Stephenson, who almost accidentally finds himself as a mature student at university, comes closer to his girlfriend Thea, with her easy talk of her family, he has to acknowledge that he has never known his father, not lived with his mother, and cannot remember what his grandparents looked like. He feels, too, that his failure to come clean about a disreputable episode in his past undermines the

good faith of their relationship. What is even more crippling is the way that his past makes him feel that all choices, actions and relationships are meaningless. It is only when he reaches an extreme inner crisis that Stephenson, in a halting way, begins to construct his own story.

In *Another Place, Another Time*, St Omer explores the circumstances in which a scholarship boy makes the decision to separate himself from his family and friends and conclude that "He had no cause nor any country now other than himself." As in all St Omer's fiction, there is a sharp focus on the inequalities of gender, and a compassionate but unwavering judgement of the failings of his male characters.

When *Shades of Grey* was first published in 1968, *The Listener* called it "one of the most genuinely daring and accomplished works of fiction... for a very long time", whilst Kenneth Ramchand concluded that St Omer's "delicacy, control and economy must surely place him in the first rank of twentieth-century novelists."

Nor Any Country
ISBN: 9781845232291; pp. 124; pub. 2013 [1969]; price £8.99

Education has taken Peter Breville away from his native St Lucia for the past eight years. Now, appointed to a university post in a bigger island to the north, he decides he must see his family on his way from England. There is his mother, whom he loves, his father with whom he has never got on, and his brother, with whom boyhood competition turned sour. And there is Phyllis, his wife, who has waited patiently for his return, determined to be a wife to him, while he has not once contacted her since he left, and has conducted two lengthy affairs.

In the week he spends with his family and meeting old friends, he discovers a St Lucia that, in the early 1960s, is on the point of emerging into the modern capitalist world, but where the disparities between the new middle class and the impoverished black majority has become ever wider. In the midst of this, he must decide what he owes Phyllis. *Nor Any Country*, first published in 1968, is a profound and elegantly written exploration of the complexities of individual moral choice and an acutely insightful study of a society in the process of change.

J—, Black Bam and the Masqueraders
ISBN: 9781845232436; pp. 136; pub. 2016 [1972]; price £8.99

This is the final instalment in the quartet of novels that explores the lives of the small St Lucian middle class in the years around independence.

In it the reader re-encounters the brothers, Peter and Paul Breville. Peter has resumed his marriage with his long abandoned wife Phyllis (the subject of *Another Country*), and is now working as a lecturer in Jamaica. His brother Paul remains in St Lucia, disgraced and sacked from professional employment by his refusal to marry his pregnant girlfriend. He has acquired a reputation for madness, though whether this is a contrived mask or an actual breakdown is left uncertain.

The novel intercuts Paul's confessional letters to Peter with the narrative of Peter's marital relationship with Phyllis, his affairs and descent into despair, drunkenness and domestic violence. In the contrast between Paul's self-lacerating honesty and Peter's self-deceptions, St Omer offers a bracingly bleak portrayal of a middle class beset with hypocrisies over race, sexism and class privilege. If sanity is at some level marked by truthful perceptions, St Omer invites us to question which of the brothers is actually sane.

No Caribbean novelist has with greater economy or elegance exposed the realities behind the masks people wear or the gaps between postcolonial rhetoric and the actuality of minds that remain deeply colonised. Though first published in 1972, St Omer's novel has lost none of its uncomfortable truth-telling power.

Prisnms
ISBN: 9781845232429; pp. 144; pub. 2015; price: £8.99

Eugene Coard is woken one morning by a phone call to report the murder of a former St Lucian friend. It throws him back to memories of their island days, and his complicated love life in London that has made necessary his relocation to the USA. Thoughts about his friend's metamorphosis from middle-class "CB" to criminal, ghetto-dwelling "Red" provoke Eugene to review his own so far profitable transformations. But just how much of Eugene's story can we believe? His confessions reveal him as probably the most unreliable and devious narrator in Caribbean fiction who has, as a writer and psychiatrist, been exploiting the confusions of race in the USA to his own advantage.

With nods to Ellison's *Invisible Man* and a witty inversion of Saul Bellow's *Sammler's Planet*, *Prisnms* is a dark comedy about the masks people wear in a racially divided society that anticipates the metafictions of a writer such as Percival Everett. In the shape-shifting figure of Eugene Coard, Garth St Omer has created a character whose admissions will bring the reader shocked and horrified delight. *Prisnms* was written in the 1980s, recently revised, but perhaps because it was so ahead of its time, not published until now.